SOURCES OF SEMIOTIC

Readings with Commentary from Antiquity to the Present

D. S. CLARKE, Jr.

Southern Illinois University Press

Carbondale and Edwardsville

Copyright © 1990 by the Board of Trustees,
    Southern Illinois University
All rights reserved
Printed in the United States of America
Edited by Robert Burdette
Designed by Kristy Robinson
Production supervised by Natalia Nadraga

Library of Congress Cataloging-in-Publication Data

Clarke, D. S. (David S.), 1936–
        Sources of semiotic: readings with commentary
from antiquity to the present / D.S. Clarke, Jr.
            p. cm.
        Includes bibliographical references.
        1. Semiotics—History. I. Title.
P99.C544   1990
302.2—dc20   89-26105
ISBN 0-8093-1613-7   CIP
ISBN 0-8093-1614-5 (pbk.)

The paper used in this publication meets the minimum requirements of American
National Standard for Information Sciences—Permanence
of Paper for Printed Library Materials, ANSI Z39.48-1984. ∞

TO

Nancy Physioc Clarke

CONTENTS

Contents

Contents

PREFACE

This volume is designed to provide students and general readers convenient access to the literature of semiotic, both past and recent, and an overview of its development. The selections are in rough chronological order, with some exceptions grouped under a common topic. They have been edited to provide consistency of punctuation and quotations and to delete footnotes, internal references, and references to supplementing literature. Original section numbering has also been deleted. A line of spaced "dots" in a selection indicates the continuation to a different page in the original edition.

The history of semiotic can be regarded as the history of key developments in philosophy—a complex, overwhelming subject indeed, one for which any selection of authors and topics must be arbitrary to some degree. Many writings on semiotic have been excluded from this sampling, not necessarily because of any shortcomings but because they would either simply restate what I consider to be the main classifications and positions developed in those that have been included or raise issues I consider less central to the development of the subject, defined in the narrow sense as the study of comparative features of signs. To the extent possible, I have attempted to restrict historical selections to those by originators of the key ideas that have been the principal sources of the development of the subject. The recent appearance of anthologies of European semiotics[1] has made it possible to be highly selective in deciding what is to be included from a vast literature that has developed in this field in the past twenty-five years. A commentary and a general introductory first chapter have been added to provide background and explanation of the reading selections. For supplemental accounts, the reader should consult the brief histories of Sebeok, Rollin, Deely, Eco, and myself.[2] At a few stages (this occurs especially in the final chapter), I depart from the role of commentator to indicate my own views on the issues raised in the selections.

1. See Robert Innis, ed., *Semiotics* (Bloomington: Indiana University Press, 1985); Marshall Blonsky, ed., *On Signs* (Baltimore: Johns Hopkins University Press, 1985); and M. Kremper et al., *Classics of Semiotics* (New York: Plenum, 1981).

2. Thomas Sebeok, "Semiotics: A Survey of the State of the Art," in *Contributions to the Doctrine of Signs* (Bloomington: Indiana University Press, 1976); Bernard Rollins, *Natural and Conventional Meaning* (The Hague: Mouton, 1976), ch. 1; John Deely, *Introducing Semiotic* (Bloomington: Indiana University Press, 1982); Umberto Eco, *Semiotics and the Philosophy of Language* (Bloomington: Indiana University Press, 1984) secs. 1.6, 1.7; and my *Principles of Semiotic* (London: Routledge and Kegan Paul, 1987), ch. 2. All these works contain extensive references to the historical and recent literature.

Readers should be forewarned of the controversial nature of our subject, controversies that are the topics of the selections and commentary in chapters 5 and 6. One of them surrounds the choice of what is employed to denote it. I have elected to use 'semiotic' in place of the term 'semiotics', which has gained wide currency in recent years. The main reason for reverting back to the term used by Locke, and later Peirce and Morris, is to emphasize the affinities of a general theory of signs to philosophical logic and the continuity of this subject with medieval classifications of signs that included natural signs, signs not used for purposes of communication. As one educated in the American analytic tradition of philosophy, I hope that the methods of logical analysis applied so successfully to both ordinary language and the specialized languages of the sciences can be extended to signs of a wider variety and that we can begin to understand the similarities and differences between different levels of signs in a way approaching our understanding of relations between different forms of sentences. Selections indicating how this might be carried out are included in the final chapter. In contrast to the medieval tradition continued by Peirce, 'semiotics', with its plural *s* ending, has been introduced to stand for a science of communication that generalizes the methods of linguistics. Methodological problems arising from attempts to construct such a general inclusive science are briefly discussed at the end of chapter 6. They are serious enough, I believe, to warrant either abandoning altogether the use of the term 'semiotics' or restricting its scope and explaining its methodology with much more exactness than is done by most currently employing it.

ACKNOWLEDGMENTS

I am grateful to Richard Lanigan and Thomas Sebeok for making valuable criticisms leading to improvements of the original manuscript version. I am also grateful to Sharon Grissom, Jean Rendleman Kelley, Sharon Langrand, Vernis Shownes, and Jay Williams for help in typing the manuscript; to editor Robert Burdette for many corrections and stylistic improvements; to Curtis Clark, Susan Wilson, and Robyn Laur of Southern Illinois University Press for their assistance in preparing the final manuscript and in obtaining permissions; and to Sadako Clarke for help in preparing the index.

Finally, I must thank the following persons, institutions, and publishers for permission to quote from the works cited below:

Antoine Arnauld, excerpt from *The Art of Thinking*. Translated by James Dickoff and Patricia James. Indianapolis: Bobbs-Merrill, 1964. Reprinted with the permission of James Dickoff and Patricia James.

St. Augustine, excerpt from *On Christian Doctrine*. Reprinted with the permission of Macmillan Publishing Company from *On Christian Doctrine*, translated by Durant Waite Robertson, Jr. Copyright © 1985 by Macmillan Publishing Company. ©1958. Excerpts from *Basic Writings of St. Augustine*, edited by Whitney Oates. New York: Random House, 1948. Copyright 1948 by Random House, Inc. Reprinted by permission of the publisher and T & T Clark, Ltd.

Roland Barthes, excerpts from *Elements of Semiology*. Translated by A. Laverson and C. Smith. New York: Hill and Wang, 1968. Translation copyright © 1967 by Jonathan Cape, Ltd. Reprinted by permission of Hill and Wang, a division of Farrar, Straus, and Giroux, Inc., and Jonathan Cape, Ltd.

Jonathan Bennett, excerpt from *Linguistic Behaviour*. Cambridge: Cambridge University Press, 1976. Copyright © by Cambridge University Press 1976. Reprinted with the permission of Cambridge University Press.

George Berkeley, excerpt from *A New Theory of Vision*. New York: Dutton, 1910. Reprinted with the permission of E. P. Dutton. Excerpt from *Three Dialogues between Hylas and Philonous*. New York: Dutton, 1910. Reprinted with the permission of E. P. Dutton.

Karl Buhler, "The Axiomatization of the Language Sciences." In R. E. Innis, *Karl Buhler*. New York: Plenum Press, 1982. Reprinted with the permission of Plenum Publishing Corporation.

Rudolph Carnap, excerpt from *Meaning and Necessity*. Chicago: University of Chicago Press, 1947. Copyright © 1947 and 1956 by the

University of Chicago Press. Reprinted with the permission of the University of Chicago Press.

Roderick Chisholm, excerpt from "Intentionality and the Theory of Signs." *Philosophical Studies* 3 (1952): 56–63. Copyright © 1952 by Kluwer Academic Publishers. Reprinted by permission of Kluwer Academic Publishers.

Noam Chomsky, excerpt from "Review of B. F. Skinner's *Verbal Behavior*." *Language* 35 (1959). Reprinted with the permission of the Linguistic Society of America and Noam Chomsky.

F. W. Galan, excerpt from "Cinema and Semiosis." *Semiotica* 44 (1983). Reprinted with the permission of Mouton de Gruyter and F. W. Galan.

Nelson Goodman, excerpt from *Languages of Art*. Indianapolis: Bobbs-Merrill, 1968. Reprinted with the permission of Hackett Publishing Company, Cambridge and Indianapolis.

H. P. Grice, excerpt from "Meaning." *Philosophical Review* 66 (1957). Reprinted with the permission of *The Philosophical Review*.

Pierre Guiraud, excerpt from *Semiology*. Translated by G. Gross. London: Routledge & Kegan Paul, 1975. Reprinted with the permission of Routledge & Kegan Paul, Ltd.

Gilbert Harman, excerpt from "Semiotics and the Cinema." *Quarterly Review of Film Studies* 2 (1977). Copyright © Harwood Academic Publishers GmbH. Reprinted with the permission of Harwood Academic Publishers and Gilbert Harman.

Hippocrates, excerpt from *Prognostic*. Translated by W. H. S. Jones. Vol. 2 in *Hippocrates*, Loeb Classical Library, 1932. Reprinted with the permission of Harvard University Press.

Louis Hjelmslev, excerpt from *Prolegomena to a Theory of Language*. Translated by F. Whitfield. Madison: University of Wisconsin Press, 1963. Copyright © by the University of Wisconsin Press. Reprinted with the permission of the University of Wisconsin Press.

Thomas Hobbes, excerpt from *De Corpore*. Translated by A. Martinich. In *Thomas Hobbes: Computatio Sive Logica*. New York: Abaris Books, 1981. Reprinted with the permission of Abaris Books, Inc.

Roman Jakobson, excerpt from *The Framework of Language*. Ann Arbor: Michigan Studies in the Humanities, 1980. Reprinted with the permission of the Jakobson Trust.

John of St. Thomas (John Poinsot), excerpts from *Ars Logica*. In *Tractis de Signis: The Semiotic of John Poinsot*. Translated by John Deely. Berkeley: University of California Press, 1985. Copyright © 1985 The

Regents of the University of California. Reprinted with the permission of the University of California Press.

Immanuel Kant, excerpt from *Anthropology from a Pragmatic Point of View*. Translated by V. L. Dowell; edited by H. Rudnick. Carbondale: Southern Illinois University Press, 1978. Reprinted with the permission of the publisher.

David Lewis, excerpts from *Convention*. Cambridge: Harvard University Press, 1969. Reprinted with the permission of Harvard University Press.

Petros Martinidis, excerpt from "Semiotics of Architectural Theories: Toward an Epistemology of Architecture." *Semiotica* 59 (1986). Reprinted with the permission of Mouton de Gruyter and Petros Martinidis.

George Herbert Mead, excerpt from *Mind, Self and Society*. Edited by C. W. Morris. Chicago: University of Chicago Press, 1934. Copyright © 1934 by the University of Chicago Press. Reprinted with the permission of the University of Chicago Press.

Charles Morris, excerpt from *Signs, Language and Behavior*. New York: Braziller, 1946. Copyright © 1955 by Charles Morris. Reprinted by permission of George Braziller, Inc.

C. K. Ogden and I. A. Richards, excerpt from *The Meaning of Meaning* by C. K. Ogden and I. A. Richards, copyright © 1923, reprinted by permission of Harcourt Brace Jovanovich, Inc.

C. E. Osgood, G. Succi, and P. Tannenbaum, excerpts from "The Logic of Semantic Differentiation" from *Psycholinguistics* by Sal Saporta, copyright © 1961 by Holt, Rinehardt and Winston, Inc., reprinted by permission of the publisher.

Charles Peirce, excerpts from *The Collected Papers of Charles Saunders Peirce*. Edited by C. Hartshorne and P. Weiss. Cambridge: Harvard University Press, 1934–1936. Reprinted with the permission of Harvard University Press.

Thomas Reid, excerpt from *An Inquiry into the Human Mind*. Vol. 1 in *Philosophical Works*. Hildesheim: Olms, 1967. Reprinted with the permission of Georg Olms Verlag.

Bertrand Russell, excerpt from *An Inquiry in Meaning and Truth*. London: Allen and Unwin, 1940. Reprinted with the permission of Unwin Hyman Limited.

Ferdinand de Saussure, excerpt from *Course in General Linguistics*. Edited by C. Bally and A. Sechetrans with A. Riedlinger. Translated by W. Baskin. New York: Philosophical Library, 1959. Reprinted with the permission of the Philosophical Library.

Thomas A. Sebeok, excerpt from *Contributions to the Doctrine of*

Signs. Bloomington: Indiana University Press, 1976. Reprinted with the permission of Inner Asian Studies, Indiana University.

Sextus Empiricus, excerpt from *Against the Logicians*. In *Sextus Empiricus*. Translated by R. G. Bury. Vol. 2 in *Sextus Empiricus*, Loeb Classical Library, 1935. Reprinted with the permission of Harvard University Press.

P. F. Strawson, excerpt from *Individuals*. London: Methuen, 1959. Reprinted with the permission of Methuen & Co.

William of Ockham, excerpts reprinted from *Summa Totius Logicae*. In *Ockham: Studies and Selections*, translated by S. Tornay, by permission of The Open Court Publishing Company, La Salle, Illinois. Copyright © by The Open Court Publishing Company, 1938.

SOURCES OF SEMIOTIC

CHAPTER ONE

Introduction

A sign is any object of interpretation, a thing or event that has significance for some interpreter. It can stand for some object for this interpreter, signify an action to be performed, arouse in the interpreter a feeling or emotion, or combine two or more of these functions. Signs include natural events such as as odors or sounds in the environments of lower animals, warning cries used in primitive forms of signaling, diagrams and drawings similar in some respects to what they represent, sentences formed according to the grammatical rules of natural languages, and segments of discourse formed by combining sentences. Semiotic is the general theory that attempts to specify the general logical features of signs and the similarities and differences between the great variety of forms they can take.

I have just stated the broad definition of 'semiotic' found in the writings of Charles Peirce at the end of the nineteenth century and guiding many earlier discussions. But writers on this subject have been far from unanimous in accepting it. Many have been skeptical of attempts to specify features common to all signs, arguing that the differences between the various kinds make any comprehensive generalizations impossible. Those that have continued the study of semiotic have tended to adopt a conception of it very different from that of Peirce and the medieval logical tradition he was continuing. Writers in recent decades have used the terms 'semiology' and 'semiotics' to stand for a descriptive discipline, modeled on linguistics, that includes within its scope language and other forms of human communication, including gestures, dress codes, and artistic forms of expression, but excludes from consideration natural events. Some in this group extend the scope of their study to primitive forms of communication found in animal communities. Many also devote their attention to complex forms of communication, such as literature, music, dance, theatre, film, and architecture, found only in the most developed human societies. Such forms are frequently the objects of interpretive studies emphasizing more personal insights and inventiveness than the kind of objectivity and consensus sought in the empirical sciences.

Contemporary semiotic thus presents us with the task of charting our own course through a maze of divergent approaches. A necessary beginning to undertaking this is a survey of the long historical development of the subject that begins with the Greeks and includes many of the key ideas that mark the transition from one historical period to its successor.

As we survey this history, we are able to distinguish five stages of development: (1) the classical Greek-medieval period in which the distinction between natural and conventional signs is developed; (2) the Renaissance period in which discussions of iconic representations are introduced and the classical conception of a natural sign extended to sensory images; (3) Peirce's development of classifications of signs, incorporating features introduced in the two preceding periods; (4) the development of an empirical program for the study of sign behavior; and (5) the program of European semiology and semiotics. The first three stages occur in historical sequence. The last two mark a divergence within the same historical period of strikingly different approaches to the study of signs. It is the seemingly irresolvable nature of this divergence that is primarily responsible for the uncertain status of semiotic as a part of present-day philosophy.

The Classical Period

The Greeks used the word 'semeion' to stand for a sign, and those who read or interpreted signs were *semeiotikos.* The earliest of these were undoubtedly those who interpreted natural events and states of affairs—the weather, positions of the heavenly bodies, entrails of animals, natural disasters—as portents of the future and the wishes of the gods. A reading of Greek plays reveals how widespread was the practice of relying on soothsayers and omen readers for information about the future and how prominent in society were the *semeiotikos* as the link between the human and the divine. Fortunately for the Greeks and for all mankind to follow, not all were content to rely on this method of securing information. The impetus for an alternative seems to have come initially from the practical need to find cures for diseases. A cure requires correctly diagnosing a disease from observed symptoms, and for this the inductive method of inferring from effects to natural causes on the basis of past experience proved to be a far better guide than the divinations of the early *semeiotikos.* Gradually the interpreter of signs came to be understood by the educated as one who makes causal inferences from observations of natural events based on inductive generalizations from past experience.

The philosophers of the time articulated this understanding. The principal philosophic tradition discussing sign interpretation in the Greek period starts with Aristotle and ends with Sextus Empiricus. For this tradition, the paradigm sign is the medical symptom as an effect from which is inferred a disease as its cause, though the concept of a sign is broadened to include also any event or state of affairs related to another as either its cause or effect. A scar observed in the present could be interpreted as an effect of a past wound that caused it, but a presently observed wound could also be interpreted as a sign of death as an effect that will follow. The *semeiotikos* for this tradition is thus one who makes inferences from observed phenomena either to their natural (not divine) causes that explain them or to predicted effects. On this all agreed. Controversies arose only regarding the form of these inferences, the extent to which inductive methods were to be applied, and the nature of the sign being interpreted.

Though there are some apparent exceptions, Greek philosophers restricted the term 'semeion' to natural events and states of affairs in the environments of their interpreters. Excluded from this heading were linguistic expressions as used in human communication. There is mention of conventional signs as arbitrarily instituted for the purposes of communication, but these are illustrated by examples such as a torch used by a sentinel to signify an approaching enemy or a bell used by a street vendor as a sign that he has meat for sale. For words and sentences, the Greeks used the term 'symbolos', translated as our 'symbol', and seem to have intended the scope of this term to contrast with that of 'semeion'. Semiotic was thus understood as the study of the interpretation of what occurs naturally in the environment. The study of language belonged to the separate disciplines of rhetoric and logic.

This separation from language continued until the time of St. Augustine in the fourth century A.D. With Augustine the term 'signum' is extended to include both natural events and words and sentences as linguistic signs. Natural events having significance for their interpreters are "natural signs" (*signa naturalia*), as contrasted to "conventional signs" (*signa data*), signs "given" or instituted by men for the purposes of communication. This natural-conventional distinction was to be employed thereafter as demarcating these basic categories of signs. While he employed this distinction to incorporate the Greek *semeia* as natural signs, however, Augustine's chief interest was clearly in linguistic signs and the way words function in communication. With this shift of attention, the earlier natural signs were retained principally to mark a contrast with the linguistic.

This preoccupation with language was reflected in an extension of the natural-conventional distinction made first by Augustine and later by William of Ockham. In contrast to the words of a language, which will differ from one linguistic community to another, both thought there were "mental words" or conceptions that occur "naturally" and are shared by all. The words used in speech and writing become, then, conventional signs that are the public expressions of the private mental words as natural signs, the means by which this mental word can be shared with others. Gradually the category of natural signs thus came to be understood as including mental items, culminating finally in eighteenth century philosophers' regarding sensory images as natural "internal" signs of the "external" objects causing them.

Modern Developments

The advent of modern philosophy with Bacon and Descartes brought some reformulations of the basic concepts of the classical philosophers. Frequently cited during this period was the early natural-conventional distinction between the *semeia* of the Greek tradition and words as arbitrarily instituted signs used for communication. Following St. Bonaventure and John of St. Thomas, Arnauld developed the conception of a sign as an iconic representation similar to the object it stands for. Included in these representations were mirror images causally related to objects and maps and pictures produced for the purposes of communication. A significant extension of this conception was made by Berkeley and Reid, who included within the category of natural signs images or "particular ideas" such as immediately experienced sights and sounds. For realists such as Locke and Reid, these images were representations of the external objects to which they were causally related, either as icons similar in some respects to these objects or as indicators of their bare existence. For Berkeley these natural signs had significance only by virtue of their correlation in past experience with other particular ideas. This realism-idealism controversy remained fundamental to philosophy until its assumptions were challenged in the twentieth century.

While such extensions of natural signs were made, the chief focus for Renaissance philosophers and their successors was on signs used for the purposes of human communication. This is reflected in Locke's restricting his discussion of signs to words as the vehicles for conveying ideas. What had been excluded by the Greeks had now become, through the influence of Augustine and later medieval treatises on logic, semiotic's principal domain. During this modern period, however, there was also a recognition by writers such as Reid and the early French anthropologist Joseph Marie de Gérando of nonlinguistic forms of communication such as gestures as a kind of "natural language" by which men, in common with lower animals, can communicate. With Kant, these nonlinguistic forms were extended to include indicators of social rank such as military insignia and family coats of arms. This emphasis on nonverbal devices used in human communication was to lay the groundwork for the later tradition of European semiology.

The end of the nineteenth century thus found philosophers embracing a wide variety of signs, but with the seeds planted for later restrictions.

Included were the natural signs of the Greek period standing in causal relations to those events and states of affairs they were interpreted as signifying. Added to the category of natural signs were also mirror images and sensory images as "private" mental items. Contrasted to these were nonlinguistic communicated signs such as maps, diagrams, and rank indicators, and most importantly words and their combinations.

Peirce's Classifications

It is on this wide variety that Peirce attempted to impose some order by means of his various classification schemes. In the process of constructing them, he introduced the terminology and many of the basic concepts that have guided subsequent developments in semiotic. His central classification of signs into icons, indices, and symbols was intended to incorporate the principal types of signs discussed in the tradition he inherited. For Peirce, *indices* are causal effects of the objects they represent for an interpreter (e.g., a fossil as a sign of past life or a bullet hole as a sign of the bullet causing it); this category thus represented the causal aspect of the Greek natural signs. *Icons* are signs that are similar in some respects to their represented objects, as a map is similar to the country it is interpreted as depicting or a drawing of a man is similar to the man being pictured; icons are thus the signs described in the writings of Arnauld. The third category, *symbols,* includes the conventional signs of the medieval philosophers.

While icon-index-symbol is his basic classification, Peirce constructed a variety of others, of varying degrees of complexity and detail, on the basis of his metaphysical categories: *firstness* (quality), *secondness* (causal interaction), and *thirdness* (mediation or law). These classifications were intended to carry out his project of developing an all-inclusive logical discipline studying the necessary features of signs as objects of interpretation.

But it is clear that Peirce's paradigm signs are sentences, with their constituent subjects and predicates as the primary vehicles of human communication and the elements of inferences used in reasoning from premises to conclusions. Earlier philosophers had placed priority on words (e.g., the noun 'man' or the adjective 'black') as the basic elements of speech and writing. For Peirce (and his contemporary Frege), a word is an incomplete symbol, a "rheme," that must be completed by a subject to convey information. The words 'man' and 'black' are regarded as parts of predicates such as '. . . is a man' and '. . . is black'. They must be complemented by subjects to form sentences such as 'Socrates is a man' or 'This stove is black' to express true or false propositions. His original formulation in his seminal "On a New List of Categories" of the basic features of sign interpretation was intended to be applied to the interpretation of singular sentences. Here the categories are derived from features such as a sentence's predicate expressing a quality, or "ground," and its singular subject referring to a correlated object. It was only later that Peirce derived the categories independently of language on the basis of direct experience through what he called "phenomenology" and extended them to a wider variety of signs through his all-embracing classification schemes.

After Peirce, semiotic was to develop in two very different directions. In the United States, the subject was linked to the attempts of experimental psychologists to find analogies between the learning of lower animals and the acquisition of languages by children. Semiotic came to be defined as the study of the behavioral processes by which all organisms, human and subhuman, learn to react differentially to the stimuli of their environments. In continental Europe, semiotic was given an anthropocentric orientation and restricted to the means by which humans communicate, including the nonverbal devices noted by Kant. It is a tribute to his pioneering work that writers in both traditions continue to appeal to Peirce's classifications and terminology.

Behavioral Semiotic

In the conditioned reflex experiments conducted by Pavlov three elements were distinguished: an unconditioned stimulus (e.g., the sight of food by a dog), a reflex response to this stimulus (e.g., salivation), and a conditioned stimulus (e.g., the sound of a bell) that after a period of trials in which it is paired by the experimenter to the unconditioned stimulus, evokes in isolation the same response originally evoked only by the unconditioned stimulus. Thus, after hearing a bell at the same time food is presented on a number of occasions, a dog reacts to the bell alone by salivating in a way similar to the way it had reacted on seeing the food. In terms of these elements, the sign and its significance were defined by the early advocates of behavioral semiotic. A sign was now understood as the conditioned stimulus (CS) that evokes a response (R) in an organism (the "interpreter") originally evoked by an unconditioned stimulus (US). The "significance" or "meaning" of the sign CS for the interpreter was now defined as this stimulus US. The significance of the bell for the dog is thus food. It is through such a process of habit formation, it was claimed, that natural events in the environment take on significance for all organisms. The natural sign that for the classical tradition had been evidence for inferring a cause or effect now became a physical stimulus evoking a characteristic response.

The extension of this definition to language was made by reasoning that in learning a word the child is confronted in experience with both utterances of the word and some object the word stands for, as a child may hear utterances of the word 'apple' and see an apple being pointed to by an adult teacher. The sight of an apple is also for the child an unconditioned stimulus evoking a reflex response, e.g., salivation, that is later, after linguistic training, evoked by utterances of the word. The "meaning" of the word 'apple' can thus be defined as the visual stimulus of apples that evokes this response.

By incorporating in this way both natural events and linguistic utterances, the proponents of behavioral semiotic maintained the medieval tradition that included within the scope of semiotic natural events and linguistic utterances as signs with significance. The earlier natural-conventional distinction now became a contrast between conditioning in physical and social environments. But while the scope of semiotic may have remained the same, the motivation was now very different from that of the earlier tradition. The behaviorists sought to convert semiotic into an empirical science for which key expressions were given operational definitions in terms of publicly observed stimuli and responses. Excluded were "private" mental items—the concepts, images, and thoughts that were central to the accounts of Augustine and his successors.

Unfortunately for this program, many difficulties were pointed out by its critics. These criticisms led to revised and more sophisticated versions developed by Charles Morris and his successors, that were in turn subject to different criticisms. Finally, Noam Chomsky's attacks on B. F. Skinner's program of extending features of instrumental learning to language acquisition led to the virtual abandonment of a comprehensive behavioral theory encompassing learning in lower animals and human language acquisition. In its place have evolved parallel studies in animal learning by experimental psychology and in human sentential processing by the newly developed field of cognitive science, using models derived from computer science. With this collapse of behavioral semiotic, one kind of attempt to develop the comprehensive theory envisioned by Peirce came to an end.

European Semiology and Semiotics

At about the same time behavioral semiotic was emerging, Ferdinand de Saussure proposed the program of semiology that in various forms has dominated European discussions since. Semiology was modeled by

Saussure after linguistics. It was intended as an extension of this science to include not only human language but all forms of communication used within society, linguistic and nonlinguistic. Just as linguistics isolates phonemes as the sounds that differentially affect meaning, morphemes as those complexes of sounds that are the minimal units of meaning, and rules for combining morphemes to form sentences, so it was thought possible to isolate comparable elements and rules for the variety of codes and other systems by which humans communicate to one another nonlinguistically. The search for such elements and combinatory rules seems to have been initially inspired by Hjelmslev and Uldall's formulation of an abstract scheme for combining sign elements. This abstract scheme was then applied by Roland Barthes to nonlinguistic codes of the kind found in food, clothing, and material possessions as means by which one's social status is conveyed to others, a means of communication similar to that noted earlier by Kant. Natural signs are explicitly excluded from semiology, as are subhuman systems of communication. In place of the behaviorists' comprehensive science of signs interpreted by all forms of organic life there is instead a humanistic study with affinities to linguistics, sociology, and anthropology.

There have been different views of the relationship between language and the nonlinguistic forms of communication studied by semiology. Saussure regarded these forms as parallel to language and thought of semiology as an inclusive science in which linguistics and the study of nonlinguistic communication constituted subdomains. Barthes has subsequently claimed the linguistic to be all-inclusive, arguing that frameworks of discourse provide the background in which nonlinguistic codes have meaning for us. This change of priorities has dramatically altered the nature of semiology, or "semiotics," as it has been more commonly referred to within the past fifteen years. Principally through the influence of the linguist Roman Jakobson, it has gradually come to include within its scope interpretive studies of nonlinguistic codes in literature and art forms such as dance, music, film, and architecture. To interpret a given artistic code is to make explicit the discourse framework providing its context. Rather than the science modeled after linguistics envisioned by Saussure, semiology or semiotics has become, at the hands of practitioners with backgrounds in literature and the arts, the vehicle by which interpretive insights are applied to complex cultural forms.

In the writings of Thomas Sebeok we find the term 'semiotics' also applied to comparative studies of human and subhuman systems of communication, thus continuing a tradition started by Karl Buhler. Such studies show affinities with the earlier behavioral program of Charles Morris, though

sign behavior now becomes behavior of animals in their natural environments of the kind described by ethologists, not the controlled laboratory
behavior studied by Pavlov and Skinner. This application of 'semiotics'
seems to be very different from that given it by those continuing Saussure's
program of describing the combinatory rules governing nonlinguistic communication and those following Jakobson's lead of extending the term to
the interpretation of art forms. The bewildering diversity of contemporary
semiotics is due in large part to the different methodologies presupposed
by these three applications.

Recent Philosophical Developments

With the abandonment of the behavioral program in the United States
and the diversity of approaches included under the umbrella term 'semiotics', the medieval tradition named 'semiotic' by Locke, Peirce, and Morris
finds itself in a very uncertain state. Many of its difficulties stem from the
careless attribution to a primitive level of signs of a property which is
language-specific. Morris, for example, claims that if a buzzer that signifies
food for a dog is sounded and the dog manages to find food, the buzzer
can be said to be "true." 'Truth' and 'falsity', however, are normative terms
that imply conformity to conventional rules governing expressions, and
their extension to nonconventional signs seems illegitimate. Faced with
such loose comparisons, some have denied the possibility of a comprehensive theory of the kind Peirce claimed semiotic to be, arguing that natural
signs, iconic representations, and sentences have such different features
and uses that it is impossible to draw any significant analogies between
them.

Such pessimism is unwarranted in my view. The remedy for semiotic's
ills is to specify more carefully the similarities and differences between the
different levels and types of signs than previously. The paradigm sign is
the sentence, which on a given occasion has both meaning and reference
for an interpreter. Semiotic should proceed by analogically extending the
basic features of meaning and reference from these conventional signs
formed according to linguistic rules to nonconventional signs, such as
gestures and drawings, and finally to natural signs, such as lightning as a
sign of thunder. This extension is made by abstracting from the linguistic
level those features unique to it. The nature of this study is logical in the
broad sense of 'logic' applied by philosophers to the study of fundamental
features of language use, as contrasted to a sense restricted to the evaluation of deductive inferences or investigations of formal semantics. A logical
study of comparative features of signs requires an understanding of the

communicative intent that serves to demarcate the level of communicated signs from natural signs, the nature of the conventional rules that distinguish spoken languages from the "natural language" of gestures, the unique referring role of a sentence's subject in comparison to more primitive forms of reference, and the special features of iconic representation. In the final chapter are some writings by recent philosophers that make some progress toward this kind of understanding.

The selections and commentary in the five chapters that precede these recent philosophic contributions are designed to trace semiotic's development and its principal conceptual and methodological issues. Many of these issues remain to be clarified and resolved before the subject can gain the central position in philosophy to which it was assigned by Peirce.

CHAPTER TWO

The Greek-Medieval Period

2.1 Aristotle's Conception of a Sign

In the writings of Aristotle we find explicitly stated for the first time the conception of a sign as an observed event or state of affairs that is evidence for its interpreter for what is at least temporarily absent. There are anticipations of this conception in the writings of pre-Socratic philosophers such as Heracleitus and Parmenides that indicate that the term 'semeion' was used in the sense of "evidence" ('tekmerion') long before Aristotle. There is also the following passage from the writings of Hippocrates in the fifth century B.C. that explains why many of Aristotle's examples of signs were later symptoms from which diseases were to be diagnosed. As this passage makes clear, at this early stage the ability to interpret a sign as symptom is valued primarily for the practical benefits accruing to the physician as interpreter.

2.1.1 Hippocrates[1]

I hold that it is an excellent thing for a physician to practise forecasting. For if he discover and declare unaided by the side of his patients the present, the past and the future, and fill in the gaps in the account given by the sick, he will be the more believed to understand the cases, so that men will confidently entrust themselves to him for treatment. Furthermore, he will carry out the treatment best if he know beforehand from the present symptoms what will take place later. Now to restore every patient to health is impossible. To do so indeed would have been better even than forecasting the future. But as a matter of fact men do die, some owing to the severity of the disease before they summon the physician, others expiring immediately after calling him in—living one day or a little longer—before the physician by his art can combat each disease. It is necessary, therefore, to learn the natures of such diseases, how much they exceed the strength of men's bodies, and to learn how to forecast them. For in this way you will justly win respect and be an able physician. For the longer time you plan to meet each emergency the greater your

---

1. The selection that follows is *Prognostic* (c. 400 B.C.), secs. I and II, in *Hippocrates*, trans. W. H. S. Jones, Loeb Library (Cambridge: Harvard University Press, 1923), vol. 2.

power to save those who have a chance of recovery, while you will be blameless if you learn and declare beforehand those who will die and those who will get better.

In acute diseases the physician must conduct his inquiries in the following way. First he must examine the face of the patient, and see whether it is like the faces of healthy people, and especially whether it is like its usual self. Such likeness will be the best sign, and the greatest unlikeness will be the most dangerous sign. The latter will be as follows. Nose sharp, eyes hollow, temples sunken, ears cold and contracted with their lobes turned outwards, the skin about the face hard and tense and parched, the colour of the face as a whole being yellow or black. If at the beginning of the disease the face be like this, and if it be not yet possible with the other symptoms to make a complete prognosis, you must go on to inquire whether the patient has been sleepless, whether his bowels have been very loose, and whether he suffers at all from hunger. And if anything of the kind be confessed, you must consider the danger to be less. The crisis comes after a day and a night if through these causes the face has such an appearance. But should no such confession be made, and should a recovery not take place within this period, know that it is a sign [*semeion*] of death. If the disease be of longer standing than three days when the face has these characteristics, go on to make the same inquiries as I ordered in the previous case, and also examine the other symptoms, both of the body generally and those of the eyes. For if they shun the light, or weep involuntarily, or are distorted, or if one becomes less than the other, if the whites be red or livid or have black veins in them, should rheum appear around the eyeballs, should they be restless or protruding or very sunken, or if the complexion of the whole face be changed—all these symptoms must be considered bad, in fact fatal. You must also examine the partial appearance of the eyes in sleep. For if a part of the white appear when the lids are closed, should the cause not be diarrhoea or purging, or should the patient not be in the habit of so sleeping, it is an unfavorable, in fact a very deadly symptom. But if, along with one of the other symptoms, eyelid, lip of nose be bent or livid, you must know that death is close at hand. It is also a deadly sign when the lips are loose, hanging, cold and very white.

Notice that Hippocrates regards symptoms as the basis for an inference to what is in the past, present, or future. The eventual Greek conception was that of a sign as either an effect of a past or contemporaneous cause or a cause of some predicted future effect. This conception was also extended from medical diagnosis and prediction to any natural event that was either a cause or effect from which an inference could be made.

With Aristotle is introduced the distinction between a sign as a necessary indication of what it signifies and a sign as only a probable indication. The context for this distinction is his discussion of inferences called "enthymemes" that lack the demonstrative certainty of the syllogism because of missing information in the premisses. A sign is for Aristotle a fact or state of affairs described by a premiss in such an inference. The following passage from the *Rhetoric* states this conception of a sign.

2.1.2 Aristotle (1)[2]

Now the materials of Enthymemes are Probabilities and Signs [*semeia*], which we can see must correspond respectively with the propositions that are generally and those that are necessarily true. A Probability is a thing that usually happens; not, however, as some definitions would suggest, anything whatever that usually happens, but only if it belongs to the class of the "contingent" or "variable." It bears the same relation to that in respect of which it is probable as the universal bears to the particular. Of Sign, one kind bears the same relation to the statement it supports as the particular bears to the universal, the other the same as the universal bears to the particular. The infallible kind is a "complete proof"; the fallible kind has no specific name. By infallible signs I mean those on which syllogisms proper may be based: and this shows us why this kind of Sign is called "complete proof": when people think that what they have said cannot be refuted, they then think that they are bringing forward a "complete Proof," meaning that the matter has now been demonstrated and completed; for the word *peras* has the same meaning (of 'end' or 'boundary') as the word *tekmar* in the ancient tongue. Now the one kind of Sign (that which bears to the proposition it supports the relation of particular to universal) may be illustrated thus. Suppose it were said, 'The fact that Socrates was wise and just is a sign that the wise are just'. Here we certainly have a Sign; but even though the proposition be true, the argument is refutable, since it does not form a syllogism. Suppose, on the other hand, it were said, 'The fact that he has a fever is a sign that he is ill', or, 'The fact that she is giving milk is a sign that she has lately borne a child'. Here we have the infallible kind of Sign, the only kind that constitutes a complete proof, since it is the only kind that, if the particular statement

2. *Rhetorica* (c. 320 b.c.), 1357b18, trans. W. Rhys Roberts, in *The Basic Works of Aristotle,* ed. R. McKeon (New York: Random House, 1941).

is true, is irrefutable. The other kind of Sign, that which bears to the proposition it supports the relation of universal to particular, might be illustrated by saying, 'The fact that he breathes fast is a sign that he has a fever'. This argument also is refutable, even if the statement about the fast breathing be true, since a man may breathe hard without having a fever.

This conception of a sign as a fact described by a premiss that could either be an "infallible" sign providing "complete proof" of the fact described by a conclusion or a fact described within a "refutable argument" was to influence all discussions by later Greek philosophers. The extent of this influence is shown by a section entitled "On Indications as Proofs" in the *Institutio Oratoria* by the Roman writer Quintilian much later in the first century A.D. Here he restates the three temporal directions of Hippocrates, Aristotle's necessary-probable distinction, and links the sign to an inferential proof of a conclusion.

2.1.3 Quintilian[3]

"Artificial" proof (proof by art) uses indications [*signa*] or arguments [*argumenta*] or examples [*exempla*]; thought indications as a rule belong to inartificial proofs (proofs without art, as a bloodstained garment or a shriek), quite analogous to documentary or oral evidence; for indications, if undoubted, leave no room for argument. The first two species of artificial proofs are those which have a necessary conclusion, and those which do not, but when the facts cannot be denied, there is no debate. The cause of a woman's child is intercourse, a matter of the past; high waves at sea are the result of wind, a matter of the future. None of these admits of debate. Some types of proof can be reversed and give the same meaning, some cannot. Other indications are only probabilities. *Signum* (sign) is also called *indicium* (suggestion) or *vestigium* (trace), and means that which helps us to infer what happened: blood suggests murder, though it might come from slaughtered animals or from nose-bleed. One indication may create suspicion; several may amount to substantial evidence tending toward certainty. Some indications serve either side, useful according to extraneous support.

Among the *signa* which are only probable Hermagoras would include

3. *Institutio Oratoria* (c. A.D. 95), bk. V, ch. IX, trans. C. Little, in *The Institutio Oratoria of Marcus Fabius Quintiliamus* (Nashville: George Peabody College for Teachers, 1951), vol. 1.

cases like this: "Atlanta cannot be a virgin as she has roamed the woods with young men." The Areopagites condemned a boy for plucking out the eyes of quails, as it indicated perverted character; and the popularity of Maelius and Manlius was held against them. This reasoning may lead us too far: lively women might thus be considered wicked, all foppish men as immoral. Signs of the weather are included, like Vergil's sign of the moon for wind and the croaking crow for rain. Vergil also infers that the atmosphere causes "that concert of bird-voices."

The examples Aristotle had earlier given of signs—a fever as a sign of illness, giving milk as a sign of having born a child, fast breathing as a sign of fever—clearly indicate that he intended them to be states of affairs or events occurring naturally, independently of human control. They do not include verbal utterances or written inscriptions, what he refers to by the term 'symbola', used in human communication.

This separation between signs and symbols was to continue throughout the Greek period. In a passage in his *De Interpretatione*, however, Aristotle seems to use the terms 'symbola' and 'semeia' interchangeably. As part of logical writings that were to be the subject of extensive commentaries in the Middle Ages, this passage was to have an important later influence.

2.1.4 Aristotle (2)[4]

Spoken expressions are symbols [*symbola*] of mental impressions, and written expressions [are symbols] of spoken expressions. And just as not all men have the same writing, so not all men make the same vocal sounds, but the things of which [all] these are primarily the signs [*semeia*] are the same mental impressions for all men, and the things of which these [mental impressions] are likenesses are ultimately the same. These have been discussed in my treatise *On the Soul*, for they belong to a different discipline.

2.2 Two Controversies

Semiotic in the Greek period following Aristotle was to be dominated by two controversies. The first, between the Stoics and Epicureans, was

4. *De Interpretatione* (c. 320 B.C.), 16a1–7, trans. H. G. Apostle, in *Aristotle's Categories and Propositions* (Grinnell: Peripatetic Press, 1980). The brackets of English expression are Apostle's; those of Greek, mine.

centered on the nature of the sign itself. The Stoics, aware of Aristotle's treatment of the sign as that from which an absent cause or effect is inferred, concluded that a sign is a proposition (*lekton*) or "expression" as the singular premiss of an inference. As such it is an intelligible conception, what is expressed by sentences such as 'It is day' or 'This man has had a viscid bronchial discharge'. These sentences occur as the antecedents of hypotheticals such as 'If it is day, it is light' and 'If this man has had a viscid bronchial discharge, he has a wound in his lungs'. When the antecedent is known to be true, the consequent is inferred by the rule of modus ponens. The form of inference is thus: A; if A then B; therefore, B. In this inference form, A is the sign and B what it signifies.

The Epicureans, in contrast, held that only sensible particulars exist and that the Stoics' propositions were fictions. The sign in their view is what can be directly experienced, and it is on the basis of direct experiences that it is interpreted. On the Stoic view, only those capable of formulating inferences and reasoning from premisses can interpret signs. The Epicureans argued that the illiterate seaman can interpret the squall he sees as a sign of an impending storm and that even a dog can interpret tracks as a sign of the animal he is tracking.

The second controversy was between the skeptics represented by Sextus Empiricus and the speculative (for the skeptics, the "dogmatic") school of medicine. The speculative school contended that it was permissible to infer from an "indicative sign" that was directly perceived to what was impossible to perceive, or what was "nonevident." As an example, there was the inference by some that sweating indicates the existence of tiny invisible pores in the skin. To see a person sweating is to infer, if one holds this theory, the invisible pores. The opposing view of narrow empiricism held that the only justifiable inference is from a perceived sign to that with which it has been correlated in past experience, as smoke is correlated with fire. These signs, related to what they signify by induction, were "commemorative" or "associative" signs. The skeptics argued that a sign should be interpreted in the same way by all. But for the indicative signs there are many competing theories about what they signify. Agreement could be reached, however, for the associative signs, and these alone should therefore be accorded the status of signs.

The passage from the writings of Sextus that follows is perhaps the best extended record we have of the classical conception of a sign. In it the Stoic-Epicurean controversy can be easily identified, and Sextus makes clear his rejection of the Stoic view. His argument against it includes a sophisticated anticipation of the modern conception of material implication as a proposition that is false only if the antecedent is true and the conclusion false. Sextus uses this to argue against the Stoic conception of a sign as the antecedent in a "valid hypothetical major premiss." Both a sign and what it signifies must be true, he argues, while a true hypothetical may have a false antecedent with either a true or a false consequent. Sextus's rejection of indicative signs as the bases of speculative inferences to hidden causes occurs in the first two paragraphs, though not in obvious form, and is returned to in the final paragraph. It is stated in the guise of the rejection of the view that signs are sensible particulars. What Sextus seems to be rejecting, however, is only the existence of indicative signs as such particulars. He does not question the existence of associative (or commemorative) signs from which inferences are made on the basis of prior inductions, for agreement can be reached for such inferences.

2.2.1 Sextus Empiricus[5]

But now, to sum up: If we claim that the sign is sensible, it must first of all be agreed and firmly established that sensibles have substantial existence, in order that it may be granted that the sign also is definitely apprehensible; or else, if it is the case that their existence has been quarrelled over eternally, we shall have to admit that the sign also partakes of the same controversial character. For just as white colour cannot be apprehended securely if the substantial existence of sensibles be not admitted, because it is itself one of the sensibles, so neither can the sign— if it belongs to the class of sensibles—be said to have stable existence so long as the conflict regarding sensibles continues. Let us suppose now that there is unanimity about sensibles and that there exists no dispute whatsoever regarding them. How, I ask, can our opponents show us that the sign is in reality sensible? For every sensible thing ought naturally to present itself alike to all who are in a like condition and be similarly apprehended. Take white colour, for instance: it is not apprehended in one way by Greeks, in another by barbarians; or in a special way by craftsmen and differently by ordinary folk; but in one and the same way by all those who have their senses unimpeded. Bitter and sweet, again, are not tasted in this way by this man and in a different way by that man, but similarly by each of those who are in a similar condition. But the sign, as sign, does not seem to affect in the same way all those who are in a similar condition; but to some it is not a sign of anything at all, although it presents itself to them plainly, while to some it is a sign, yet not of the

5. *Against the Logicians* (c. A.D. 200), II, 186–194, 244–274, in *Sextus Empiricus*, trans. R. G. Bury, Loeb Library (Cambridge: Harvard University Press, 1935), vol. 2.

same thing but of something different; thus in medicine, for instance, the same appearances are signs of one thing to this man (such as Erasistratus), but of another to that man (say, Herophilus), and of another to a third (such as Asclepiades). We must not, then, say that the sign is sensible; for if the sensible affects all similarly, but the sign does not affect all similarly, the sign will not be sensible.—Again, if the sign is sensible, it ought to follow that, just as fire, which is sensible, burns all those capable of being burnt, and snow, being sensible, chills all those capable of being chilled, so also the sign, if it belongs to the sensibles, leads all to the same signified thing. But, in fact, it does not so lead them; therefore it is not sensible.—Furthermore, if the sign is sensible, the things non-evident are either apprehensible by us or non-apprehensible. If, then, they are non-apprehensible by us, the sign disappears; for things being of two kinds, some evident, others non-evident, if neither the evident thing possesses a sign owing to its being self-revealed, nor the non-evident things because they are non-apprehensible, there is no sign. But if the non-evident things are apprehensible, it ought to follow again that, since the sign is sensible and the sensible affects all men alike, the things non-evident are apprehended by all. But some—like the Empirical doctors and the Sceptic philosophers—assert that they are not apprehended, and others that they are apprehended but not equally. The sign, therefore, is not sensible.

"Yes," they reply, "but just as fire, being sensible, exhibits different potencies owing to differences in the material subjected to it, and when applied to wax melts it, to clay hardens it, to wood burns it; so likewise it is probable that the sign also, being sensible, should serve to indicate different things according to the differences in those who apprehend it. Nor is this paradoxical, since this is also seen to happen even in the case of commemorative signs; for the raising high of a torch signifies to some the approach of enemies, but to others indicates the arrival of friends; and the sound of a bell is to some a sign of the selling of meat, but to others of the need for watering the roads. Therefore the indicative sign also, having a sensible nature, will be capable of revealing things of different sorts."—But here, too, one might require those who make use of the inference from fire to prove that what happens to take place in the case of fire takes place also in the case of the sign.

. . . .

In reply, then, to those who maintain that the sign is sensible let this much be said by way of objection; but let us also examine the view opposed to theirs—I mean that of those who conceive it to be intelligible. But perhaps it will be proper for us first to deal shortly with the view they accept, according to which the sign is, they maintain, a proposition, and on this account an intelligible. Thus, in describing it, they say that "The Sign is an antecedent proposition in a valid hypothetical major premiss, which serves to reveal the consequent." And while there are, they say, many other tests of such a valid major, there is one above all—and even it not be agreed upon—which shall be described. Every hypothetical major either begins with truth and ends in truth, or begins with falsehood and ends in falsehood, or proceeds from truth to falsehood or from falsehood to truth. The premiss 'If there are gods, the world is ordered by the gods' providence' begins with truth and ends in truth; and 'If the earth flies, the earth has wings' proceeds from falsehood to falsehood; and 'If the earth flies, the earth exists' from falsehood to truth; and 'If this man moves, this man walks' from truth to falsehood, when he is not walking but is moving. As, then, there are four combinations of the major premiss—when it begins with truth and ends in truth, or when it proceeds from falsehood to falsehood, or when it proceeds from falsehood to truth, or conversely from truth to falsehood,—in the first three modes the premiss, they say, is true (for if it begins with truth and ends in truth it is true, and if it begins with falsehood and ends in falsehood it is again true, and so likewise when it passes from falsehood to truth); and in one mode only is it false, namely, when it begins with truth and ends in falsehood. And this being so, one should not look, they say, for the sign in this unsound major premiss but in the sound one; for it is called "a proposition which is the antecedent in a valid major premiss." But since there is not one valid major but three—namely, that which begins with truth and ends with truth, and that which proceeds from falsehood to falsehood, and that which proceeds from falsehood to truth—one has to inquire whether possibly the sign should be sought in all the valid premisses, or in some, or in one. So then, if the sign must be true and indicative of truth, it will not reside either in that which begins with falsehood and ends in falsehood or in that which passes from falsehood to truth. Thus it only remains for it to exist in that which both begins with truth and ends in truth, since it really exists itself and the thing signified also must co-exist with it. So then, when the sign is said to be "a proposition which is the antecedent in a valid major premiss," one shall have to understand that it is an antecedent in that valid major only which begins with truth and ends in truth. Moreover, not every proposition which is an antecedent in a valid major beginning with truth and ending in truth is a sign. Such a major premiss as this, for instance—'If it is day, it is light'—begins with the truth 'It is day' and ends in the truth 'It is light', but it does not contain any antecedent proposition which is a sign of the consequent; for 'It is day' does not serve to reveal that 'It is light'; for just as the latter truth was perceived by means of itself, so also 'It is light' was comprehended owing to its own obviousness. The sign, therefore, must not only be the antecedent in a valid major premiss—that is, in one that begins with truth and ends in truth—but must also possess a character which serves to reveal the consequent; as, for example, the antecedent in premisses such as these—'If this woman has milk in her breasts, she has conceived'; and 'If this man has had a viscid bronchial discharge, he has a wound in his lungs'. For this premiss is valid, as it begins with the truth 'This man has had a viscid bronchial discharge', and ends in the truth 'He has a wound in his lungs'; and, besides, the first serves to reveal the second; for by observing the former we come to an apprehension of the latter.

Further, they say, the sign must be a present sign of a present thing. For some people erroneously claim that a present thing may also be a sign of a past thing, as in the case of 'If this man has a scar, he has had a wound' (for if he has a scar it is present, for it is apparent, but his having had a wound is past, for there is no longer a wound), and that a present thing may be the sign of a future thing, as for instance that included in such a premiss as this—'If this man is wounded in the heart, he will die', for they say that the wound in the heart exists already, but death is in the future. But those who make such statements are ignorant of the fact that though things past and things future are different, yet even in these cases the sign is a present sign of a present thing. For in the former premiss— 'If this man has a scar, he has had a wound'—the wound has existed already and is past, but the statement that this man has had a wound, which is a proposition, is present, being stated about a thing which has existed. And in the premiss 'If the man is wounded in the heart, he will die', his death is in the future, but the proposition 'He will die' is present, though a statement about the future, inasmuch as it is true even now. So that the sign is a proposition, and also it is the antecedent in a valid major premiss which begins with truth and ends in truth, and it serves to reveal the consequent, and always it is a present sign of a present thing.

Now that these things have been explained according to their own rules of logic, it is proper to reply to them, first, in this wise: If the sign is sensible according to some, but intelligible according to others, and the dispute on this point is undecided up till now, we must declare that the sign is as yet non-evident. And being non-evident, it needs things to reveal it and ought not to be capable itself of revealing other things.—Moreover, if the sign is, according to them, classed, as to its "substance," under the head of "expression," and if the existence of "expressions" is a matter of inquiry, it is absurd to take the particular as securely fixed before the genus is agreed upon. And we see that there are some who have denied the real existence of "expressions," and these not only men of other Schools, such as the Epicureans, but even Stoics like Basileides who held that nothing incorporeal exists. So, then, we must preserve suspension of judgement regarding Sign. But, say they, when we have first proved the real existence of "expressions" we shall have the reality of the sign also securely established. "Yes," one will reply, "when you have proved it, then assume also that the existence of the sign is to be believed; but so long as you remain merely promising, we too must necessarily remain in an attitude of suspension." And further, how is it possible to prove the existence of "expressions"? For one will have to do this either by means of a sign or by proof. But neither by means of a sign nor by proof is it possible to do this; for these, being themselves "expressions," are matters of inquiry like the other "expressions," and are so far from being capable of establishing anything firmly that, on the contrary, they themselves require something to establish them. The Stoics, too, have unwittingly fallen into the fallacy of circular reasoning. For in order that "expressions" may be agreed to, proof and sign must exist; and in order that proof and sign may really pre-exist, the reality of "expressions" must be previously confirmed. As these lean, then, on one another and await confirmation from one another, they are equally untrustworthy.

But let it be supposed and gratuitously conceded, for the sake of advancing our inquiry, that "expressions" are in existence, although the battle regarding them remains unending. If, then, they exist, the Stoics will declare that they are either corporeal or incorporeal. Now they will not say that they are corporeal; and if they are incorporeal, either— according to them—they effect something, or they effect nothing. Now they will not claim that they effect anything; for, according to them, the incorporeal is not of a nature either to effect anything or to be affected. And since they effect nothing, they will not even indicate and make evident the thing of which they are signs; for to indicate anything and make it evident is to effect something. But it is absurd that the sign should neither indicate nor make evident anything; therefore the sign is not an intelligible thing, nor yet a proposition.

Moreover, as we have frequently shown in many places, some things signify, others are signified. Vocal sounds signify, but "expressions" are signified, and they include also propositions. And as propositions are signified, but not signifying, the sign will not be a proposition.

Again, let it be conceded that "expressions" are of an incorporeal nature. Yet, since they assert that the sign is the antecedent in a valid major premiss, the valid major will have to be tested and scrutinized beforehand, whether it be what is valid according to Philo, or according to Diodorus, or through congruence, or judged by some other criterion; for since on this point also there are many rival views it is impossible to have a firm grasp of the sign so long as the dispute remains unsettled.

Further, in addition to the foregoing arguments, even if we grant that the valid criterion is agreed upon and that it is incontestably of the kind the Stoics claim, none the less they must necessarily agree that the premiss containing the sign is uncertain. For they hold that the thing signified is either pre-evident or non-evident. And if it is pre-evident, it will not admit of being signified, nor will be perceived of itself; while if it is non-evident, it certainly cannot be known whether it is true or false, since when it is known which of these it is it will become pre-evident. The premiss, then, which contains the sign and the thing signified, as it ends in what is non-evident, is of necessity uncertain. For that it begins with truth is known, but it ends in the unknown. But in order to pass judgement upon it we must first of all learn wherein it ends, so that if it ends in truth we may pronounce it true because it begins with truth and ends in truth, but if it ends in falsehood, we may, contrariwise, declare it to be false because it begins with truth and ends in falsehood. So then, the sign should not be said to be a proposition, or an antecedent in a sound premiss.

To these objections it should be added that those who champion this opinion are in conflict with evident facts. For if the sign is a judgement and an antecedent in a valid major premiss, those who have no conception at all of a judgement, and have made no study of logical technicalities, ought to have been wholly incapable of interpreting by signs. But this is not the case; for often illiterate pilots, and often farmers unskilled in logical theorems, interpret by signs excellently—the former of the sea prognosticating squalls and calms, stormy weather and fair, and the latter on the farm foretelling good crops and bad crops, droughts and rainfalls. Yet why do we talk of men, when some of the Stoics have endowed even irrational animals with understanding of the sign? For, in fact, the dog, when he tracks a beast by its footprints, is interpreting by signs; but he does not therefore derive an impression of the judgement 'If this is a footprints, a beast is here'. The horse, too, at the prod of a goad or the crack of a whip leaps forward and starts to run, but he does not frame a judgement logically in a premiss such as this—'If a whip has cracked, I must run'. Therefore the sign is not a judgement, which is the antecedent in a valid major premiss.

Let these special arguments be stated against those who hold that the sign is intelligible; but it will be possible also to use against them the general arguments we have brought against those who assert that it is sensible. For if the sign is an antecedent proposition in a valid major premiss, and in every major the consequent follows the antecedent, and these connexions are between things present, then the sign and the thing signified, both being present at one and the same time, will necessarily co-exist and neither of them will serve to disclose the other, but both will be known of themselves.

Further, the sign serves to reveal the thing signified, and the thing signified is revealed by the sign. And these are not absolute things but relative; for the thing revealed is conceived in relation to that which is reveals, and that which reveals is conceived in relation to that which is revealed. But if both, being relative things, are present at the same time, both co-exist; and if they co-exist, each of them is apprehensible of itself and neither of them through the other.—This, too, may be said: Whatever be the character of the sign, either it is itself of such a nature as to indicate and disclose the non-evident, or we are capable or remembering the things laid bare together with it. But it does not possess a nature capable of indicating non-evident things, since, if so, it ought to indicate non-evident things to all men equally. Therefore it depends upon the state of our memory what view we take about the real nature of things.

2.3 St. Augustine

To St. Augustine we owe an important change in the conception of a sign. The term 'signum' as the Latin translation of 'semeion' came to take on in his writings a generic sense that includes both the evidential signs of the Greeks and words as linguistic signs used in communication. There are for Augustine two kinds of signs. Natural signs (*signa naturalia*) are those that "without any desire or intention of signifying, make us aware of something beyond themselves, like smoke which signifies fire." Included within this class are facial expressions signifying unseen emotions. Linguistic signs, in contrast, are included within the category of conventional signs (*signa data*), signs that are "given" or arbitrarily introduced for the purposes of communication. In the passage that follows, Augustine characterizes them as signs "which living creatures show to one another for the purpose of conveying, in so far as they are able, the motions of their spirits or something which they have sensed or understood." Augustine notes communication between animals, but whether animal signals such as mating calls "express the motion of the spirit without intention" and hence are not genuine signs is left an open question.

2.3.1 St. Augustine (1)[6]

I

Just as I began, when I was writing about things, by warning that no one should consider them except as they are, without reference to what they signify beyond themselves, now when I am discussing signs I wish it understood that no one should consider them for what they are but rather for their value as signs which signify something else. A sign is a thing which causes us to think of something beyond the impression the thing itself makes upon the senses. Thus if we see a track, we think of the animal that made the track; if we see smoke, we know that there is a fire which causes it; if we hear the voice of a living being, we attend to the emotion it expresses; and when a trumpet sounds, a soldier should know whether it is necessary to advance or to retreat, or whether the battle demands some other response.

Among signs, some are natural and others are conventional. Those are natural which, without any desire or intention of signifying, make us aware of something beyond themselves, like smoke which signifies fire. It does this without any will to signify, for even when smoke appears alone, observation and memory of experience with things bring a recognition of an underlying fire. The track of a passing animal belongs to this class, and the face of one who is wrathful or sad signifies his emotion even when he does not wish to show that he is wrathful or sad, just as other emotions are signified by the expression even when we do not deliberately set out to show them. But it is not proposed here to discuss signs of this type. Since the class formed a division of my subject, I could not disregard it completely, and this notice of it will suffice.

II

Conventional signs are those which living creatures show to one another for the purpose of conveying, in so far as they are able, the motion of their spirits or something which they have sensed or understood. Nor is there any other reason for signifying, or for giving signs, except for bringing forth and transferring to another mind the action of the mind in the person who makes the sign. We propose to consider and to discuss this class of signs in so far as men are concerned with it, for even signs given by God and contained in the Holy Scriptures are of this type also,

6. *On Christian Doctrine* (c. 427), bk. II, trans. D. W. Robertson, Jr. (New York: Macmillan, 1986).

since they were presented to us by the men who wrote them. Animals also have signs which they use among themselves, by means of which they indicate their appetites. For a cock who finds food makes a sign with his voice to the hen so that she runs to him. And the dove calls his mate with a cry or is called by her in turn, and there are many similar examples which may be adduced. Whether these signs, or the expression or cry of a man in pain, express the motion of the spirit without intention of signifying or are truly shown as signs is not in question here and does not pertain to our discussion, and we remove this division of the subject from this work as superfluous.

III

Among the signs by means of which men express their meanings to one another, some pertain to the sense of sight, more to the sense of hearing, and very few to the other senses. For when we nod, we give a sign only to the sight of the person whom we wish by that sign to make a participant in our will. Some signify many things through the motions of their hands, and actors give signs to those who understand with the motions of all their members as if narrating things to their eyes. And banners and military standards visibly indicate the will of the captains. And all of these things are like so many visible words. More signs, as I have said, pertain to the ears, and most of these consist of words. But the trumpet, the flute, and the harp make sounds which are not only pleasing but also significant, although as compared with the number of verbal signs the number of signs of this kind are few. For words have come to be predominant among men for signifying whatever the mind conceives if they wish to communicate it to anyone. However, Our Lord gave a sign with the odor of the ointment with which His feet were anointed; and the taste of the sacrament of His body and blood signified what He wished; and when the woman was healed by touching the hem of His garment, something was signified. Nevertheless, a multitude of innumerable signs by means of which men express their thoughts is made up of words. And I could express the meaning of all signs of the type here touched upon in words, but I would not be able at all to make the meanings of words clear by these signs.

IV

But because vibrations in the air soon pass away and remain no longer that they sound, signs of words have been constructed by means of letters. Thus words are shown to the eyes, not in themselves but through certain signs which stand for them. These signs could not be common to all peoples because of the sin of human dissension which arises when one people seizes the leadership for itself. A sign of this pride is that tower erected in the heavens where impious men deserved that not only their minds but also their voices should be dissonant.

Besides formulating this generic sense of 'signum', Augustine formulated a distinction that was to have in conjunction with a similar distinction of Aristotle's (cf. 2.1.4) a profound impact on later medieval and early Renaissance philosophers. This was the distinction between an internal private mental word, a word originating in a person's mind, and a public word as a *signum datum*. The private mental word is common to all men; the public word, in contrast, is formulated within a specific language and used in communication to convey this mental word from one mind to another. In the following passage, Augustine is concerned with the problem of distinguishing the mental word of a person from the eternal Word that is in God's mind.

2.3.2 St. Augustine (2)[7]

Whoever, then, is able to understand a word, not only before it is uttered in sound, but also before the images of its sounds are considered in thought—for this it is which belongs to no tongue, to wit, of those which are called the tongues of nations, of which our Latin tongue is one—whoever, I say, is able to understand this, is able now to see through this glass and in this enigma some likeness of that Word of whom it is said, "In the beginning was the Word, and the Word was with God, and the Word was God." For of necessity, when we speak what is true, i.e. speak what we know, there is born from the knowledge itself which the memory retains, a word that is altogether of the same kind with that knowledge from which it is born. For the thought that is formed by the thing which we know, is the word which we speak in the heart: which word is neither Greek nor Latin, nor of any other tongue. But when it is needful to convey this to the knowledge of those to whom we speak, then some sign is assumed whereby to signify it. And generally a sound, sometimes a nod, is exhibited, the former to the ears, the latter to the eyes, that the word which we bear in our mind may become known also by bodily signs to the bodily senses. For what is to nod or beckon, except to speak in some way to the sight? And Holy Scripture gives its testimony

---

7. *On the Trinity*, bk. XV, 10, 15, trans. A. W. Haddan, in *Basic Writings of Saint Augustine*, ed. W. J. Oates (New York: Random House, 1948), vol. 2.

to this; for we read in the *Gospel according to John:* "Verily, verily, I say
unto you, that one of you shall betray me. Then the disciples looked one
upon another, doubting of whom He spake. Now there was leaning on
Jesus' breast one of His disciples whom Jesus loved. Simon Peter therefore
beckons to him, and says to him, Who is it of whom He speaks?" Here
he spoke by beckoning what he did not venture to speak by sounds. But
whereas we exhibit these and the like bodily signs either to ears or eyes
of persons present to whom we speak, letters have been invented that we
might be able to converse also with the absent; but these are signs of
words, as words themselves are signs in our conversation of those things
which we think.

· ·

And hence it comes to pass, that if there can be in the mind any
knowledge that is eternal, while the thought of that knowledge cannot be
eternal, and any inner and true word of ours is only said by our thought,
then God alone can be understood to have a Word that is eternal, and co-
eternal with Himself. Unless, perhaps, we are to say that the very possibility of thought—since that which is known is capable of being truly
thought, even at the time when it is not being thought—constitutes a
word as perpetual as the knowledge itself is perpetual. But how is that a
word which is not yet formed in the vision of the thought? How will it be
like the knowledge of which it is born, if it has not the form of that
knowledge, and is only now called a word because it can have it? For it
is much as if one were to say that a word is to be so called because it can
be a word. But what is this that can be a word, and is therefore already
held worthy of the name of a word? What, I say, is this thing that is
formable, but not yet formed, except a something in our mind, which we
toss to and fro by revolving it this way or that, while we think of first one
thing and then another, according as they are found by or occur to us?
And the true word then comes into being, when, as I said, that which we
toss to and fro by revolving it arrives at that which we know, and is formed
by that, in taking its entire likeness; so that in what manner each thing
is known, in that manner also it is thought, i.e. is said in this manner in
the heart, without articulate sound, without thought of articulate sound,
such as no doubt belongs to some particular tongue. And hence if we
even admit, in order not to dispute laboriously about a name, that this
something of our mind, which can be formed from our knowledge, is to
be already called a word, even before it is so formed, because it is, so to say,
already formable, who would not see how great would be the unlikeness
between it and that Word of God, which is so in the form of God, as not
to have been formable before it was formed, or to have been capable at

any time of being formless, but is a simple form, and simply equal to Him from whom it is, and with whom it is wonderfully co-eternal?

2.4 Later Medieval Philosophers

Augustine's natural-conventional distinction was to dominate discussions of later medieval philosophers. In the passage that follows, Peter of Spain extends the concept of a natural sign to nonverbal significant sounds or "voices." Significant voices can be interpreted, unlike meaningless sounds. They consist of two kinds: those that have meaning by convention and are understood only by members of a common linguistic community and those that signify "naturally" and have the same meaning for all.

2.4.1 Peter of Spain [8]

A sound is whatever is properly perceived by hearing; for though a man or a bell may be heard, this is only by means of sound. Of sounds, one is voice, another not voice. Sound-voice is the same as voice; so voice is sound produced from the mouth of an animal, formed by the natural organs. . . . Of voices, one is literate, another not literate. Literate voice is that which can be written, e.g. 'man'; not literate is that which cannot be written. Of literate voices one is significant, another not significant. Significant voice is that which represents something to the hearing, e.g. 'man' or the groans of the sick which signify pain. Not significant voice is that which represents nothing nothing to the hearing, e.g. 'bu', 'ba'. Of significant voices, one signifies naturally, another conventionally. Conventionally significant voice is that which represents something at the will of one who originates it, e.g. 'man'. Naturally significant voice is that which represents the same thing to all, e.g., the groans of the sick, the bark of the dogs.

This passage suggests that nonconventional natural signs such as groans and barks are involuntary, not at the "will" of their originators. There seems to be no recognition of the possibility of there being nonconventional signs intentionally produced for the purposes of communication.

This classification is reflected in William of Ockham's inclusion of sounds such as groans and laughter among the class of natural signs.

8. Peter of Spain, *The Summulae Logicales* (c. 1246), trans. I. M. Bochenski, in *A History of Formal Logic* (South Bend: Notre Dame University Press, 1961), p. 153.

2.4.2 William of Ockham (1)[9]

The universal is two fold: natural and conventional. The first is a natural sign predicable of many things, as smoke naturally signifies fire, and a groan the pain of the sick man, and laughter a certain interior joy. The conventional universal is one by voluntary institution. Such is the spoken word which is an actual quality, numerically one, and universal because of its being a voluntarily instituted sign for the signification of many things.

Ockham also struggles with the problem of specifying the relationship between utterances or words and Augustine's mental words or "concepts of the mind." We find him explicitly rejecting the view that utterances signify these mental words. He argues that a mental word constitutes a distinct type of natural sign that itself has meaning. Public utterances are the "external" means of communication by which this same meaning is conveyed to others.

2.4.3 William of Ockham (2)[10]

All who treat of Logic intend to establish by arguments that syllogisms are composed of propositions, and propositions of terms. A term, therefore, is nothing else than the extreme part of a proposition. For Aristotle, defining the term, says in the First Part of the *Prior Analytics:* I call a term that into which a proposition is resolved, such as the predicate or that of which the predicate is stated by adding or removing the 'is' or the 'is not'. But, although every term is called the extreme part of a proposition, or may become such, not all terms are of the same nature. For that reason, to obtain a perfect knowledge of terms we have first to get acquainted with certain distinctions of terms.

It is to be known, then, that to follow Boethius in the first part of his *On Interpretation,* just as there are three kinds of discourse: written, spoken, and conceived, this latter being in the mind only; in the same manner, the term, too, is threefold: written, spoken, and conceived. The written term is a part of a written proposition, which is seen, or may be

9. William of Ockham, *Super Quatuor Libros Sententarium Subtilissimae Earumdenque Decisiones* (1495), II, qu. 25, trans. S. Tornay, in *Ockham: Studies and Selections* (LaSalle: Open Court, 1938), p. 19.

10. Ockham, *Summa Totius Logicae* (1488), Pt. I, Ch. I, also in Tornay's *Ockham*, pp. 91–95.

seen, with the physical eye. (The spoken term is a part of the proposition pronounced by the mouth and meant to be heard by physical hearing. The conceived term is an intention, or passion of the soul, which by its nature signifies or co-signifies something, and is meant to be a part of a mental proposition.) Now these conceived terms and the propositions composed of them are those mental words which Saint Augustine says in the fifth book *On the Trinity* to be of no language. These words remain in the mind only and cannot be brought to light externally, although words, as signs subordinated to them, are pronounced externally. For we call words signs subordinated to concepts or intentions of the soul. The word 'sign' is not used here in the proper sense, as if words signify concepts originally and properly speaking. Rather we mean to imply that words are used to signify those same things that are signified by the concepts of the mind, in such manner that first the concept signifies something naturally, and secondly the word signifies that same thing. And the dependence goes so far that the word, after it was instituted to signify something which is signified by the concept of the mind, should that concept change its signified object, at the same time the word, too, without a new institution would also change its signified object. And to this fact can be referred Aristotle's statement that words are marks of such passions which are in the soul. This is also the meaning of Boethius' statement that words signify concepts; and, generally, the same is meant by all authors who say that words signify the passions of the soul, or are marks of them. (Their intention is nothing else than to say that words are signs which signify secondarily those things that are primarily presented by the passions.) To be sure, some words present primarily certain passions of the soul or concepts, which words, however, secondarily, present other intentions of the soul, as we shall show later. And what was said of words with regard to passions, intentions, or concepts, can be said similarly about written signs with reference to words.

Now these terms present certain differences. One is that the concept or the passion of the soul naturally signifies whatever it signifies. The pronounced or written term, on the other hand, does not signify anything save by voluntary institution. (From this fact another difference follows, namely, that the spoken or written term can change its signified object at discretion, whereas the concept-term never changes its signification at anyone's pleasure.) For the sake of those who are not initiated, it is to be known that 'sign' is taken in a twofold manner, in one way for anything that as apprehended, conveys something else to cognition. To be sure, the sign does not lead to the first cognition of the object, as it is shown elsewhere. It leads to the actual knowledge of what has been previously known. And in this way it signifies something naturally, as every effect signifies at least its own cause. Thus, the disk signifies wine in the tavern. However, I am not speaking of the sign as generally used. To use that word in another way, the sign is taken for that which conveys something to cognition and is meant to stand for that thing or which is to be added in a proposition, such as syncategorematic words, verbs, and other parts of speech which do not have a definite signification. 'Sign' is also everything which is meant to be compounded out of these parts, such as discourse or the proposition. Taking the word 'sign' in this sense, the word is not a natural sign for anything.

This medieval notion of a mental word as a "private" sign was to survive as late as Thomas Hobbes after the end of the Middle Ages. Like Augustine and Ockham, Hobbes distinguishes between public and private sensible "tokens" (*sensibilia*) of words. First, there are "marks" (*notae*) which are devices for our remembering our own thoughts, a type of mental word which remains unexpressed. Conventional signs, in contrast, are the public means by which we communicate our thoughts to others. Of note is Hobbes's use of the Stoics' conception of a natural sign as an "antecedent" and his extension of conventional signs to include such nonverbal communicative devices as a bush hung to signify the selling of wine and stones standing for a boundary.

2.4.4 Thomas Hobbes [11]

The necessity of having sensible tokens or marks for memory. So fluctuating and frail are the thoughts of men, and so fortuitous is the recovery of them, that the most indubitable experiences can be lost to anyone. For no one is able to remember quantities without sensible and present measures, nor colors without sensible and present samples, nor numbers without the names of numbers (arranged and committed to memory). Therefore, without some such help, whatever a man will have put together in his mind by reasoning will immediately slip away, nor can it be recalled except by repeating the effort. From this it follows that for the acquisition of philosophy some sensible tokens are necessary, to which past thought can be reduced, and which can be registered in their own order, as it were.

Definition of a mark. Tokens of this kind are what we call *marks,*

11. *De Corpore* (1650), pt. I, ch. 2, secs. 1, 2, trans. A. Martinich, in *Thomas Hobbes: Computatio Sive Logica* (New York: Abaris Books, 1981), pp. 193–198.

namely, *sensible things employed by our own decision, so that at the sensation of these things, thoughts can be recalled to the mind, similar to those thoughts for the sake of which they were summoned.*

The necessity of having marks to signify the conceptions of the mind. Moreover, even if some one man, although of great ability, passes all this time partly in reasoning and partly in inventing and memorizing marks to help his memory, who will not see that he will not benefit himself much and others not at all? For unless the tokens which he may have invented for himself be common to others also, his scientific knowledge will perish with him. But if the same tokens or marks are common to many and the ones which are invented by one man have been handed down to others, then scientific knowledge is able to increase in usefulness for the entire human race. Therefore, it is necessary for the acquisition of philosophy that there should be some signs by which what has been contrived by some might be disclosed and made known to others. Signs however are customarily called *the antecedents of consequences and the consequences of antecedents, since we generally experience them in a similar way preceding or following one another in a similar fashion.* For example, a dense cloud is a sign of consequent rain and rain a sign of an antecedent cloud, for the reason that we know from experience that there is rarely a dense cloud without consequent rain, and never rain without an antecedent cloud. Of signs, however, some are natural of which type we have just discussed an example. Others are conventional, namely, those which are applied of our own accord; of this type are: a bush hung for signifying that wine is for sale, a stone for signifying the boundaries of a field, and human vocal sounds connected in a certain way for signifying the thoughts and motions of the mind. The difference between a mark and a sign, therefore, is that the former is instituted for our own sake, the latter for the sake of others.

Names perform both of these functions. Human vocal sounds, so connected as to be the signs of thoughts, are speech, but the individual parts are called names. Both marks and signs (marks so that we might be able to remember our thoughts, signs so that we might be able to make them known) are necessary to philosophy, as we have said; names perform both jobs. But they perform the function of marks before that of signs. For they would serve a man as a memory aid even if he existed alone in the world, when they would not be able to serve him for making things known unless there were someone else for whom he might be making it known. Moreover, names in themselves are individual marks, for they recall thoughts even alone, while they are not signs except insofar as they are arranged in speech and are its parts. For example, the vocal sound 'man' evokes the idea of man in the hearer, but does not signify that some idea was in the speaker's mind (unless he adds, 'is an animal', or something equivalent); but it signifies that he wanted to say something, which could indeed begin with the vocal sound 'man' but also could begin with the vocal sound 'manageable'. Therefore, the nature of a name consists primarily in this, that it is a mark, employed for the sake of remembering; but it happens that it also serves for those things to be signified and made known, which we hold in our memory. Therefore we will define a name in this way:

The definition of a name. A name is a human vocal sound employed by a decision of man, so that there might be a mark by which a thought similar to a previous thought might be aroused in the mind, and which, ordered in speech and uttered to others, might be a sign to them that such a thought either previously occurred or did not occur in the speaker. I have assumed that names have arisen from a decision of men and I think that this matter is hardly doubtful and can be assumed for the sake of brevity; for who can come to think that the natures of things display themselves in their names, when he sees new words born daily, old ones destroyed, different words in use in different nations, and, finally, when he sees neither any similarity between words and things nor any establishable comparison? For although God taught certain names of animals and other things, which our first parents used, still he ordained them by his own decision; and later, first at the tower of Babel and then now and then in the passage of time, they fell into disuse and were forgotten, and other words, invented and accepted by a decision of men, succeeded in their place.

The extent of emphasis on the linguistic during the Middle Ages is shown by some philosophers taking language as the model for natural signs. Turning from the empiricism of Sextus, medieval thinkers thought of the primary evidence being the testimony of some source, with the primary source being the Scriptures. The authority of the source determined how reliable the testimony was to be regarded. Natural events and states of affairs came to be regarded as God's testimony to man, and to correctly interpret them was to be able to read nature as God's "Book."[12]

The following passage from the writings of St. Bonaventure sets forth this conception. One way of knowing God's nature, Bonaventure claims, is to infer from "shadows," "traces," and "images" that God makes available

12. Cf. Ian Hacking, *The Emergence of Probability* (London: Cambridge University Press, 1975), pp. 42, 43.

to us. Appeal to these types of signs is a historically early reference to iconic representations, which signify by virtue of a similarity to what they stand for.

2.4.5 St. Bonaventure [13]

To the objection which is raised that there are always infinite steps, it must be said that the ascent to God can be in two ways: either with respect to the *sight of the presence;* and in that way every creature is formed naturally to lead to God, nor are there infinite steps that way; or with respect to *equality of equivalence;* and in that way it is true that there are infinite steps, for the created good, howsoever much it be doubled, is never equal to the uncreated.

The *first* step, however, in respect to the ascent to the sight of the presence is in the consideration of visible things, the *second* in the consideration of invisible things, as of the soul or of another spiritual substance; the *third* is from the soul to God, because *the image is formed by truth itself and is joined immediately to God.*

To the inquiry which was made last *concerning the difference of trace and image,* some make this difference, that the trace is in sensible things, the image in spiritual. But this distinction and position does not hold, because the trace is also in spiritual things. For unity, truth, goodness, in which there is a trace, are conditions in the highest degree universal and intelligible.

Others say that the trace is so called because it represents in respect to the part, but the image in respect to the whole. But this difference again does not hold because, as God is simple, he has no representative in respect to part; again since he is infinite, he can be represented with respect to the whole by absolutely no creature, not even by the whole world.

And therefore it must be understood that since the creature leads to the knowledge of God by the mode of *shadow,* by the mode of *trace,* and by the mode of *image,* the better known difference of these modes by which likewise they are named, is taken from the *mode of representing.* For *shadow* is spoken of in so far as it represents in a certain removal and confusion; *trace* in so far as it represents in removal but distinction; but *image* in so far as it represents in nearness and distinction.

---

13. *Commentary on the Four Books of Sentences of Peter Lombard* (c. 1251), pt. I, qu. II, trans. R. McKeon, in *Selections from Medieval Philosophers*, (New York: Scribner's, 1930), vol. 2, pp. 133, 134.

We shall see in the next section how this conception provides the background for Berkeley's claim that sensory images are a kind of "natural language" instituted by God.

Most discussions of signs by medieval logicians employed the concept of a sign as a means of introducing logical discussions about terms, sentences, and inferences as linguistic signs. No exception to this is the *Ars Logica* of John of St. Thomas (or John Poinsot, his given name) where the sign is introduced as a means for a logic student to "know his tools." But this work is exceptional in its thoroughness in discussing the nature of signs within a metaphysical framework typical of the later Scholastic period. For St. Thomas, this framework consists of four types of causes of knowledge, the productive (Aristotle's efficient cause), the objective, the formal, and the instrumental. In terms of these causes, a complex classification of signs is generated that anticipates Peirce's later classifications in terms of his metaphysical categories. Noteworthy is the inclusion of iconic representations standing for objects by virtue of some similarity, as a picture of Julius Caesar might be a sign of the Roman emperor.

2.4.6 John of St. Thomas (John Poinsot) (1)[14]

A term, no less than a statement and a proposition, and any other logical instrument, is defined by means of signification. This is due to the fact that the understanding knows by means of the signification of concepts, and expresses what it knows by means of the signification of sounds, so that, without exception, all the instruments which we use for knowing and speaking are signs. Therefore, if the student of logic is to know his tools—namely, terms and statements—in an exact manner, it is necessary that he should also know what a sign is. *The sign, therefore, admits of the following general definition:* "That which represents something other than itself to a cognitive power."

To better understand this definition, one must consider that there is a fourfold cause of knowledge namely, a productive, objective, formal, and instrumental cause. The productive or efficient cause is the power itself which elicits an act of knowledge, for example, the eye, the ear, the understanding. The object is the thing which stimulates or toward which a cognition tends, as when I see a stone or a man. The formal cause is the awareness itself whereby a power is rendered cognizant, as the sight

---

14. John of St. Thomas, *Ars Logica* (1632), pt. I, ch. 2, trans. John Deely, in *Tractatus de Signis: The Semiotic of John Poinsot* (Berkeley: University of California Press, 1985), pp. 25–27.

itself of the stone or of the man. The instrumental cause is the means by which the object is represented to the power, as a picture of Caesar represents Caesar. The object is threefold, to wit, stimulative only, terminative only, both stimulative and terminative at once. An object that is only a stimulus is one that arouses a power to form an awareness not of the stimulating object itself, but of another object, as, for example, the picture of the emperor, which moves the power to know the emperor. An object that is terminative only is a thing known through an awareness produced by some other object, for example, the emperor known through the picture. An object that is simultaneously terminative and stimulative is one that arouses a power to form a cognition of the very object stimulating, as when the wall is seen in itself.

Thus, 'making cognizant' has wider extension than does 'representing', and 'representing' more than 'signifying'. For *to make cognizant* is said of every cause concurring in the production of knowledge; and so it is said in *four* ways, namely, effectively, objectively, formally, and instrumentally. *Effectively,* as of the power itself eliciting cognition and of the causes concurring in that production, as of God moving, the understanding acting or producing specifying forms, the inclinations of habit, etc. *Objectively,* as of the very thing which is known. For example, if I know a man, the man as an object makes himself known by presenting himself to the power. *Formally,* as of the awareness itself, which as a form, makes the power know. *Instrumentally,* as of the very medium or means bearing object to power, as the picture of the emperor conveys the emperor to the understanding as a medium, and this means we call the instrument. To *represent* is said of each factor which makes anything become present to a power, and so is said in *three* ways, namely, *objectively, formally,* and *instrumentally.* For an object such as the wall represents itself objectively, an awareness represents formally, a footprint instrumentally. To *signify* is said of that by which something distinct from itself becomes present, and so is said in only *two* ways, namely, formally and instrumentally.

Hence arises the twofold *division of the sign.* For insofar as signs are ordered *to a power,* they are divided into formal and instrumental signs; but insofar as signs are ordered *to something signified,* they are divided according to the cause of that ordering into natural and stipulative and customary. A formal sign is the formal awareness which represents of itself, not by means of another. An instrumental sign is one that represents something other than itself from a pre-existing cognition of itself as an object, as the footprint of an ox represents an ox. And this definition is usually given for signs generally. A natural sign is one that represents from the nature of a thing, independently of any stipulation and custom whatever, and so it represents the same for all, as smoke signifies a fire burning. A stipulated sign is one that represents something owing to an imposition by the will of a community, like the linguistic expression 'man'. A customary sign is one that represents from use alone without any public imposition, as napkins upon the table signify a meal.

Of interest in St. Thomas's extended discussions of signs is his distinction between conventional (or stipulative) and natural signs in terms of their dependence on a mind to interpret them. A sign is by definition any object "which represents something to a knowing power." In this sense all signs, including natural signs, require some mind to interpret them. But St. Thomas reasons (in the complex, contrived way characteristic of later Scholasticism) that a natural sign is also a term of a causal relation, either as cause or effect. This causal relation considered in itself will hold whether or not there is a mind to interpret the events. Thus, smoke is the effect of fire, and clouds cause rain, whether or not there is a knowing subject to interpret the smoke or clouds as signifying fire or rain. Further, an iconic representation, he seems to want to claim (much less plausibly), is similar to the object it represents independently of a mind recognizing this similarity. In contrast, a conventional sign, since its meaning is the result of an arbitrary stipulation, is necessarily dependent on a mind to interpret it.

2.4.7 John of St. Thomas (John Poinsot) (2)[15]

To get to the point of difficulty, it is necessary to distinguish the several relations which can concur in a sign. There is no doubt that some of these relations could exist in a natural sign independently of mind, yet they are not the formal and definitive relation of sign. A sign by its definition is "that which represents something to a knowing power." If the sign is outside the cognitive power, in order to represent another it must have in itself the rationale of an object knowable in itself, so that the cognitive power might arrive at another by knowing the sign. If, on the other hand, the sign is a formal sign and within the power, in order to represent another it must be an intentional representation independent of being itself known objectively, which in the physical order is a kind of quality, yet one with a relation of similitude to that of which it is a representation, and with an order to the power.

Similarly, for a sign to be said to represent this rather than that, there

---

15. *Ars Logica*, pt. II, bk. I, qu. 2, in Deely, *Tractatus de Signis*, pp. 135–137.

has to be in it some congruence or proportion and connection with the given significate. This proportion or congruence can take several forms. Sometimes it is one of an effect to a cause or of cause to effect, as, for example, smoke as an effect signifies fire, clouds or wind as a cause signify rain. Sometimes it is one of similitude or of an image or of whatever other proportion. But in the case of stipulated signs, it is the imposition and appointment, the acceptance, by common usage. In a word: since a sign functions relative to a significate and to a cognitive power, the respects or rationales which habilitate it to the power or those which habilitate it to the signified can precede the forming of the rationale of a sign. But the formal and definitive rationale of a sign does not consist in these, nor does its relation to the thing signified, since indeed they can be separated and found apart from the rationale of a sign. For the rationale of an object is found without the rationale of a sign; and the rationale of an effect or cause or similitude or image can also be found apart from the rationale of a sign. Again because a relation to some thing bespeaks diverse fundaments and formal rationales, as, for example: the relation to an effect or a cause, which is founded on an action; or the relation of an image, which is founded on a similarity of imitation without an order to a cognitive power; or the relation of a sign, which is founded on the measured's being relative to its measure in the mode of a representative substituting for another in an order to a cognitive power, which the other relations do not respect.

We ask, therefore, whether that formal and most proper sign-relation, which is found in addition to or as arising from all those involved in the habilitation of a sign to its significate or to a cognitive power, is a mind-independent relation in the case of physical or natural signs. And we certainly acknowledge that the relation of object to power, which precedes the sign-relation in the case of the instrumental sign, whether by way of stimulating or of terminating, is not a mind-independent relation, because an object does not respect a power by a relation that is mind-independent according to the way it has being, but rather the power respects the object and depends upon and is specified by it. And supposing that the relation of object to power were mind-independent, and that the object reciprocally respects the power in just the way that the power respects the object (which is certainly an assumption contrary to fact, since the object is the measure and the power the measured), this relation still would not be the relation nor the rationale of the sign, because the rationale of an object formally and directly respects or is respected by the power in such a way that the respect between the two is immediate; but the rationale of a sign directly respects a signified and a power indirectly, because it respects the thing signified as that which is to be manifested to a cognitive power. Therefore there is a different line and order of respecting in an object inasmuch as it is an object, and in a sign inasmuch as it is a sign, although for it to be a sign, an object must be supposed.

I answer the question before us therefore by saying: The relation of a natural sign to its significate by which the sign is constituted in being as a sign, is mind-independent and not mind-dependent, considered in itself and by virtue of its fundament and presupposing the existence of the terminus and the other conditions for a mind- independent or physical relation.

CHAPTER THREE

Modern Philosophy

3.1 Locke and Arnauld

Despite their inclusion of the classical evidential signs within the generic category of signs, for Augustine and the later medieval tradition, the primary sign was the word as the primary means of communication among humans. The extent to which this type of linguistic sign became the paradigm is shown in Book IV of Locke's *Essay Concerning Human Understanding*. Here he defines semiotic as the general theory of signs, of which logic is a subbranch.

3.1.1 John Locke[1]

The third branch may be called *semeiotike,* or *the Doctrine of Signs,* the most usual whereof being Words, it is aptly enough termed also *logike,* Logick; the business whereof, is to consider the Nature of Signs, the Mind makes use of for the understanding of Things, or conveying its Knowledge to others. For since the Things, the Mind contemplates, are none of them, besides it self, present to the Understanding, 'tis necessary that something else, as a Sign or Representation of the thing it considers, should be present to it: And these are *Ideas.* And because the Scene of *Ideas* that makes one Man's Thoughts, cannot be laid open to the immediate view of another, nor laid up any where but in the Memory, a no very sure Repository: Therefore to communicate our Thoughts to one another, as well as record them for our own use, Signs of our *Ideas* are also necessary. Those which Men have found most convenient, and therefore generally make use of, are articulate Sounds.

But while he acknowledges semiotic as the more general theory, Locke's exclusive attention in Book IV is to the subject matter of logic, to words as the "most usual kind of signs." Ignored completely are the classical evidential signs. Substituting for the mental words of Augustine and Ockham are abstract ideas for which speech and writing provide the means of communication.

1. John Locke, *Essay Concerning the Human Understanding* (1690), bk. IV, ch. XXI, sec. 4 (New York: Dover, 1959).

More faithful to the medieval tradition is Arnauld's discussion of signs in his *Art of Thinking* where the classical evidential signs are explicitly retained, along with Aristotle's distinction between necessary and probable signs and Augustine's natural-conventional distinction. Also prominent in Arnauld's account are natural occurrences as signs of the divine, as the rainbow signified for the believers of the period God's promise not to destroy the human race. There is also explicit mention of the iconic representations introduced towards the end of the Middle Ages by St. Bonaventure and St. Thomas. For Arnauld, these can be natural signs, as for a mirror image, or conventional signs depending on the "whim of man," as for a map or picture.

3.1.2 Antoine Arnauld[2]

Ideas of Things and Ideas of Signs

When one considers an object in itself and according to its own being, then he thinks of that object simply as a thing; but when he considers an object as representing some other object, then the first object is being thought of as a sign. Maps and pictures are ordinarily regarded as signs. Thus, when we consider an object as sign, we consider two things; the sign as thing, and the thing signified by the sign. It is of the nature of a sign that the idea of the sign excites the idea of the things signified by the sign.

Signs may be divided in various ways, but we will be satisfied here with giving three very useful divisions of signs:

1. There are some signs whose presence insures the existence of the things signified—for example, respiration is a sure sign of life in animals. There are other signs from whose presence we can infer only the probable existence of the thing signified—for instance; paleness is only a probable sign of pregnancy in a woman.

Many rash judgments result from our taking a probable sign as a sure sign. Misinterpreting a sign may lead us to infer from the presence of a certain effect a certain cause even though that effect may stem from another cause.

2. Signs may be divided accordingly as that signified is copresent with the sign or not copresent. The expression of the face considered as a sign of mental attitude is a sign which is copresent with the thing

2. Antoine Arnauld, *The Art of Thinking* (1662), ch. 4, trans. J. Dickoff and P. James (Indianapolis: Bobbs-Merrill, 1964).

signified. Similarly, the symptoms of a disease considered as signs are copresent with the disease. Let us consider some nobler examples. The ark taken as a sign of the Church was in Noah's day a sign copresent with the thing signified, since Noah and his children were the Church in the days of the ark. Similarly, our cathedrals considered as signs of the faithful are signs copresent with the thing signified; the dove, the sign of the Holy Ghost, copresent with the Holy Ghost; and, finally, the waters of baptism, the sign of the spiritual rebirth copresent with this rebirth.

Considered as signs of Christ immolated, the sacrifices of the Ancient Law are signs not copresent with the signified.

This second division of signs is the basis for the following maxims:

a. From the presence of a sign we cannot always infer the presence of the thing signified; nor from the presence of a sign can we always infer the absence of the thing signified. Each sign must be considered according to its own nature.

b. Every sign must be somehow distinct from what it signifies, but one state of a thing may be considered as a sign of some other state of that same thing. Thus, it is quite possible that a man in his own apartments be a sign of himself preaching.

c. Those who say that nothing can be manifest by what hides it advance a poorly founded maxim. For a sign considered as thing may be very different from and yet a sign of the thing signified. A thing can be considered both as a thing and as a sign. Warm ashes as thing hide the fire; as sign, show forth the fire. Similarly, when the angels assumed human forms, these forms as things hid the angels but as signs showed forth the angels. And again, the Eucharistic symbols as things hide the body of Christ but as signs show forth his body.

d. By nature a sign is such that the idea of the sign excites the idea of the thing signified. So long as the idea of the sign excites the idea of the signified, the sign subsists even though the sign as thing does not exist. That is, insofar as the one idea excites the other, the sign subsists—even when the sign as thing altered in its essential nature. The rainbow is taken as God's sign that he will never again destroy the human race by flood. Whether or not the rainbow is a real thing, the rainbow remains a sign of God's promise so long as the idea of a rainbow excites in us the idea of God's promise. Similarly, the Eucharistic bread will remain the sign of Christ's body as the nourishment of our souls and the union among the faithful, no matter what form the bread takes—so long as the idea of the bread excites the idea of nourishment for the soul and bond of the faithful.

3. Signs may be divided into natural signs and conventional signs.

Natural signs do not depend on the whim of man—an image in a mirror is a natural sign of the person mirrored. A conventional sign is a sign established by convention and may, but need not, have any connection with the thing signified. Words are conventional signs of thoughts, and written characters are conventional signs of words.

3.2 Berkeley and Reid

The so-called representative theory of perception, first formulated explicitly by Locke, proposes a type of iconic representation different from any recognized by Arnauld. According to this theory, perception of objects involves two stages. We first directly perceive a sensory image or "particular idea," e.g., a whitish visual image of a rectangular shape. We then infer from this perceived image to the nature and existence of the object causing it. On seeing the whitish visual image present to me, for example, I would then normally infer to a piece of paper as its cause, according to this theory. The paper is similar in certain respects (for Locke, similar with respect to a primary quality such as shape) to the image as its iconic representation.

It is to this realist theory that George Berkeley developed his own alternative theory of subjective idealism. The outlines of this theory can be found in his *A New Theory of Vision* where he analyzes the relationship between visual and tactual images. He attacks the "prejudice" that visual images suggest "by a natural resemblance" those objects we touch. Instead, the relationship between sight and touch "has been learnt at our first entrance into the world," becoming so habitual through regular associations in prior experience that we become unaware of this background. Berkeley compares the manner in which particular ideas signify to that of conventional signs "of human appointment." Particular ideas constitute "a universal language of the Author of nature" produced by this Author in order to guide his creatures through the affairs of life.

3.2.1 George Berkeley (1)[3]

It must be confessed that we are not so apt to confound other signs with the things signified, or to think them of the same species, as we are visible and tangible ideas. But a little consideration will show us how this may be, without our supposing them of a like nature. These signs are constant and universal; their connexion with tangible ideas has been

3. George Berkeley, *A New Theory of Vision* (1709), secs. CXLIV–CXLVII (New York: Dutton, 1910).

learnt at our first entrance into the world; and ever since, almost every moment of our lives, it has been occurring to our thoughts, and fastening and striking deeper in our minds. When we observe that signs are variable, and of human institution; when we remember, there was a time they were not connected in our minds, with those things they now so readily suggest; but that their signification was learned by the slow steps of experience; this preserves us from confounding them. But when we find the same signs suggest the same things all over the world; when we know they are not of human institution, and cannot remember that we ever learned their signification, but think that at first sight they would have suggested to us the same things they do now: all this persuades us they are of the same species as the things respectively represented by them, and that it is by a natural resemblance they suggest them to our minds.

Add to this, that whenever we make a nice survey of any object, successively directing the optic axis to each point thereof; there are certain lines and figures described by the motion of the head or eye, which being in truth perceived by feeling, do nevertheless so mix themselves, as it were, with the ideas of sight, that we can scarce think but they appertain to that sense. Again, the ideas of sight enter into the mind, several at once, more distinct and unmingled, than is usual in the other senses beside the touch. Sounds, for example, perceived at the same instant, are apt to coalesce, if I may so say, into one sound, but we can perceive at the same time great variety of visible objects, very separate and distinct from each other. Now tangible extension being made up of several distinct co-existent parts, we may hence gather another reason, that may dispose us to imagine a likeness or analogy between the immediate objects of sight and touch. But nothing, certainly, doth more contribute to blend and confound them together, than the strict and close connexion they have with each other. We cannot open our eyes, but the ideas of distance, bodies, and tangible figures are suggested by them. So swift, and sudden, and unperceived is the transition from visible to tangible ideas, that we can scarce forbear thinking them equally the immediate object of vision.

The prejudice, which is grounded on these, and whatever other cause may be assigned thereof, sticks so fast, that it is impossible, without obstinate striving and labour of the mind, to get entirely clear of it. But then the reluctancy we find, in rejecting any opinion, can be no argument of its truth, to whoever considers what has been already shown, with regard to the prejudices we entertain concerning the distance, magnitude, and situation of objects; prejudices so familiar to our minds, so confirmed and inveterate, as they will hardly give way to the clearest demonstration.

Upon the whole, I think we may fairly conclude, that the proper objects of vision constitute a universal language of the Author of nature, whereby we are instructed how to regulate our actions, in order to attain those things that are necessary to the preservation and well-being of our bodies, as also to avoid whatever may be hurtful and destructive of them. It is by their information that we are principally guided in all the transactions and concerns of life. And the manner wherein they signify, and mark unto us the objects which are at a distance, is the same with that of languages and signs of human appointment, which do not suggest the things signified, by any likeness or identity of nature, but only by an habitual connexion, that experience has made us to observe between them.

The representative theory of perception is explicitly criticized by Berkeley in *Three Dialogues between Hylas and Philonous.* In the dialogue Hylas represents the views of Locke's realism; Philonous is idealism's advocate. The following passage from it presents Berkeley's comparison between interpreting a picture of Julius Caesar as a sign of the historical figure (St. Thomas's example in 2.4.6) and interpreting the sound of the coach as a sign of the coach itself. In both cases it is "reason and memory" that enables interpretation. In the case of the sound of the coach, interpretation is made possible only by the association in prior experience between the sound of the coach and the sight of it. There is no inference to an object that is the physical cause of the sound.

3.2.2 George Berkeley (2)[4]

Hyl. To speak the truth, Philonous, I think there are two kinds of objects, the one perceived immediately, which are likewise called ideas; the other are real things or external objects perceived by the mediation of ideas, which are their images and representations. Now I own, ideas do not exist without the mind; but the latter sort of objects do. I am sorry I did not think of this distinction sooner; it would probably have cut short your discourse.

Phil. Are those external objects perceived by sense, or by some other faculty?

Hyl. They are perceived by sense.

---

4. *Three Dialogues between Hylas and Philonous,* (1713) I (New York: Dutton, 1910).

Phil.   How! Is there anything perceived by sense, which is not immediately perceived?

Hyl.   Yes, Philonous, in some sort there is. For example, when I look on a picture or statue of Julius Caesar, I may be said after a manner to perceive him (though not immediately) by my senses.

Phil.   It seems then, you will have our ideas, which alone are immediately perceived, to be pictures of external things: and that these also are perceived by sense, inasmuch as they have a conformity or resemblance to our ideas.

Hyl.   That is my meaning.

Phil.   And in the same way that Julius Caesar, in himself invisible, is nevertheless perceived by sight; real things, in themselves imperceptible, are perceived by sense.

Hyl.   In the very same.

Phil.   Tell me, Hylas, when you behold the picture of Julius Caesar, do you see with your eyes any more than some colors and figures, with a certain symmetry and composition of the whole?

Hyl.   Nothing else.

Phil.   And would not a man, who had never known anything of Julius Caesar, see as much?

Hyl.   He would.

Phil.   Consequently he hath his sight, and the use of it, in as perfect a degree as you.

Hyl.   I agree with you.

Phil.   Whence comes it then that your thoughts are directed to the Roman emperor, and his are not? This cannot proceed from the sensations or ideas of sense by you then perceived; since you acknowledge you have no advantage over him in that respect. It should seem therefore to proceed from reason and memory: should it not?

Hyl.   It should.

Phil.   Consequently it will not follow from that instance, that anything is perceived by sense which is not immediately perceived. Though I grant we may in one acceptation be said to perceive sensible things mediately by sense: that is, when from a frequently perceived connection, the immediate perception of ideas of one sense suggests to the mind others, perhaps belonging to another sense, which are wont to be connected with them. For instance, when I hear a coach drive along the street, immediately I perceive only the sound; but from the experience I have had that such a sound in connected with a coach, I am said to hear the coach. It is nevertheless evident, that in truth and strictness, nothing can be heard but sound: and the coach is not then properly perceived by sense, but suggested from experience. So likewise when we are said to see a red-hot bar of iron; the solidity and heat of the iron are not the objects of sight, but suggested to the imagination by the color and figure, which are properly perceived by that sense. In short, those things alone are actually and strictly perceived by any sense, which would have been perceived, in case that same sense had then been first conferred on us. As for other things, it is plain they are only suggested to the mind by experience grounded on former perceptions. But to return to your comparison of Caesar's picture, it is plain, if you keep to that, you must hold the real things, or archetypes of our ideas, are not perceived by sense, but by some internal faculty of the soul, as reason or memory. I would therefore fain know, what arguments, you can draw from reason for the existence of what you call real things or material objects. Or whether you remember to have seen them formerly as they are in themselves? Or if you have heard or read of any one that did.

The issue between Locke and Berkeley is one of those treated by Thomas Reid in his discussion of signs in his *Inquiry into the Human Mind.* But Reid has much wider interests, and his treatment of signs can be regarded as the most extensive after Sextus, unrivaled until Peirce's classifications more than a century later. In the first section of the passage that follows, Reid distinguishes between the "artificial" or conventional language of speech and writing and the "natural" language used by lower animals and as a "common language" among men. A natural language is more effective than an artificial for expressing "the passions, the affections of the will" and is utilized in the fine arts. In contrast to the medieval tradition, Reid regards signs from this natural language as intentionally produced for purposes of communication.

In the second section, Reid develops a classification of natural signs as distinguished from artificial signs. Included in natural signs are the signs of the natural language described earlier. These are noted to be often iconic representations of the objects they stand for, in contrast to a word such as 'gold' that "has no similitude to the substance signified by it." Included also in this broad class are the classical evidential signs "whose connection with the thing signified is established by nature, but discovered only by experience." Finally, sensations or sensory images are regarded by Reid as natural signs that "by a natural kind of magic" indicate the existence of the objects that cause them. Reid concedes to both Berkeley and Hume, "the Bishop of Cloyne and the author of the *Treatise on Human Nature,*" that the relation of a sensation to an object must be established by prior experience in which ideas are associated. Nevertheless, Reid maintains the more restricted realist position that "sensations are invariably connected with the conception and belief of external objects." If we cannot infer the nature of objects from the resembling sensations they cause in us, we can at least infer their bare existence.

3.2.3 Thomas Reid[5]

Of Natural Language

One of the noblest purposes of sound undoubtedly is language, without which mankind would hardly be able to attain any degree of improvement above the brutes. Language is commonly considered as purely an invention of men, who by nature are no less mute than the brutes; but, having a superior degree of invention and reason, have been able to contrive artificial signs of their thoughts and purposes, and to establish them by common consent. But the origin of language deserves to be more carefully inquired into, not only as this inquiry may be of importance for the improvement of language, but as it is related to the present subject, and tends to lay open some of the first principles of human nature. I shall, therefore, offer some thoughts upon this subject.

By language I understand all those signs which mankind use in order to communicate to others their thoughts and intentions, their purposes and desires. And such signs may be conceived to be of two kinds: First, such as have no meaning but what is affixed to them by compact or agreement among those who use them—these are artificial signs; Secondly, such as, previous to all compact or agreement, have a meaning which every man understands by the principles of his nature. Language, so far as it consists of artificial signs, may be called *artificial;* so far as it consists of natural signs, I call it *natural.*

Having premised these definitions, I think it is demonstrable, that, if mankind had not a natural language, they could never have invented an artificial one by their reason and ingenuity. For all artificial language supposes some compact or agreement to affix a certain meaning to certain signs; therefore, there must be compacts or agreements before the use of artificial signs; but there can be no compact or agreement without signs, nor without language; and, therefore, there must be a natural language before any artificial language can be invented: which was to be demonstrated.

---

5. Thomas Reid, *An Inquiry into the Human Mind* (1764), pt. II, ch. 5, secs. II, III, in *Philosophical Works* (Hildesheim: Olms, 1967), vol. 1.

Had language in general been a human invention, as much as writing or printing, we should find whole nations as mute as the brutes. Indeed, even the brutes have some natural signs by which they express their own thoughts, affections, and desires, and understand those of others. A chick, as soon as hatched, understands the different sounds whereby its dam calls it to food, or gives the alarm of danger. A dog or a horse understands, by nature, when the human voices caresses, and when it threatens him. But brutes, as far as we know, have no notion of contracts or covenants, or of moral obligation to perform them. If nature had given them these notions, she would probably have given them natural signs to express them. And where nature has denied these notions, it is as impossible to acquire them by art, as it is for a blind man to acquire the notion of colours. Some brutes are sensible of honour or disgrace; they have resentment and gratitude; but none of them, as far as we know, can make a promise or plight their faith, having no such notions from their constitution. And if mankind had not these notions by nature, and natural signs to express them by, with all their wit and ingenuity they could never have invented language.

The elements of this natural language of mankind, or the signs that are naturally expressive of our thoughts, may, I think, be reduced to these three kinds: modulations of the voice, gestures, and features. By means of these, two savages who have no common artificial language, can converse together; can communicate their thoughts in some tolerable manner; can ask and refuse, affirm and deny, threaten and supplicate; can traffic, enter into covenants, and plight their faith. This might be confirmed by historical facts of undoubted credit, if it were necessary.

Mankind having thus a common language by nature, though a scanty one, adapted only to the necessities of nature, there is no great ingenuity required in improving it by the addition of artificial signs, to supply the deficiency of the natural. These artificial signs must multiply with the arts of life, and the improvements of knowledge. The articulations of the voice seem to be, of all signs, the most proper for artificial language; and as mankind have universally used them for that purpose, we may reasonably judge that nature intended them for it. But nature probably does not intend that we should lay aside the use of the natural signs; it is enough that we supply their defects by artificial ones. A man that rides always in a chariot, by degrees loses the use of his legs; and one who uses artificial signs only, loses both the knowledge and the use of the natural. Dumb people retain much more of the natural language than others, because necessity obliges them to use it. And for the same reason, savages have much more of it than civilized nations. It is by natural signs chiefly that we give force and energy to language; and the less language has of them, it is the less expressive and persuasive. Thus, writing is less expressive than reading, and reading less expressive than speaking without book; speaking without the proper and natural modulation force, and variations of the voice, is a frigid and dead language, compared with that which is attended with them; it is still more expressive when we add the language of the eyes and features; and is then only in its perfect and natural state, and attended with its proper energy, when to all these we superadd the force of action.

Where speech is natural, it will be an exercise, not of the voice and lungs only, but of all the muscles of the body; like that of dumb people and savages whose language, as it has more of nature, is more expressive, and is more easily learned.

Is it not pity that the refinements of a civilized life, instead of supplying the defects of natural language, should root it out and plant in its stead dull and lifeless articulations of unmeaning sounds, or the scrawling of insignificant characters? The perfection of language is commonly thought to be, to express human thoughts and sentiments distinctly by these dull signs; but if this is the perfection of artificial language, it is surely the corruption of the natural.

Artificial signs signify, but they do not express; they speak to the understanding, as algebraical characters may do, but the passion, the affections, and the will, hear them not: these continue dormant and inactive, till we speak to them in the language of nature, to which they are all attention and obedience.

It were easy to shew, that the fine arts of the musician, the painter, the actor, and the orator, so far as they are expressive—although the knowledge of them requires in us a delicate taste, a nice judgment, and much study and practice—yet they are nothing else but the language of nature, which we brought into the world with us, but have unlearned by disuse, and so find the greatest difficulty in recovering it.

Abolish the use of articulate sounds and writing among mankind for a century, and every man would be a painter, an actor, and an orator. We mean not to affirm that such an expedient is practicable; or if it were, that the advantage would counterbalance the loss; but that, as men are led by nature and necessity to converse together, they will use every mean in their power to make themselves understood; and where they cannot do this by artificial signs, they will do it, as far as possible, by natural ones: and he that understands perfectly the use of natural signs, must be the best judge in all the expressive arts.

Of Natural Signs

As in artificial signs there is often neither similitude between the sign and thing signified, nor any connection that arises necessarily from the nature of the things, so it is also in natural signs. The word gold has no similitude to the substance signified by it; nor is it in its own nature more fit to signify this than any other substance; yet, by habit and custom, it suggests this and no other. In like manner, a sensation of touch suggests hardness, although it hath neither similitude to hardness, nor, as far as we can perceive, any necessary connection with it. The difference betwixt these two signs lies only this—that, in the first, the suggestion is the effect of habit and custom; in the second it is not the effect of habit, but of the original constitution of our minds.

It appears evident from what hath been said on the subject of language, that there are natural signs as well as artificial; and particularly, that the thoughts, purposes, and dispositions of the mind, have their natural signs in the features of the face, the modulation of the voice, and the motion and attitude of the body: that, without a natural knowledge of the connection between these signs and the things signified by them, language could never have been invented and established among men: and, that that the fine arts are all founded upon this connection, which we may call *the natural language of mankind*. It is now proper to observe, that there are different orders of natural signs, and to point out the different classes into which they may be distinguished, that we may more distinctly conceive the relation between our sensations and the things they suggest, and what we mean by calling sensations signs of external things.

The first class of natural signs comprehends those whose connection with the thing signified is established by nature, but discovered only by experience. The whole of genuine philosophy consists in discovering such connections, and reducing them to general rules. The great Lord Verulam had a perfect comprehension of this, when he called it *an interpretation of nature*. No man ever more distinctly understood or happily expressed the nature and foundation of the philosophic art. What is all we know of mechanics, astronomy, and optics, but connections established by nature, and discovered by experience or observation, and consequences deduced from them? All the knowledge we have in agriculture, gardening, chemistry, and medicine, is built upon the same foundation. And if ever our philosophy concerning the human mind is carried so far as to deserve the name of science, which ought never to be despaired of, it must be by observing facts, reducing them to general rules, and drawing just conclusions from them. What we commonly call natural *causes* might, with more propriety, be called natural *signs,* and what we call *effects,* the things signified. The causes have no proper efficiency or causality, as far as we know; and all we can certainly affirm is, that nature hath established a constant conjunction between them and the things called their effects; and hath given to mankind a disposition to observe those connections, to confide in their continuance, and to make use of them for the improvement of our knowledge, and increase of our power.

A second class is that wherein the connection between the sign and thing signified, is not only established by nature, but discovered to us by a natural principle, without reasoning or experience. Of this kind are the natural signs of human thoughts, purposes, and desires, which have been already mentioned as the natural language of mankind. An infant may be put into a fright by an angry countenance, and soothed again by smiles and blandishments. A child that has a good musical ear, may be put to sleep or to dance, may be made merry or sorrowful, by the modulation of musical sounds. The principles of all the fine arts, and of what we call a *fine taste,* may be resolved into connections of this kind. A fine taste may be improved by reasoning and experience; but if the first principles of it were not planted in our minds by nature, it could never be acquired. Nay, we have already made it appear, that a great part of this knowledge, which we have by nature, is lost by the disuse of natural signs, and the substitution of artificial in their place.

A third class of natural signs comprehends those which, though we never before had any notion or conception of the thing signified, do suggest it, or conjure it up, as it were, by a natural kind of magic, and at once give us a conception and create a belief of it. I shewed formerly, that our sensations suggest to us a sentient being or mind to which they belong—a being which hath a permanent existence, although the sensations are transient and of short duration—a being which is still the same, while its sensation and other operations are varied ten thousand ways—a being which hath the same relation to all that infinite variety of thoughts, purposes, actions, affections, enjoyments, and sufferings, which we are conscious of, or can remember. The conception of a mind is neither an idea of sensation nor of reflection; for it is neither like any of our sensations, nor like anything we are conscious of. The first conception of it, as well as the belief of it, and of the common relation it bears to all that we are conscious of, or remember, is suggested to every thinking being, we do not know how.

The notion of hardness in bodies, as well as the belief of it, are got in a similar manner; being, by an original principle of our nature, annexed to that sensation which we have when we feel a hard body. And so naturally and necessarily does the sensation convey the notion and belief of hardness, that hitherto they have been confounded by the most acute inquirers into the principles of human nature, although they appear upon accurate reflection, not only to be different things, but as unlike as pain is to the point of a sword.

It may be observed, that, as the first class of natural signs I have mentioned is the foundation of true philosophy, and the second the foundation of the fine arts, or of taste—so this last is the foundation of common sense—a part of human nature which hath never been explained.

I take it for granted, that the notion of hardness; and the belief of it, is first got by means of that particular sensation which, as far back as we can remember, does invariably suggest it; and that, if we had never had such a feeling, we should never have had any notion of hardness. I think it is evident that we cannot, by reasoning from our sensations, collect the existence of bodies at all, far less any of their qualities. This hath been proved by unanswerable arguments by the Bishop of Cloyne, and by the author of the *Treatise of Human Nature*. It appears as evident that this connection between our sensations and the conception and belief of external existences cannot be produced by habit, experience, education, or any principle of human nature that hath been admitted by philosophers. At the same time, it is a fact that such sensations are invariably connected with the conception and belief of external existences. Hence, by all rules of just reasoning, we must conclude, that this connection is the effect of our constitution, and ought to be considered as an original principle of human nature, till we find some more general principle into which it may be resolved.

3.3 Gérando

Reid's conception of a "natural language of mankind," providing the foundation for both the development of conventional languages and the fine arts, was to enjoy wide currency, with many theories proposed to explain the evolution of language from primitive forms of communication. Also proposed by the French anthropologist Joseph Marie de Gérando was a method for coming to understand the expressions of primitive peoples by first communicating with them through a natural "language of gestures" shared by all people. The three basic kinds of signs within such a language are indexical pointing gestures or "demonstrative signs," iconic or imitative gestures or "descriptive signs," and "metaphorical signs" relying on common associations of ideas.

3.3.1 *Joseph Marie de Gérando*[6]

The main object, therefore, that should today occupy the attention and zeal of a truly philosophical traveller would be the careful gathering of all means that might assist him to penetrate the thought of the peoples among whom he would be situated, and to account for the order of their actions and relationships. This is not only because such study is in itself the most important of all, it is also because it must stand as a necessary preliminary and introduction to all the others. It is a delusion to suppose that one can properly observe a people whom one cannot understand and with whom one cannot converse. The first means to the proper knowledge of the Savages, is to become after a fashion like one of them; and it is by learning their language that we shall become their fellow citizens.

The most important thing to observe in the study of the signs of Savages, is the order of the enquiry.

Since the articulate language of savage peoples, according to the information which we have about it, is composed of signs almost as arbitrary and conventional as our own, it is clear that to establish an initial intercourse with them, we need to go back to signs which are closest to nature; with them, as with children, we must begin with the language of action.

In the language of action or gesture, three kinds of sign must be distinguished; demonstrative signs, whose only function is to fix the attention on an object that is present; descriptive signs with which, when the object is not present, we imitate its shape, its size, its movements; and finally, metaphorical signs, which help us, when we cannot imitate and depict an object, to reproduce at least the circumstances connected with it in our memory, recalling, for example, the effect by its cause, or the whole by one of its parts.

Of these three kinds of sign, the *demonstrative* is that whose effect is most sure, and least subject to ambiguity, when it can be used. It is with such signs, therefore, that we should begin; it is to them that we must have recourse in cases of doubt. We must think of *describing* only when we cannot *point out*.

The usefulness of *descriptive* signs will depend on how effective the

6. Joseph Marie de Gérando, *The Observation of Savage Peoples* (1800), trans. F. C. T. Moore (Berkeley: University of California Press, 1969), pp. 70–72.

descriptions are. Now the effectiveness of a description depends on the skill with which three conditions have been observed: the imitation first of the most striking and obvious qualities of objects, secondly of those most peculiar to them, qualities which are thus more suitable to distinguish the objects with which they could be confounded; and finally of those which must have been particularly noticeable to the individuals with whom one is speaking, whether by the nature of their dispositions or by the effect of the circumstances in which they were placed.

Metaphorical signs are most of all liable to uncertainty, and most difficult to interpret in a precise way. Yet one is often compelled to have recourse to them. Accordingly, if the explorer used them, he will overlook nothing that could make them more expressive; he will avoid supposing too readily that the Savage entertains associations of ideas analogous to his own. If it is the Savage who is using them, the explorer will be careful to encompass faithfully all the accompanying circumstances, and to adduce previously known habits of the people, which may assist explanation.

3.4 Kant

Immanuel Kant cannot be considered one of the main contributors to the development of semiotic. Like Locke, his almost exclusive attention is directed toward topics of logic, to the neglect of a more general theory of signs. Nevertheless, Kant provides an important anticipation of the direction semiotic was to take in continental Europe, arising from his recognition of devices such as insignia used in human communication that serve to indicate the social status of persons engaged in communication rather than to convey propositional information. Such signs are included in the following listing of types of signs.

3.4.1 Immanuel Kant[7]

> *We can divide signs into voluntary (artificial), natural and miraculous signs.*

To the first type belong 1) signs of gesticulation (imitative, which are also partly natural); 2) characters (letters, which are signs for sounds); 3) tone signs (notes); 4) signs agreed upon between individuals, for the

---

7. *Anthropology from a Pragmatic Point of View* (1798), bk. I, sec. 39, trans. V. L. Dowdell, ed. H. Rudnick (Carbondale: Southern Illinois University Press, 1978).

purposes of communication (ciphers); 5) class signs of free men honored with hereditary superiority (coats of arms); 6) signs of service, in prescribed costume (uniforms and livery); 7) badges of honor, for service (ribbons awarded by orders); 8) signs of dishonor (brandings and so forth). To this type also belong the literary signs of pause, question or emotion, and astonishment (signs of punctuation) in written material.

All language is a signification of thought; the supreme way of indicating thought is by language, the greatest instrument for understanding ourselves and others. Thinking is speaking to ourselves. (The Indians of Tahiti call it "the language inside the body.") Consequently, there is also hearing ourselves inwardly (by means of the reproductive imagination). To the man born deaf, speaking is a feeling of play of lips, tongue, and jaw; and it is hardly possible to imagine that he does more when speaking than carry on a play with physical feelings, without thinking or having real concepts. Yet even those who can speak and hear do not always understand either themselves or others. This is to be attributed to the lack of the power of designation, or to its faulty use (when signs are taken for things, and vice versa), and to the fact that men, especially where reason is concerned, who speak the same language are miles apart in regard to concepts. This is manifest only by chance, when each person is dealing with his own concepts.

Concerning the natural signs, the relation of signs to things signified is, depending on the time, either demonstrative, or remonstrative, or prognostic.

The pulse signifies to the physician the presence of a feverish condition in the patient, just as smoke signifies fire. Reagents reveal to the chemist elements concealed in water, just as the weathercock reveals the wind, and so forth. However, whether blushing betrays consciousness of guilt, or rather a delicate sense of honor, or just a response to the imputation of something of which one would have to be ashamed, is quite uncertain in particular instances.

Burial mounds and tombs are signs of remembrance of the dead, just as pyramids are perpetual reminders of the former great power of a king. The layers of shells in districts situated far from the sea, the holes of the Pholades in the high Alps, or volcanic residue [in places] where fire no longer bursts forth from the earth, signify to us the ancient condition of the world and provide the basis for an archeology of nature, though, to be sure, they are not so plainly visible as the scars of a wounded warrior. The ruins of Palmyra, Balbek, and Persepolis are telling monuments of the state of art in ancient nations, as well as sad indications of the change of all things.

Prognostic signs are the most interesting of all, because the present is but a moment in the series of changes, and human desire leads us to ponder the present only for the sake of future consequences (*ob futura consequentia*), thus making us especially attentive to these signs. In regard to future events in the world, the surest prognosis is in astronomy. But it is childish and fantastic when heavenly configurations, conjunctions, and altered positions of plants are represented (in the *Astrologia Judiciaria*) as allegorical signs in the heavens of impending human destinies.

Natural, prognostic signs of an impending illness or convalescence, or (like the *facies Hippocratics*) of imminent death, are phenomena which, based upon long and frequent experience, serve the physician as a guide in administering his cure even after the discovery of the relation between cause and effect. The same holds true for the so-called critical days. Yet the auguries and haruspices, set up by the Romans for political purposes, were a superstition sanctioned by the government in order to direct the people in perilous times.

Among the miraculous signs (events in which the nature of things reverses itself), apart from those of which we do not yet make anything (monstrosities among men and animals), there are signs and wonders in the sky—comets, balls of light shooting through the high atmosphere, northern lights, solar and lunar eclipses. It is especially when several such signs coincide, and are accompanied by war, pestilence, and so forth, that they are thought by the great terrified populace to herald the imminent doomsday and the end of the world.

CHAPTER FOUR

Peirce's Classifications

4.1 The Definition of 'Semiotic'

Peirce can be rightfully regarded as the founder of semiotic as understood in recent times. He defined the scope of the subject, introduced the basic terminology that has been employed since, and produced classifications that, if not presently followed in all details, continue to be suggestive and warrant study. For Peirce, semiotic is a logical discipline, not one of the empirical sciences. It describes necessary features of signs as used by any organism capable of learning from experience, not contingent features as described by the empirical sciences. Its subject matter is a sign as a thing or event that stands for some object for some interpreter. The "interpretant" of a sign for Peirce is another sign that has the same meaning for its interpreter as the original.

4.1.1 Charles Peirce (1)[1]

Logic, in its general sense, is, as I believe I have shown, only another name for *semiotic* (semiotike), the quasi-necessary, or formal, doctrine of signs. By describing the doctrine as "quasi-necessary," or formal, I mean that we observe the characters of such signs as we know, and from such an observation, by a process which I will not object to naming Abstraction, we are led to statements, eminently fallible, and therefore in one sense by no means necessary, as to what *must be* the characters of all signs used by a "scientific" intelligence, that is to say, by an intelligence capable of learning by experience. As to that process of abstraction, it is itself a sort of observation. The faculty which I call abstractive observation is one which ordinary people perfectly recognize, but for which the theories of philosophers sometimes hardly leave room. It is a familiar experience to

1. C. Hartshorne and P. Weiss, eds., *The Collected Papers of Charles Saunders Peirce*, 6 vols. (Cambridge: Harvard University Press, 1934–36), paragraphs 2.227–2.232. The passages that follow are writings, many unpublished, from different periods. The first part of this passage was written about 1897, the second in 1910. In the passages that follow, paragraph numbers have been deleted from the edited edition, along with the editors' footnotes and some bracketed editorial additions. Original Greek expressions have been replaced by their Roman equivalents and punctuation and quotes made consistent with those in preceding sections.

every human being to wish for something quite beyond his present means, and to follow that wish by the question, "Should I wish for that thing just the same, if I had ample means to gratify it?" To answer that question, he searches his heart, and in doing so makes what I term an abstractive observation. He makes in his imagination a sort of skeleton diagram, or outline sketch, of himself, considers what modifications the hypothetical state of things would require to be made in that picture, and then examines it, that is, *observes* what he has imagined, to see whether the same ardent desire is there to be discerned. By such a process, which is at bottom very much like mathematical reasoning, we can reach conclusions as to what *would be* true of signs in all cases, so long as the intelligence using them was scientific. The modes of thought of a God, who should possess an intuitive omniscience superseding reason, are put out of the question. Now the whole process of development among the community of students of those formulations by abstractive observation and reasoning of the truths which *must* hold good of all signs used by a scientific intelligence is an observational science, like any other positive science, notwithstanding its strong contrast to all the special sciences which arises from its aiming to find out what *must be* and not merely what *is* in the actual world.

A sign, or *representamen*, is something which stands to somebody for something in some respect or capacity. It addresses somebody, that is, creates in the mind of that person an equivalent sign, or perhaps a more developed sign. That sign which it creates I call the *interpretant* of the first sign. The sign stands for something, its *object*. It stands for that object, not in all respects, but in reference to a sort of idea, which I have sometimes called the *ground* of the representamen. 'Idea' is here to be understood in a sort of Platonic sense, very familiar in everyday talk; I mean in that sense in which we say that one man catches another man's idea, in which we say that when a man recalls what he was thinking of at some previous time, he recalls the same idea, and in which when a man continues to think anything, say for a tenth of a second, in so far as the thought continues to agree with itself during that time, that is to have a *like* content, it is the same idea, and is not at each instant of the interval a new idea.

In consequence of every representamen being thus connected with three things, the ground, the object, and the interpretant, the science of semiotic has three branches. The first is called by Duns Scotus *grammatica speculativa*. We may term it *pure grammar*. It has for its task to ascertain what must be true of the representamen used by every scientific intelligence in order that they may embody any *meaning*. The second is logic proper. It is the science of what is quasi-necessarily true of the representamina of any scientific intelligence in order that they may hold good of any *object*, that is, may be true. Or say, logic proper is the formal science of the conditions of the truth of representations. The third, in imitation of Kant's fashion of preserving old associations of words in finding nomenclature for new conceptions, I call *pure rhetoric*. Its task is to ascertain the laws by which in every scientific intelligence one sign gives birth to another, and especially one thought brings forth another.

. . . .

The word Sign will be used to denote an Object perceptible, or only imaginable, or even unimaginable in one sense—for the word '*fast*', which is a Sign, is not imaginable, since it is not *this word itself* that can be set down on paper or pronounced, but only *an instance* of it, and since it is the very same word when it is written as it is when it is pronounced, but is one word when it means "rapidly" and quite another when it means "immovable," and a third when it refers to abstinence. But in order that anything should be a Sign, it must "represent," as we say, something else, called its *Object*, although the condition that a Sign must be other than its Object is perhaps arbitrary, since, if we insist upon it we must at least make an exception in the case of a Sign that is a part of a Sign. Thus nothing prevents the actor who acts a character in an historical drama from carrying as a theatrical "property" the very relic that that article is supposed merely to represent, such as the crucifix that Bulwer's Richelieu holds up with such effect in his defiance. On a map of an island laid down upon the soil of that island there must, under all ordinary circumstances, be some position, some point, marked or not, that represents *qua* place on the map, the very same point *qua* place on the island. A sign may have more than one Object. Thus, the sentence 'Cain killed Abel', which is a Sign, refers at least as much to Abel as to Cain, even if it be not regarded as it should, as having "*a killing*" as a third Object. But the set of objects may be regarded as making up one complex Object. In what follows and often elsewhere Signs will be treated as having but one object each for the sake of dividing difficulties of the study. If a Sign is other than its Object, there must exist, either in thought or in expression, some explanation or argument or other context, showing how—upon what system or for what reason the Sign represents the Object or set of Objects that it does. Now the Sign and the Explanation together make up another Sign, and since the explanation will be a Sign, it will probably require an additional explanation, which taken together with the already enlarged Sign will make up a still larger Sign; and proceeding in the same way, we shall, or should, ultimately reach a Sign of itself, containing its own explanation and those of all its significant parts; and according to this explanation each such part has some other part as its Object. According to this every sign has, actually or virtually, what we may call a *precept* of explanation according to which it is to be understood as a sort of emanation, so to speak, of its Object. (If the Sign be an Icon, a scholastic might say that the "*species*" of the Object emanating from it found its matter in the Icon. If the Sign be an Index, we may think of it as a fragment torn away from the Object, the two in their Existence being one whole or a part of such whole. If the Sign is a Symbol, we may think of it as embodying the "*ratio*," or reason, of the Object that has emanated from it. These, of course, are mere figures of speech; but that does not render them useless.)

The Sign can only represent the Object and tell about it. It cannot furnish acquaintance with or recognition of that Object; for that is what is meant in this volume by the Object of a Sign; namely, that with which it presupposes an acquaintance in order to convey some further information concerning it. No doubt there will be readers who will say they cannot comprehend this. They think a Sign need not relate to anything otherwise known, and can make neither head nor tail of the statement that every Sign must relate to such an Object. But if there be anything that conveys information and yet has absolutely no relation nor reference to anything with which the person to whom it conveys the information has, when he comprehends that information, the slightest acquaintance, direct or indirect—and a very strange sort of information that would be—the vehicle of that sort of information is not, in this volume, called a Sign.

Two men are standing on the seashore looking out to sea. One of them says to the other, 'That vessel there carries no freight at all, but only passengers'. Now, if the other, himself, sees no vessel, the first information he derives from the remark has for its Object the part of the sea that he does see, and informs him that a person with sharper eyes than his, or more trained in looking for such things, can see a vessel there; and then, that vessel having been thus introduced to his acquaintance, he is prepared to receive the information about it that it carries passengers exclusively. But the sentence as a whole has, for the person supposed, no other Object than that with which it finds him already acquainted. The Objects—for a Sign may have any number of them—may each be a single known existing thing or thing believed formerly to have existed or expected to exist, or a collection of such things, or a known quality or relation or fact, which single Object may be a collection, or whole of parts, or it may have some other mode of being, such as some act permitted whose being does not prevent its negation from being equally permitted, or something of a general nature desired, required, or invariably found under certain general circumstances.

In the above passage, Peirce specifies semiotic to be a general science which includes within it the "speculative grammar" of medieval logicians, as well as logic and rhetoric. Elsewhere, Peirce lists semiotic as the primary branch of logic as one of the normative sciences. Distinct from semiotic, but dependent on it for its basic principles, are two other branches of logic, one evaluating inferences in terms of their validity, the other evaluating the methodologies of the different sciences. Semiotic as part of logic is, in turn, dependent for its principles on what Peirce calls "phenomenology," that branch of philosophy that on the basis of a direct inspection of the immediate facts of experience specifies its basic categories.

4.1.2 Charles Peirce (2)[2]

Philosophy is divided into *a*. Phenomenology; *b*. Normative Science; *c*. Metaphysics.

Phenomenology ascertains and studies the kinds of elements universally present in the phenomenon; meaning by the *phenomenon*, whatever is present at any time to the mind in any way. Normative science distinguishes what ought to be from what out not to be, and makes many other divisions and arrangements subservient to its primary dualistic distinction. Metaphysics seeks to give an account of the universe of mind and matter. Normative science rests largely on phenomenology and on mathematics; metaphysics on phenomenology and on normative science.

. . . .

Normative science has three widely separated divisions: i. Esthetics; ii. Ethics; iii. Logic.

Esthetics is the science of ideals, or of that which is objectively admirable without any ulterior reason. I am not well acquainted with this science; but it ought to repose on phenomenology. Ethics, or the science of right or wrong, must appeal to Esthetics for aid in determining the *summum bonum*. It is the theory of self-controlled, or deliberate, conduct. Logic is the theory of self-controlled, or deliberate, thought; and as such, must appeal to ethics for its principles. It also depends upon phenomenology and upon mathematics. All thought being performed by means of signs, logic may be regarded as the science of the general laws of signs.

2. *Collected Papers*, 1.186, 1.191 (1903).

It has three branches: 1, Speculative Grammar, or the general theory of the nature and meanings of signs, whether they be icons, indices, or symbols; 2, Critic, which classifies arguments and determines the validity and degree of force of each kind; 3, Methodeutic, which studies the methods that ought to be pursued in the investigation, in the exposition, and in the application of truth. Each division depends on that which precedes it.

4.2 Icon, Index, and Symbol

Peirce's classifications of signs are confusing and sometimes inconsistent. He was attempting to combine in them three projects. First, he wanted to conform to his abstract metaphysical scheme of three categories: *firstness* (qualitative possibility), *secondness* (causal correlations and existence), and *thirdness* (representation, thought, or law). Second, he was attempting to incorporate the variety of signs described in the tradition preceding him. These included the classical evidential signs, the iconic representations of Arnauld, and conventional linguistic signs. Finally, as a logician, his goal was to specify the basic elements of sentences and their different functions. The often confusing nature of the classifications illustrates the difficulties of combining all three projects.

Peirce's primary classification of signs is into three classes: icons, indices, and symbols. Examples of icons are Arnauld's maps and diagrams, signs that represent objects by virtue of their similarity to them. Symbols are the conventional signs of the medieval tradition, Reid's "artificial" signs. Indices are more difficult to characterize. He intends them to incorporate the classical evidential signs causally related to what they signify; as examples he gives a bullet hole as a sign of the bullet causing it and a fossil as a sign of past life. But his logical interest in the subject-predicate structure of sentences also leads him to characterize indices as devices used by the speaker that serve to direct the attention of the hearer to the object being referred to. Thus, in the sentence 'This stove is black', the demonstrative 'this' would be an index indicating the object referred to by the sentence's subject 'this stove'. The function of the predicate 'is black' is to express the quality being ascribed to this object.

Peirce's "On a New List of Categories" is his earliest complete exposition of his categories and his icon-index-symbol classification of signs. In this early work, the categories are listed as quality (or ground), correlation, and interpretant. They are derived, not from the phenomena of direct experience as in his later writings, but from features of sign interpretation. The following excerpt from this very abstract and in many places puzzling work reveals how important were his logical interests in developing both his scheme of categories and his classification of signs.

4.2.1 Charles Peirce (3)[3]

The conception of *being* arises upon the formation of a proposition. A proposition always has, besides a term to express the substance, another to express the quality of that substance; and the function of the conception of being is to unite the quality to the substance. Quality, therefore, in its very widest sense, is the first conception in order in passing from being to substance.

Quality seems at first sight to be given in the impression. Such results of introspection are untrustworthy. A proposition asserts the applicability of a mediate conception to a more immediate one. Since this is *asserted*, the more mediate conception is clearly regarded independently of this circumstance, for otherwise the two conceptions would not be distinguished, but one would be thought through the other, without this latter being an object of thought, at all. The mediate conception, then, in order to be *asserted* to be applicable to the other, must first be considered without regard to this circumstance, and taken immediately. But, taken immediately, it transcends what is given (the more immediate conception), and its applicability to the latter is hypothetical. Take, for example, the proposition, 'This stove is black'. Here the conception of *this stove* is the more immediate, that of *black* the more mediate, which latter, to be predicated of the former, must be discriminated from it and considered *in itself,* not as applied to an object, but simply as embodying a quality, *blackness.* Now this *blackness* is a pure species or abstraction, and its application to *this stove* is entirely hypothetical. The same thing is meant by 'the stove is black', as by 'there is blackness in the stove'. *Embodying blackness* is the equivalent of *black.* The proof is this. These conceptions are applied indifferently to precisely the same facts. If, therefore, they were different, the one which was first applied would fulfill every function of the other; so that one of them would be superfluous. Now a superfluous conception is an arbitrary fiction, whereas elementary conceptions arise only upon the requirement of experience; so that a superfluous elementary conception is impossible. Moreover, the conception of a pure abstraction is indispensable, because we cannot comprehend an agreement of two things, except as an agreement in some *respect*, and this respect is such a pure abstraction as blackness. Such a pure abstraction, reference

3. *Collected Papers,* 1.551–1.553, 1.558 (1868).

to which constitutes a *quality* or general attribute, may be termed a *ground*.

Reference to a ground cannot be prescinded from being, but being can be prescinded from it.

Empirical psychology has established the fact that we can know a quality only by means of its contrast with or similarity to another. By contrast and agreement a thing is referred to a correlate, if this term may be used in a wider sense than usual. The occasion of the introduction of the conception of reference to a ground is the reference to a correlate, and this is, therefore, the next conception in order.

Reference to a correlate cannot be prescinded from reference to a ground; but reference to a ground may be prescinded from reference to a correlate.

The occasion of reference to a correlate is obviously by comparison. This act has not been sufficiently studied by the psychologists, and it will, therefore, be necessary to adduce some examples to show in what it consists. Suppose we wish to compare the letters p and b. We may imagine one of them to be turned over on the line of writing as an axis, then laid upon the other, and finally to become transparent so that the other can be seen through it. In this way we shall form a new image which mediates between the images of the two letters, inasmuch as it represents one of them to be (when turned over) the likeness of the other. Again, suppose we think of a murderer as being in relation to a murdered person; in this case we conceive the act of the murder, and in this conception it is represented that corresponding to every murderer (as well as to every murder) there is a murdered person; and thus we resort again to a mediating representation which represents the relate as standing for a correlate with which the mediating representation is itself in relation. Again, suppose we look up the word *homme* in a French dictionary; we shall find opposite to it the word *man*, which, so placed, represents *homme* as representing the same two-legged creature which *man* itself represents. By a further accumulation of instances, it would be found that every comparison requires, besides the related thing, the ground, and the correlate, also *a mediating representation which represents the relate to be a representation of the same correlate which this mediating representation itself represents*. Such a mediating representation may be termed an *interpretant*, because it fulfills the office of an interpreter, who says that a foreigner says the same thing which he himself says. The term representation is here to be understood in a very extended sense, which can be explained by instances better than by a definition. In this sense, a word represents a thing to the conception in the mind of the hearer, a portrait represents the person for whom it is intended to the conception of recognition, a weathercock represents the direction of the wind to the conception of him who understands it, a barrister represents his client to the judge and jury whom he influences.

Every reference to a correlate, then, conjoins to the substance the conception of a reference to an interpretant; and this is, therefore, the next conception in order in passing from being to substance.

Reference to an interpretant cannot be prescinded from reference to a correlate; but the latter can be prescinded from the former. . . .

A quality may have a special determination which prevents its being prescinded from reference to a correlate. Hence there are two kinds of relation.

First. That of relates whose reference to a ground is a prescindible or internal quality.

Second. That of relates whose reference to a ground is an unprescindible or relative quality.

In the former case, the relation is a mere *concurrence* of the correlates in one character, and the relate and correlate are not distinguished. In the latter case the correlate is set over against the relate, and there is in some sense an *opposition*.

Relates of the first kind are brought into relation simply by their agreement. But mere disagreement (unrecognized) does not constitute relation, and therefore relates of the second kind are only brought into relation by correspondence in fact.

A reference to a ground may also be such that it cannot be prescinded from a reference to an interpretant. In this case it may be termed an *imputed* quality. If the reference of a relate to its ground can be prescinded from reference to an interpretant, its relation to its correlate is a mere concurrence or community in the possession of a quality, and therefore the reference to a correlate can be prescinded from reference to an interpretant. It follows that there are three kinds of representations.

First. Those whose relation to their objects is a mere community in some quality, and these representations may be termed *likenesses*.

Second. Those whose relation to their objects consists in a correspondence in fact, and these may be termed *indices* or *signs*.

Third. Those the ground of whose relation to their objects is an imputed character, which are the same as *general signs*, and these may be termed *symbols*.

In the following passage from later writings, Peirce develops his basic classification of signs. Note that under the heading of "hypoicons" he lists images as a kind of iconic representation in a manner reminiscent of Reid. His class of indices seems to combine inconsistent elements. His first illustration of an index is a bullet hole that is an effect of the bullet, "whether anybody has the sense to attribute to it a shot or not." In this he agrees with St. Thomas's conception of a natural sign as "mind- independent" (cf. 2.4.7). But then he immediately also uses the demonstrative 'here' as an example of an index, though one which is not a causal effect, and goes so far as to include within this class letters as used in mathematics.

4.2.2 Charles Peirce (4)[4]

A *sign*, or *Representamen*, is a First which stands in such a genuine triadic relation to a Second, called its *Object*, as to be capable of determining a Third, called its *Interpretant*, to assume the same triadic relation to its Object in which it stands itself to the same Object. The triadic relation is *genuine*, that is its three members are bound together by it in a way that does not consist in any complexus of dyadic relations. That is the reason the Interpretant, or Third, cannot stand in a mere dyadic relation to the Object, but must stand in such a relation to it as the Representamen itself does. Nor can the triadic relation in which the Third stands be merely similar to that in which the First stands, for this would make the relation of the Third to the First a degenerate Secondness merely. The Third must indeed stand in such a relation, and thus must be capable of determining a Third of its own; but besides that, it must have a second triadic relation in which the Representamen, or rather the relation thereof to its Object, shall be its own (the Third's) Object, and must be capable of determining a Third to this relation. All this must equally be true of the Third's Thirds and so on endlessly; and this, and more, is involved in the familiar idea of a Sign; and as the term Representamen is here used, nothing more is implied. A *Sign* is a Representamen with a mental Interpretant. Possibly there may be Representamens that are not Signs. Thus, if a sunflower, in turning towards the sun, becomes by that very act fully capable, without further condition, of reproducing a sunflower which turns in precisely corresponding ways toward the sun, and of doing so with the same reproductive power, the sunflower would become a Representamen of the sun. But *thought* is the chief, if not the only mode of representation.

. . . The most fundamental [division of signs] is into *Icons, Indices,* and *Symbols*. Namely, while no Representamen actually functions as

4. *Collected Papers*, 2.274–2.302 (c. 1893, 1895, 1902).

such until it actually determines an Interpretant, yet it becomes a Representamen as soon as it is fully capable of doing this; and its Representative Quality is not necessarily dependent upon its ever actually determining an Interpretant, nor even upon its actually having an Object.

An *Icon* is a Representamen whose Representative Quality is a Firstness of it as a First. That is, a quality that it has *qua* thing renders it fit to be a representamen. Thus, anything is fit to be a *Substitute* for anything that it is like. (The conception of "substitute" involves that of a purpose, and thus of genuine thirdness.) Whether there are other kinds of substitutes or not we shall see. A Representamen by Firstness alone can only have a similar Object. Thus, a Sign by Contrast denotes its object only by virtue of a contrast, or Secondness, between two qualities. A sign by Firstness is an image of its object and, more strictly speaking, can only be an *idea*. For it must produce an Interpretant idea; and an external object excites an idea by a reaction upon the brain. But most strictly speaking, even an idea, except in the sense of a possibility, or Firstness, cannot be an Icon. A possibility alone is an Icon purely by virtue of its quality; and its object can only be a Firstness. But a sign may be *iconic*, that is, may represent its object mainly by its similarity, no matter what its mode of being. If a substantive be wanted, an iconic representamen may be termed a *hypoicon*. Any material image, as a painting, is largely conventional in its mode of representation; but in itself, without legend or label it may be called a *hypoicon*.

Hypoicons may be roughly divided according to the mode of Firstness of which they partake. Those which partake of simple qualities, or First Firstnesses, are *images;* those which represent the relations, mainly dyadic, or so regarded, of the parts of one thing by analogous relations in their own parts, are *diagrams;* those which represent the representative character of a representamen by representing a parallelism in something else, are *metaphors*.

The only way of directly communicating an idea is by means of an icon; and every indirect method of communicating an idea must depend for its establishment upon the use of an icon. Hence, every assertion must contain an icon or set of icons, or else must contain signs whose meaning is only explicable by icons. The idea which the set of icons (or the equivalent of a set of icons) contained in an assertion signifies may be termed the *predicate* of the assertion.

Turning now to the rhetorical evidence, it is a familiar fact that there are such representations as icons. Every picture (however conventional its method) is essentially a representation of that kind. So is every diagram, even although there be no sensuous resemblance between it and its object, but only an analogy between the relations of the parts of each. Particularly deserving of notice are icons in which the likeness is aided by conventional rules. Thus, an algebraic formula is an icon, rendered such by the rules of commutation, association, and distribution of the symbols. It may seem at first glance that it is an arbitrary classification to call an algebraic expression an icon; that it might as well, or better, be regarded as a compound conventional sign. But it is not so. For a great distinguishing property of the icon is that by the direct observation of it other truths concerning its object can be discovered than those which suffice to determine its construction. Thus, by means of two photographs a map can be drawn, etc. Given a conventional or other general sign of an object, to deduce any other truth than that which it explicitly signifies, it is necessary, in all cases, to replace that sign by an icon. This capacity of revealing unexpected truth is precisely that wherein the utility of algebraical formulae consists, so that the iconic character is the prevailing one.

That icons of the algebraic kind, though usually very simple ones, exist in all ordinary grammatical propositions is one of the philosophic truths that the Boolean logic brings to light. In all primitive writing, such as the Egyptian hieroglyphics, there are icons of a non-logical kind, the ideographs. In the earliest form of speech, there probably was a large element of mimicry. But in all languages known, such representations have been replaced by conventional auditory signs. These, however, are such that they can only be explained by icons. But in the syntax of every language there are logical icons of the kind that are aided by conventional rules. . . .

Photographs, especially instantaneous photographs, are very instructive, because we know that they are in certain respects exactly like the objects they represent. But this resemblance is due to the photographs having been produced under such circumstances that they were physically forced to correspond point by point to nature. In that aspect, then, they belong to the second class of signs, those by physical connection. The case is different if I surmise that zebras are likely to be obstinate, or otherwise disagreeable animals, because they seem to have a general resemblance to donkeys, and donkeys are self-willed. Here the donkey serves precisely as a probable likeness of the zebra. It is true we suppose that resemblance has a physical cause in heredity; but then, this hereditary affinity is itself only an inference from the likeness between the two animals, and we have not (as in the case of the photograph) any independent knowledge of the circumstances of the production of the two species. Another example of the use of a likeness is the design an artist draws of a statue, pictorial composition, architectural elevation, or piece of decoration, by the contemplation of which he can ascertain whether what he proposes will be beautiful and satisfactory. The question asked is thus answered almost with certainty because it relates to how the artist will himself be affected. The reasoning of mathematicians will be found to turn chiefly upon the use of likenesses, which are the very hinges of the gates of their science. The utility of likenesses to mathematicians consists in their suggesting in a very precise way, new aspects of supposed states of things. . . .

Many diagrams resemble their objects not at all in looks; it is only in respect to the relations of their parts that their likeness consists. Thus, we may show the relation between the different kinds of signs by a brace, thus:

$$\text{Signs:} \quad \left\{ \begin{array}{l} \text{Icons,} \\ \text{Indices,} \\ \text{Symbols.} \end{array} \right.$$

This is an icon. But the only respect in which it resembles its object is that the brace shows the classes of *icons, indices,* and *symbols* to be related to one another and to the general class of signs, as they really are, in a general way. When in algebra, we write equations under one another in a regular array, especially when we put resembling letters for corresponding coefficients, the array is an icon. Here is an example:

$$a_1 x + b_1 y = n_1$$
$$a_2 x + b_2 y = n_2$$

This is an icon, in that it makes quantities look alike which are in analogous relations to the problem. In fact, every algebraical equation is an icon, in so far as it *exhibits,* by means of the algebraical signs (which are not themselves icons), the relations of the quantities concerned.

It may be questioned whether all icons are likenesses or not. For example, if a drunken man is exhibited in order to show, by contrast, the excellence of temperance, this is certainly an icon, but whether it is a likeness or not may be doubted. The question seems somewhat trivial.

An *Index* or *Seme* (*sema*) is a Representamen whose Representative character consists in its being an individual second. If the Secondness is an existential relation, the Index is *genuine.* If the Secondness is a reference, the Index is *degenerate.* A genuine Index and its Object must be existent individuals (whether things or facts), and its immediate Interpretant must be of the same character. But since every individual must have characters, it follows that a genuine Index may contain a firstness, and so an Icon as a constituent part of it. Any individual is a degenerate Index of its own characters.

Subindices or *Hyposemes* are signs which are rendered such principally by an actual connection with their objects. Thus a proper name, personal demonstrative, or relative pronoun or the letter attached to a diagram, denotes what it does owing to a real connection with its object but none of these is an Index, since it is not an individual.

Let us examine some examples of indices. I see a man with a rolling gait. This is a probable indication that he is a sailor. I see a bowlegged man in corduroys, gaiters, and a jacket. These are probable indications that he is a jockey or something of the sort. A sundial or a clock *indicates* the time of day. Geometricians mark letters against the different parts of their diagrams and then use these letters to indicate those parts. Letters are similarly used by lawyers and others. Thus, we may say: If A and B are married to one another and C is their child while D is brother of A, then D is uncle of C. Here A, B, C, and D fulfill the office of relative pronouns, but are more convenient since they require no special collocation of words. A rap on the door is an index. Anything which focusses the attention is an index. Anything which startles us is an index, in so far as it marks the junction between two portions of experience. Thus a tremendous thunderbolt indicates that *something* considerable happened, though we may not know precisely what the event was. But it may be expected to connect itself with some other experience.

. . . A low barometer with a moist air is an index of rain; that is we suppose that the forces of nature establish a probable connection between the low barometer with moist air and coming rain. A weathercock is an index of the direction of the wind; because in the first place it really takes the self-same direction as the wind, so that there is a real connection between them, and in the second place we are so constituted that when we see a weathercock pointing in a certain direction it draws our attention to that direction, and when we see the weathercock veering with the wind, we are forced by the law of mind to think that direction is connected with the wind. The pole star is an index, or pointing finger, to show us which way is north. A spirit-level, or a plumb bob, is an index of the vertical direction. A yard-stick might seem, at first sight, to be an icon of a yard; and so it would be, if it were merely intended to show a yard as near as it can be seen and estimated to be a yard. But the very purpose of a yard-stick is to show a yard nearer than it can be estimated by its appearance. This it does in consequence of an accurate mechanical comparison made with the bar in London called the yard. Thus it is a real connection which gives the yard-stick its value as a representamen; and thus it is an *index*, not a mere *icon*.

When a driver to attract the attention of a foot passenger and cause him to save himself, calls out 'Hi!' so far as this is a significant word, it is as will be seen below, something more than an index; but so far as it is simply intended to act upon the hearer's nervous system and to rouse him to get out of the way, it is an index, because it is meant to put him in real connection with the object, which is his situation relative to the approaching horse. Suppose two men meet upon a country road and one of them says to the other, 'The chimney of that house is on fire'. The other looks about him and descries a house with green blinds and a verandah having a smoking chimney. He walks on a few miles and meets a second traveller. Like a Simple Simon he says, 'The chimney of that house is on fire'. 'What House?' asks the other. 'Oh, a house with green blinds and a verandah', replies the simpleton. 'Where is the house?' asks the stranger. He desires some *index* which shall connect his apprehension with the house meant. Words alone cannot do this. The demonstrative pronouns, 'this' and 'that', are indices. For they call upon the hearer to use his powers of observation, and so establish a real connection between his mind and the object; and if the demonstrative pronoun does that—without which its meaning is not understood—it goes to establish such a connection; and so is an index. The relative pronouns, *who* and *which,* demand observational activity in much the same way, only with them the observation has to be directed to the words that have gone before. Lawyers use A, B, C, practically as very effective relative pronouns. To show how effective they are, we may note that Messrs. Allen and Grenough in their admirable (though in the edition of 1877, too small) Latin Grammar, declare that no conceivable syntax could wholly remove the ambiguity of the following sentence, 'A replied to B that he thought C (his brother) more unjust to himself than to his own friend'. Now, any lawyer would state that with perfect clearness, by using A, B, C, as relatives, thus:

A replied to B that he $\frac{(A)}{(B)}$, thought C (his $\frac{(A's)}{(B's)}$ brother) more unjust

to himself, $\frac{(A)}{(B)}$ than to his $\frac{(A's)}{(B's)}$ own friend. The terminations which in any $\frac{(C)}{}$ $\frac{(C's)}{}$

inflected language are attached to words "governed" by other words, and which serve to show which the governing word is, by repeating what is elsewhere expressed in the same fore, are likewise *indices* of the same relative pronoun character. Any bit of Latin poetry illustrates this, such as the twelve-line sentence beginning, '*Jam satis terris*'. Both in these terminations and in the A, B, C, a likeness is relied upon to carry the attention to the right object. But this does not make them icons, in any important way; for it is of no consequence how the letters A, B, C, are shaped or what the terminations are. It is not merely that one occurrence of an A is like a previous occurrence that is the important circumstance, but that *there is an understanding that like letters shall stand for the same thing,* and this acts as a force carrying the attention from one occurrence of A to the previous one. A possessive pronoun is two ways an index: first it indicates the possessor, and, second, it has a modification which syntactically carries the attention to the word denoting the thing possessed.

Some indices are more or less detailed directions for what the hearer is to do in order to place himself in direct experiential or other connection with the thing meant. Thus, the coast Survey issues "Notices to Mariner," giving the latitude and longitude, four or five bearings of prominent objects, etc., and saying *there* is a rock, or a shoal, or buoy, or lightship. Although there will be other elements in such directions, yet in the main they are indices.

Along with such indexical directions of what to do to find the object meant, ought to be classed those pronouns which should be entitled *selective* pronouns because they inform the hearer how he is to pick out one of the objects intended, but which grammarians call by the very indefinite designation of *indefinite* pronouns. Two varieties of these are particularly important in logic, the *universal selectives,* such as *quivis, quilibet, quisquam, ullus, nullus, nemo, quisque, uterque,* and in English, *any, every, all, no, none, whatever, whoever, everybody, anybody, nobody.* These mean that the hearer is at liberty to select any instance he likes within limits expressed or understood, and the assertion is intended to apply to that one. The other logically important variety consists of the *particular selectives, quis, quispiam, nescio quis, aliquis, quidam,* and in English, *some, something, somebody, a, a certain, some or other, a suitable, one.*

Allied to the above pronouns are such expressions as *all but one, one or two, a few, nearly all, every other one,* etc. Along with pronouns are to be classed adverbs of place and time, etc.

Not very unlike these are, *the first, the last, the seventh, two-thirds of, thousands of,* etc.

Other indexical words are prepositions, and prepositional phrases, such as, 'on the right (or left) of'. Right and left cannot be distinguished by any general description. Other prepositions signify relations which may, perhaps, be described; but when they refer, as they do oftener than would be supposed, to a situation relative to the observed, or assumed to be experientially known, place and attitude of the speaker relatively to that of the hearer, then the indexical element is the dominant element.

Icons and indices assert nothing. If an icon could be interpreted by a sentence, that sentence must be in a "potential mood," that is, it would merely say, "Suppose a figure has three sides," etc. Were an index so interpreted, the mood must be imperative, or exclamatory, as 'See there!' or 'Look out!'. But the kind of signs which we are now coming to consider are, by nature, in the "indicative," or, as it should be called, the *declarative* mood. Of course, they can go to the expression of any other mood, since we may declare assertions to be doubtful, or mere interrogations, or imperatively requisite.

A *Symbol* is a Representamen whose Representative character consists precisely in its being a rule that will determine its Interpretant. All words, sentences, books, and other conventional signs are Symbols. We speak of writing or pronouncing the word 'man'; but it is only a *replica*, or embodiment of the word, that is pronounced or written. The word itself has no existence although it has a real being, *consisting in* the fact that existents *will* conform to it. It is a general mode of succession of three sounds or representamens of sounds, which becomes a sign only in the fact that a habit, or acquired law, will cause replicas of it to be interpreted as meaning a man or men. The word and its meaning are both general rules; but the word alone of the two prescribes the qualities of its replicas in themselves. Otherwise the 'word' and its 'meaning' do not differ, unless some special sense be attached to 'meaning'.

A Symbol is a law, or regularity of the indefinite future. Its Interpretant must be of the same description; and so must be also the complete immediate Object, or meaning. But a law necessarily governs, or "is embodied in" individuals, and prescribes some of their qualities. Consequently, a constituent of a Symbol may be an Index, and a constituent may be an Icon. A man walking with a child points his arm up into the air and says, 'There is a balloon'. The pointing arm is an essential part of the symbol without which the latter would convey no information. But if the child asks, 'What is a balloon', and the man replies, 'It is something like a great big soap bubble', he makes the image a part of the symbol. Thus, while the complete object of a symbol, that is to say, its meaning, is of the nature of a law, it must *denote* an individual and must *signify* a character. A *genuine* symbol is a symbol that has a general meaning. There are two kinds of degenerate symbols, the *Singular Symbol* whose Object is an existent individual, and which signifies only such characters as that individual may realize; and the *Abstract Symbol,* whose only Object is a character.

Although the immediate Interpretant of an Index must be an Index, yet since its Object may be the Object of an Individual Symbol, the Index may have such a Symbol for its indirect Interpretant. Even a genuine Symbol may be an imperfect Interpretant of it. So an *icon* may have a degenerate Index, or an Abstract Symbol, for an indirect Interpretant, and a genuine Index or Symbol for an imperfect Interpretant.

A *Symbol* is a sign naturally fit to declare that the set of objects which is denoted by whatever set of indices may be in certain ways attached to it is represented by an icon associated with it. To show what this complicated definition means, let us take as an example of a symbol the word 'loveth'. Associated with this word is an idea, which is the mental icon of one person loving another. Now we are to understand that 'loveth' occurs in a sentence; for what it may mean by itself, if it means anything, is not the question. Let the sentence, then, be 'Ezekiel loveth Huldah'. Ezekiel and Huldah must, then, be or contain indices; for without indices it is impossible to designate what one is talking about. Any mere description would leave it uncertain whether they were not mere characters in a ballad; but whether they be so or not, indices can designate them. Now the effect of the word 'loveth' is that the pair of objects denoted by the pair of indices Ezekiel and Huldah is represented by the icon, or the image we have in our minds of a lover and his beloved.

The same thing is equally true of every verb in the declarative mood; and indeed of every verb, for the other moods are merely declarations of a fact somewhat different from that expressed by the declarative mood. As for a noun, considering the meaning which it has in the sentence, and not as standing by itself, it is most conveniently regarded as a portion of a symbol. Thus the sentence, 'every man loves a woman' is equivalent to 'whatever is a man loves something that is a woman'. Here 'whatever' is a universal selective index, 'is a man' is a symbol, 'loves' is a symbol, 'something that' is a particular selective index, and 'is a woman' is a symbol. . . .

The word *Symbol* has so many meanings that it would be an injury to the language to add a new one. I do not think that the signification I attach to it, that of a conventional sign, or one depending upon habit (acquired or inborn), is so much a new meaning as a return to the original meaning. Etymologically, it should mean a thing thrown together, just as [an] *embolum* is a thing thrown into something, a bolt, and [a] *parabolum* is a thing thrown besides, collateral security, and [a] *hypobolum* is a thing thrown underneath, an antenuptial gift. It is usually said that in the word *symbol* the throwing together is to be understood in the sense of 'to conjecture'; but were that the case, we ought to find that *sometimes* at least it meant a conjecture, a meaning for which literature may be searched in vain. But the Greeks used 'throw together' *Symballein* very frequently to signify the making of a contract or convention. Now, we do find symbol *symbolum* early and often used to mean a convention or contract. Aristotle calls a noun a "symbol," that is a conventional sign. In Greek, watch-fire is a "symbol"; a church creed is called a "symbol," because it serves as a badge or shibboleth; a theatre ticket is called a "symbol"; any ticket or check entitling one to receive anything is a "symbol." Moreover, any expression of sentiment was called a "symbol." Such were the principal meanings of the word in the original language. The reader will judge whether they suffice to establish my claim that I am not seriously wrenching the word in employing it as I propose to do.

Any ordinary word, as 'give', 'bird', 'marriage', is an example of a symbol. It is *applicable to whatever may be found to realize the idea connected with the word;* it does not, in itself, identify those things. It does not show us a bird, nor enact before our eyes a giving or a marriage, but supposes that we are able to imagine those things, and have associated the word with them.

A regular progression of one, two, three may be remarked in the three orders of signs, Icon, Index, Symbol. The Icon has no dynamical connection with the object it represents; it simply happens that its qualities resemble those of that object, and excite analogous sensations in the mind for which it is a likeness. But it really stands unconnected with them. The index is physically connected with its object; they make an organic pair, but the interpreting mind has nothing to do with this connection, except remarking it, after it is established. The symbol is connected with its object by virtue of the idea of the symbol-using mind, without which no such connection would exist.

Every physical force reacts between a pair of particles, either of which may serve as an index of the other. On the other hand, we shall find that every intellectual operation involves a triad of symbols.

A symbol, as we have seen, cannot indicate any particular thing; it denotes a kind of thing. Not only that, but it is itself a kind and not a single thing. You can write down the word 'star' but that does not make you the creator of the word, nor if you erase it have you destroyed the word. The word lives in the minds of those who use it. Even if they are all asleep, it exists in their memory. So we may admit, if there be reason to do so, that generals are mere words without at all saying, as Ockham supposed, that they are really individuals.

Symbols grow. They come into being by development out of other signs, particularly from icons, or from mixed signs partaking of the nature of icons and symbols. We think only in signs. These mental signs are of mixed nature; the symbol-parts of them are called concepts. If a man makes a new symbol, it is by thoughts involving concepts. So it is only out of symbols that a new symbol can grow. *Omne symbolum de symbolo.* A symbol, once in being, spreads among the peoples. In use and in experience, its meaning grows. Such words as *force, law, wealth, marriage,* bear for us very different meanings from those they bore to our barbarous ancestors. The symbol may, with Emerson's sphynx, say to man,

Of thine eye I am eyebeam.

4.3 Other Classifications

More complex classifications are developed by Peirce in which the icon-index-symbol distinction is incorporated into a broader classification scheme based on the categories. This is in accordance with the classification scheme outlined above in 4.1.2 in which semiotic is claimed to be dependent on phenomenology for its fundamental conceptions. This extended classification divides signs into trichotomies consisting of three basic divisions, each with three branches. The result is nine subclasses of signs. The distinction between "sinsign" and "legisign" is elsewhere termed by Peirce the distinction between a sign "token" and sign "type," and in this form has persisted into the present.

4.3.1 Charles Peirce (5)[5]

Signs are divisible by three trichotomies; first, according as the sign in itself is a mere quality, is an actual existent, or is a general law; secondly, according as the relation of the sign to its object consists in the sign's having some character in itself, or in some existential relation to that object, or in its relation to an interpretant; thirdly, according as its Interpretant represents it as a sign of possibility or as a sign of fact or a sign of reason.

According to the first division, a Sign may be termed a *Qualisign,* a *Sinsign,* or a *Legisign.*

A Qualisign is a quality which is a Sign. It cannot actually act as a

5. *Collected Papers,* 2.243–2.252 (c. 1903).

sign until it is embodied; but the embodiment has nothing to do with its character as a sign.

A *Sinsign* (where the syllable *sin* is taken as meaning "being only once," as in *single, simple,* Latin *semel,* etc.) is an actual existent thing or event which is a sign. It can only be so through its qualities; so that it involves a qualisign, or rather, several qualisigns. But these qualisigns are of a peculiar kind and only form a sign through being actually embodied.

A *Legisign* is a law that is a Sign. This law is usually established by men. Every conventional sign is a legisign. It is not a single object, but a general type which, it has been agreed, shall be significant. Every legisign signifies through an instance of its application, which may be termed a *Replica* of it. Thus, the word 'the' will usually occur from fifteen to twenty-five times on a page. It is in all these occurrences one and the same word, the same legisign. Each single instance of it is a Replica. The Replica is a Sinsign. Thus, every Legisign requires Sinsigns. But these are not ordinary Sinsigns, such as are peculiar occurrences that are regarded as significant. Nor would the Replica be significant if it were not for the law which renders it so.

According to the second trichotomy, a Sign may be termed an *Icon,* an *Index,* or a *Symbol.*

An *Icon* is a sign which refers to the Object that it denotes merely by virtue of characters of its own, and which it possesses, just the same, whether any such Object actually exists or not. It is true that unless there really is such an Object, the Icon does not act as a sign; but this has nothing to do with its character as a sign. Anything whatever, be it quality, existent individual, or law, is an Icon of anything, in so far as it is like that thing and used as a sign of it.

An *Index* is a sign which refers to the Object that it denotes by virtue of being really affected by that Object. It cannot, therefore, be a Qualisign, because qualities are whatever they are independently of anything else. In so far as the Index is affected by the Object, it necessarily has some Quality in common with the Object, and it is in respect to these that it refers to the Object. It does, therefore, involve a sort of Icon, although an Icon of a peculiar kind; and it is not the mere resemblance of its Object, even in these respects which makes it a sign, but it is the actual modification of it by the Object.

A *Symbol* is a sign which refers to the Object that it denotes by virtue of a law, usually an association of general ideas, which operates to cause the Symbol to be interpreted as referring to that *Object.* It is thus itself a general type or law, that is, is a Legisign. As such it acts through a Replica. Not only is it general itself, but the Object to which it refers is of a general nature. Now that which is general has its being in the instances which it will determine. There must, therefore, be existent instances of what the Symbol denotes, although we must here understand by "existent," existent in the possibly imaginary universe to which the Symbol refers. The Symbol will indirectly, through the association or other law, be affected by those instances; and thus the Symbol will involve a sort of Index, although an Index of a peculiar kind. It will not, however, be by any means true that the slight effect upon the Symbol of those instances accounts for the significant character of the Symbol.

According to the third trichotomy, a Sign may be termed a *Rheme,* a *Dicisign* or *Dicent Sign* (that is, a proposition or quasi-proposition), or an *Argument.*

A *Rheme* is a Sign which, for its Interpretant, is a Sign of qualitative Possibility, that is, is understood as representing such and such a kind of possible Object. Any Rheme, perhaps, will afford some information; but it is not interpreted as doing so.

A *Dicent Sign* is a Sign, which, for its Interpretant, is a Sign of actual existence. It cannot, therefore, be an Icon, which affords no ground for an interpretation of it as referring to actual existence. A Dicisign necessarily involves, as a part of it, a Rheme, to describe the fact which it is interpreted as indicating. But this is a peculiar kind of Rheme; and while it is essential to the Dicisign, it by no means constitutes it.

An *Argument* is a Sign which, for its Interpretant, is a Sign of law. Or we may say that a Rheme is a sign which is understood to represent its object in its characters merely; that a Dicisign is a sign which is understood to represent its object in respect to actual existence; and that an Argument is a Sign which is understood to represent its Object in its character as Sign. Since these definitions touch upon points at this time much in dispute, a word may be added in defence of them. A question often put is: What is the essence of a Judgment? A judgment is the mental act by which the judger seeks to impress upon himself the truth of a proposition. It is much the same as an act of asserting the proposition, or going before a notary and assuming formal responsibility for its truth, except that those acts are intended to affect others, while the judgment is only intended to affect oneself. However, the logician, as such, cares not what the psychological nature of the act of judging may be. The question for him is: What is the nature of the sort of sign of which a principal variety is called a proposition, which is the matter upon which the act of judging is exercised? The proposition need not be asserted or judged. It may be contemplated as a sign capable of being asserted or denied. This sign itself retains its full meaning whether it be actually asserted or not. The peculiarity of it, therefore, lies in its mode of meaning; and to say this is to say that its peculiarity lies in its relation to its interpretant. The proposition professes to be really affected by the actual existent or real law to which it refers. The argument makes the same pretension, but that is not the principal pretension of the argument. The rheme makes no such pretension.

Peirce seems to intend his nine subclasses to stand for aspects of signs that are combined in the actual signs we encounter in experience. Some of these combinations are listed in this extended classification.

4.3.2 Charles Peirce (6)[6]

The three trichotomies of Signs result together in dividing Signs into *TEN CLASSES OF SIGNS,* of which numerous subdivisions have to be considered. The ten classes are as follows:

First: A *Qualisign* is any quality in so far as it is a sign. Since a quality is whatever it is positively in itself, a quality can only denote an object by virtue of some common ingredient or similarity; so that a Qualisign is necessarily an Icon. Further, since a quality is a mere logical possibility, it can only be interpreted as a sign of essence, that is, as a Rheme.

Second: An Iconic Sinsign [e.g., an individual diagram] is any object of experience in so far as some quality of it makes it determine the idea of an object. Being an Icon, and thus a sign by likeness purely, of whatever it may be like, it can only be interpreted as a sign of essence, or Rheme. It will embody a Qualisign.

Third: A Rhematic Indexical Sinsign is any object of direct experience so far as it directs attention to an Object by which its presence is caused. It necessarily involves an Iconic Sinsign of a peculiar kind, yet is quite different since it brings the attention of the interpreter to the very Object denoted.

Fourth: A Dicent Sinsign is any object of direct experience, in so far as it is a sign, and, as such, affords information concerning its Object. This it can only do by being really affected by its Object; so that it is necessarily an Index. The only information it can afford is of actual fact. Such a Sign must involve an Iconic Sinsign to embody the information and a Rhematic Indexical Sinsign to indicate the Object to which the information refers. But the mode of combination, or *Syntax,* of these two must also be significant.

6. *Collected Papers,* 2.254–2.259 (c. 1903).

Fifth: An Iconic Legisign is any general law or type, in so far as it requires each instance of it to embody a definite quality which renders it fit to call up in the mind the idea of a like object. Being an Icon, it must be a Rheme. Being a Legisign, its mode of being is that of governing single Replicas, each of which will be an Iconic Sinsign of a peculiar kind.

Sixth: A Rhematic Indexical Legisign is any general type or law, however established, which requires each instance of it to be really affected by its Object in such a manner as merely to draw attention to that Object. Each Replica of it will be a Rhematic Indexical Sinsign of a peculiar kind. The Interpretant of a Rhematic Indexical Legisign represents it as an Iconic Legisign; and so it is, in a measure—but in a very small measure.

Seventh: A Dicent Indexical Legisign is any general type or law, however established, which requires each instance of it to be really affected by its Object in such a manner as to furnish definite information concerning that Object. It must involve an Iconic Legisign to signify the information and a Rhematic Indexical Legisign to denote the subject to that information. Each Replica of it will be a Dicent Sinsign of a peculiar kind.

Eighth: A Rhematic Symbol or Symbolic Rheme is a sign connected with its Object by an association of general ideas in such a way that its Replica calls up an image in the mind which image, owing to certain habits or dispositions of that mind, tends to produce a general concept, and the Replica is interpreted as a Sign of an Object that is an instance of that concept. Thus, the Rhematic Symbol either is, or is very like, what the logicians call a General Term. The Rhematic Symbol, like any Symbol, is necessarily itself of the nature of a general type, and is thus a Legisign. Its Replica, however, is a Rhematic Indexical Sinsign of a peculiar kind, in that the image it suggests to the mind acts upon a Symbol already in that mind to give rise to a General Concept. In this it differs from other Rhematic Indexical Sinsigns, including those which are Replicas of Rhematic Indexical Legisigns. Thus, the demonstrative pronoun 'that' is a Legisign, being a general type; but it is not a Symbol, since it does not signify a general concept. Its Replica draws attention to a single Object, and is a Rhematic Indexical Sinsign. A Replica of the word 'camel' is likewise a Rhematic Indexical Sinsign, being really affected, through the knowledge of camels, common to the speaker and auditor, by the real camel it denotes, even if this one is not individually known to the auditor; and it is through such real connection that the word 'camel' calls up the idea of a camel. The same thing is true of the word 'phoenix'. For although no phoenix really exists, real descriptions of the phoenix are well known to the speaker and his auditor; and thus the word is really affected by the Object denoted. But not only are the Replicas of Rhematic Symbols very different from ordinary Rhematic Indexical Sinsigns, but so likewise are Replicas of Rhematic Indexical Legisigns. For the thing denoted by 'that' has not affected the replica of the word in any such direct and simple manner as that in which, for example, the ring of a telephone- bell is affected by the person at the other end who wants to make a communication. The Interpretant of the Rhematic Symbol often represents it as a Rhematic Indexical Legisign; at other times as as Iconic Legisign; and it does in a small measure partake of the nature of both.

Ninth: A Dicent Symbol, or ordinary Proposition, is a sign connected with its object by an association of general ideas, and acting like a Rhematic Symbol, except that its intended interpretant represents the Dicent Symbol as being, in respect to what it signifies, really affected by its Object, so that the existence or law which it calls to mind must be actually connected with the indicated Object. Thus, the intended Interpretant looks upon the Dicent Symbol as a Dicent Indexical Legisign; and if it be true, it does partake of this nature, although this does not represent its whole nature. Like the Rhematic Symbol, it is necessarily a Legisign. Like the Dicent Sinsign it is composite inasmuch as it necessarily involves a Rhematic Symbol (and thus is for its Interpretant an Iconic Legisign) to express its information and a Rhematic Indexical Legisign to indicate the subject of that information. But its Syntax of these is significant. The Replica of the Dicent Symbol is a Dicent Sinsign of a peculiar kind. This is easily seen to be true when the information the Dicent Symbol conveys is of actual fact. When that information is of a real law, it is not true in the same fullness. For a Dicent Sinsign cannot convey information of law. It is, therefore, true of the Replica of such a Dicent Symbol only in so far as the law has its being in instances.

Tenth: An Argument is a sign whose interpretant represents its object as being an ulterior sign through a law, namely, the law that the passage from all such premisses to such conclusions tends to the truth. Manifestly, then, its object must be general; that is, the Argument must be a Symbol. As a Symbol, it must, further, be a Legisign. Its Replica is a Dicent Sinsign.

The interpretant of a sign, as we have seen, is for Peirce another sign aroused in the mind of the interpreter, a kind of mental sign analogous to the mental words of the medieval tradition. This interpretant becomes in turn a sign for another interpretant in a process that can continue in many successive stages. But this process cannot continue indefinitely, he reasons, and its termination comes in the formation of a habit.

4.3.3 Charles Peirce (7)[7]

In advance of ascertaining the nature of this effect, it will be convenient to adopt a designation for it, and I will call it the *logical interpretant*, without as yet determining whether this term shall extend to anything beside the meaning of a general concept, though certainly closely related to that, or not. Shall we say that this effect may be a thought, that is to say, a mental sign? No doubt, it may be so; only, if this sign be of an intellectual kind—as it would have to be—it must itself have a logical interpretant; so that it cannot be the *ultimate* logical interpretant of the concept. It can be proved that the only mental effect that can be so produced and that is not a sign but is of a general application is a *habit-change;* meaning by a habit-change a modification of a person's tendencies toward action, resulting from previous experiences or from previous exertions of his will or acts, or from a complexus of both kinds of cause. It excludes natural dispositions, as the term 'habit' does, when it is accurately used; but it includes beside associations, what may be called "transsociations," or alterations of association, and even includes *dissociation*, which has usually been looked upon by psychologists (I believe mistakenly), as of deeply contrary nature to association.

The program of behavioral semiotic that was to follow embraced this concept of an "ultimate logical interpretant" and regarded sign interpretation itself as the activation of a previously formed habit.

Peirce pays almost exclusive attention to "logical" interpretation where the sign stands for an object. But he also acknowledges that there are other functions of signs.

4.3.4 Charles Peirce (8)[8]

Now the problem of what the "meaning" of an intellectual concept is can only be solved by the study of the interpretants, or proper significate effects, of signs. These we find to be of three general classes with some important subdivisions. The first proper significate effect of a sign is a feeling produced by it. There is almost always a feeling which we come

7. *Collected Papers*, 5.476 (c. 1905).
8. *Collected Papers*, 5.475 (c. 1905).

to interpret as evidence that we comprehend the proper effect of the sign, although the foundation of truth in this is frequently very slight. This "emotional interpretant," as I call it, may amount to much more than that feeling of recognition; and in some cases, it is the only proper significate effect that the sign produces. Thus, the performance of a piece of concerted music is a sign. It conveys, and is intended to convey, the composer's musical ideas; but these usually consist merely in a series of feelings. If a sign produces any further proper significate effect, it will do so through the mediation of the emotional interpretant, and such further effect will always involve an effort. I call it the energetic interpretant. The effort may be a muscular one, as it is in the case of the command to ground arms; but it is much more usually an exertion upon the Inner World, a mental effort. It never can be the meaning of an intellectual concept, since it is a single act, [while] such a concept is of a general nature. But what further kind of effect can there be?

Peirce's "energetic interpretant" seems to be the first acknowledgment of a prescriptive function of signs since Sextus's example of the horse leaping at the crack of a whip (2.2.1).

CHAPTER FIVE

Behavioral Semiotic

5.1 Direct-Response Theories

The behavioral program for semiotic undertook to translate the mentalistic terminology of the tradition into a terminology that referred only to publicly observable stimuli and responses. This terminology was formulated in a way general enough to apply to both the responses of lower animals to events in their environments and human responses to verbal utterances. Environmental stimuli were conceived of as replacing the classical natural signs; verbal utterances were the traditional conventional signs. The task was seen as constructing a framework inclusive of both.

An early version of a behavioral analysis of sign behavior is found in C. K. Ogden and I. A. Richards's *The Meaning of Meaning*. In this work, sign interpretation is conceived as the activation of a habit whose physiological basis is an "engram" formed from previous experiences. The sign is defined as a substitute stimulus, a stimulus that is a part of a complex whole to which the organism as interpreter responds in a way similar to its original reflex response to the whole. Thus, the visual stimulus of the caterpillar as associated with its bitter taste becomes a sign insofar as it evokes in isolation the rejection response evoked by a whole including both sight and taste.

5.1.1 C. K. Ogden and I. A. Richards[1]

The effects upon the organism due to any sign, which may be any stimulus from without, or any process taking place within, depend upon the past history of the organism, both generally and in a more precise fashion. In a sense, no doubt, the whole past history is relevant: but there will be some among the past events in that history which more directly determine the nature of the present agitation than others. Thus when we strike a match, the movements we make and the sound of the scrape are present stimuli. But the excitation which results is different from what it would be had we never struck matches before. Past strikings have left, in our organization, engrams, residual traces, which help to determine what

1. C. K. Ogden and I. A. Richards, *The Meaning of Meaning* (New York: Harcourt and Brace, 1923), pp. 139, 140.

the mental process will be. For instance, this mental process is among other things an awareness that we are striking a *match*. Apart from the effects of similar previous situations we should have no such awareness. Suppose further that the awareness is accompanied by an expectation of a flame. This expectation again will be due to the effects of situations in which the striking of a match has been followed by a flame. The expectation is the excitation of part of an engram complex, which is called up by a stimulus (the scrape) similar to a part only of the original stimulus-situation.

A further example will serve to make this clearer. The most celebrated of all caterpillars, whose history is in part recorded in the late Professor Lloyd Morgan's *Habit and Instinct*, was striped yellow and black and was seized by one of the professor's chickens. Being offensive in taste to the chicken he was rejected. Thenceforth the chicken refrained from seizing similar caterpillars. Why? Because the sight of such a caterpillar, a part that is of the whole sight-seize-taste context of the original experience, now excites the chicken in a way sufficiently like that in which the whole context did, for the seizing at least not to occur, whether the tasting (in images) does or not.

This simple case is typical of all interpretation, the peculiarity of interpretation being that when a context has affected us in the past the recurrence of merely a part of the context will cause us to react in the way in which we reacted before. A sign is always a stimulus similar to some part of an original stimulus and sufficient to call up the engram formed by that stimulus.

An engram is the residual trace of an adaptation made by the organism to a stimulus. The mental process due to the calling up of an engram is a similar adaptation: so far as it is cognitive, what it is adapted to is its referent, and is what the sign which excites it stands for or signifies.

The term 'adapted', though convenient, requires expansion if this account is to be made clear—and to this expansion the remainder of the present chapter is devoted. Returning to our instance, we will suppose that the match ignites and that we have been expecting a flame. In this case the flame is what we are adapted to. More fully, the mental process which is the expectation is similar to processes which have been caused by flames in the past, and further it is "directed to" the future. If we can discover what this 'directed to' stands for we shall have filled in the chief part of our account of interpretation.

Besides being "directed to" the future our expectation is also "directed to" flame. But here 'directed to' stands for nothing more than 'similar *to what has been caused by*'. A thought is directed to flame when it is similar in certain respects to thoughts which have been caused by flame. As has been pointed out above, we must not allow the defects of causal language either to mislead us here or alternatively to make us abandon the method of approach so indicated. We shall find, if we improve this language, both that this kind of substitute for "directed to" loses its strangeness, and also that the same kind of substitution will meet the case of "direction to the future" and will in fact explain the "direction" or reference of thinking processes in general.

This account was to be refined by others to exclude any reference to thinking or mental processes. The significance or meaning of a sign became then defined as the stimulus (e.g., the gustatory stimulus caused by the caterpillar) evoking a reflex, unlearned response similar to that which after associations and learning is evoked by the sign as a substitute for it. The extension to language was made by reasoning that linguistic expressions evoke responses similar to the responses evoked by the objects they signify. Hence, the "meaning" of a word is defined as the stimuli correlated to objects to which the word is associated in linguistic behavior. Apples evoke in us, let us say, salivation responses. The meaning of the word 'apple' would be the visual stimuli from apples if utterances of the word came to evoke similar responses. An early version of the view that words are substitute stimuli is stated by the psychologist John Watson.

5.1.2 John Watson[2]

The fact that every object and situation in the external environment is *named* is of vast importance. Words not only can and do call out other words, phrases and sentences, but when the human being is properly organized they can call out all of his manual activity. The words function in the matter of calling out responses exactly as did the objects for which the words serve as substitutes. Wasn't it Dean Swift who had one of his characters who couldn't or wouldn't speak carry around in a bag all the objects of common use so that instead of having to say words to influence the behavior of others, he pulled out the actual object from his bag and showed it? The world would be in this situation today if we did not have this *equivalence for reaction* between objects and words. You get something of the helpless state humanity would be in unless you had this *equivalence* in your own household when you by chance employ a

2. John Watson, *Behaviorism* (Chicago: University of Chicago Press, 1930), p. 233.

Roumanian nurse, a German cook and a French butler and you yourself speak only English.

Bertrand Russell also states with characteristic clarity the outlines of this theory.

5.1.3 Bertrand Russell[3]

The meaning of an object-word can only be learned by hearing it frequently pronounced in the presence of the object. The association between word and object is just like any other habitual association, e.g., that between sight and touch. When the association has been established, the object suggests the word, and the word suggests the object, just as an object seen suggests sensations of touch, and an object touched in the dark suggests sensations of sight. Association and habit are not specially connected with language; they are characteristics of psychology and physiology generally. How they are to be interpreted is, of course, a difficult and controversial question, but it is not a question which specially concerns the theory of language.

As soon as the association between an object-word and what it means has been established, the word is "understood" in the absence of the object, that is to say, it "suggests" the object in exactly the same sense in which sight and touch suggest one another.

Suppose you are with a man who suddenly says 'fox' because he sees a fox, and suppose that, though you hear him, you do not see the fox. What actually happens to you as a result of your understanding the 'fox'? You look about you, but this you would have done if he had said 'wolf' or 'zebra'. You may have an image of a fox. But what, from the observer's standpoint, shows your understanding of the word, is that you behave (within limits) as you would have done if you had seen the fox.

Generally, when you hear an object-word which you understand, your behaviour is, up to a point, that which the object itself would have caused. This may occur without any "mental" intermediary, by the ordinary rules of conditioned reflexes, since the word has become associated with the object. In the morning you may be told 'breakfast is ready', or you may smell the bacon. Either may have the same effect upon your actions. The association between the smell and the bacon is "natural," that is to say it is not a result of any human behaviour. But the association

3. Bertrand Russell, *An Inquiry into Meaning and Truth* (London: Allen and Unwin, 1940), pp. 67, 68.

between the word 'breakfast' and breakfast is a social matter, which exists only for English-speaking people. This, however, is only relevant when we are thinking of the community as a whole. Each child learns the language of its parents as it learns to walk. Certain associations between words and things are produced in it by daily experience, and have as much the appearance of natural laws as have the properties of eggs or matches; indeed they are exactly on the same level so long as the child is not taken to a foreign country.

One obvious difficulty with this theory arises from the fact that few verbal utterances evoke detectable responses from us, and those that are evoked usually seem to be unrelated to the objects they stand for. In an attempt to overcome this difficulty, C. E. Osgood and his collaborators have proposed a version of this theory that defines the relevant responses as "representational mediational responses" evoked by the sign that are part of the responses evoked by the "significate" as the unconditioned stimulus. These mediational responses can include neural processes that as are yet undetectable. Critics were quick to point out that postulating such unobservables is simply an ad hoc attempt to save the theory and undermines its empirical claims.

5.1.4 C. E. Osgood et alia[4]

Certain stimulus patterns have a "wired-in" connection with certain behavior patterns (unconditional reflexes) and additional stimuli have acquired the capacity (conditional reflexes). Food powder in the mouth regularly and reliably elicits a complex pattern of foodtaking reactions in the hungry animal (including salivating, swallowing and the like); a shock to the foot-pads regularly and reliably elicits a complex pattern of escape reactions (leaping, running, urinating, autonomic "fear" reactions, and the like). We may define a *significate*, then, as any stimulus which in a given situation, regularly and reliably produces a predictable pattern of behavior. For the naive organism, there are multitudes of stimuli which do not have this capacity—a buzzer sound does not reliably produce escape behavior like the shock does; the sound of a metronome does not reliably produce food-taking reactions, initially; the auditory effects of hearing 'hammer' do not produce behavior in any way relevant to HAM-

4. C. E. Osgood, G. Succi, and P. Tannenbaum, "The Logic of Semantic Differentiation," in *Psycholinguistics*, ed. S. Saporta, (New York: Holt, 1965); the excerpted passage is from pp. 286–288.

MER object in the pre-verbal child. How can each initially meaningless stimuli become meaningful signs for the organisms affected by them?

We have seen that ordinary single-stage conditioning does not provide a satisfactory answer—reactions made to signs are seldom identical with those made to the objects signified. But if we look at the conditioning situation more carefully, a possible solution to the problem may be seen. Many experiments of the details of the conditioning process combine to support the following conclusion: Components of the total unconditioned reaction vary in their dependence on the unconditioned stimulus and hence in the ease with which they may become conditioned to another stimulus. Typically, the less energy-expending a reaction component (e.g., "light-weight" components like glandular changes and animal postural adjustments) and the less interfering a reaction component with ongoing overt behavior (e.g., components which do not hinder overt approaches, avoidances, manipulations, and the like), the more promptly it appears in the conditioned reaction and hence the more readily available it is for the mediation function. The argument thus far may be summarized as follows: *Whenever some stimulus other than the significate is contiguous with the significate, it will acquire an increment of association with some portion of the total behavior elicited by the significate as a representational mediation process. . . .*

Whereas Morris linked sign and significate through partial identity of significate-produced and "disposition"-produced behaviors, we have linked sign and significate through partial identity of the "disposition" itself (r_m) with the behavior produced by the significate. Thus, according to this view, words represent things because they produce in human organisms some replica of the actual behavior toward these things, as a mediation process. This is the crucial identification, the mechanism that ties particular signs to particular significates rather than others. Stating the proposition formally: *A pattern of stimulation which is not the significate is a sign of that significate if it evokes in the organism a mediating process, this process* (a) *being some fractional part of the total behavior elicited by the significate and* (b) *producing responses which would not occur without the previous contiguity of non-significate and significate patterns of stimulation.* It will be noted that in this statement we have chosen the term 'mediating process' rather than 'mediating reaction'; this is to leave explicitly open the question of the underlying nature of such representational mediators—they may well be purely neural events rather than actual muscular contractions or glandular secretions in the traditional sense of "reaction." In any case, in the formal statement of the theory they are presumed to have all the functional properties of stimulus-producing reactions. The above definition of a sign-process may be somewhat cumbersome, but all the limiting conditions seem necessary. The mediational process must include some part of the same behavior produced by the significate if the sign is to have its particularistic representing property; the presence of this property must depend upon the prior contiguity of non-significate and significate patterns of stimulation in the experience of the organism if the definition is to include the criterion that sign-processes are learned.

5.2 Mead and Morris

Besides the difficulty of identifying a response to a sign raised in the preceding selection, the direct-response theory suffers from a serious omission—any reference to communicative behavior and the problem of distinguishing such behavior from reflex responses that trigger responses in other organisms because of innate or "wired-in" mechanisms that are the product of a long evolutionary development. Stickleback fish exhibit elaborate courtship behavior, movements of the male coordinated with the female in an extended sequence of responses to the other's behavior. But is this communication, and is there any analogy between this behavior and the use of signs to communicate? To this question George Herbert Mead gave a negative answer by distinguishing between a "significant symbol" or "significant gesture" used to communicate and a "non-significate gesture" triggered as a reflex response to environmental stimuli and occurring without communicative intent. The bristling of the hairs on a dog's back during a dogfight is such a reflex response and may be evidence for us of an imminent attack by the dog and a criterion for ascribing anger or fear to it. The bristling has "meaning" for us insofar as we can anticipate the future attack. But there is no "conscious determination" by the dog to convey this to us, Mead claims, and the bristling thus does not represent communication. In contrast, when someone shakes his fist at another, there is "some idea behind it," and it "calls out in the individual making it the same attitude toward it . . . that it calls out in the other individuals" to whom it is addressed. It is thus used to communicate and is a "significate symbol."

Mead's distinction between bristling as coordinative behavior and genuine communication can be regarded as an early anticipation of the more elaborate attempts by Grice and Bennett to solve the same problem that will be outlined in the final chapter. All formulate this problem as that of distinguishing between evidence for an event or state of affairs (e.g., the dog's bristling as evidence for us of attack) and a sign used for communication. Mead's solution is presented by combining a behavioral methodology with use of mentalistic terms such as 'idea' and 'consciousness'.

5.2.1 *George Herbert Mead*[5]

The primitive situation is that of the social act which involves the interaction of different forms, which involves, therefore, the adjustment of the conduct of these different forms to each other, in the social process. Within that process one can find what we term gestures, those phases of the act which bring about the adjustment of the response to the other form. These phases of the act carry with them the attitude as the observer recognizes it and also what we call the inner attitude. The animal may be angry or afraid. There are such emotional attitudes which lie back of these acts, but these are only part of the whole process that is going on. Anger expresses itself in attack; fear expresses itself in flight. We can see, then, that the gestures mean these attitudes on the part of the form, that is, they have that meaning for us. We see that an animal is angry and that he is going to attack. We know that that is in the action of the animal and is revealed by the attitude of the animal. We cannot say the animal means it in the sense that he has a reflective determination to attack. A man may strike another before he means it; a man may jump and run away from a loud sound behind his back before he knows what he is doing. If he has the idea in his mind, then the gesture not only means this to the observer but it also means the idea which the individual has. In one case the observer sees that the attitude of the dog means attack, but he does not say that it means a conscious determination to attack on the part of the dog. However, should somebody shake his fist in your face you assume that he has not only a hostile attitude but that he has some idea behind it. You assume that it means not only a possible attack, but that the individual has an idea in his experience.

When, now, that gesture means this idea behind it and it arouses that idea in the other individual, then we have a significant symbol. In the case of the dogfight we have a gesture which calls out appropriate response; in the present case we have a symbol which answers to a meaning in the experience of the first individual and which also calls out that meaning in the second individual. Where the gesture reaches that situation it has become what we call "language." It is now a significant symbol, and it signifies a certain meaning.

5. George Herbert Mead, *Mind, Self and Society*, ed. C. W. Morris, (Chicago: University of Chicago Press, 1934), pp. 45-47.

The gesture is that phase of the individual act to which adjustment takes place on the part of other individuals in the social process of behavior. The vocal gesture becomes a significant symbol (unimportant, as such, on the merely affective side of experience) when it has the same effect on the individual making it that it has on the individual to whom it is addressed or who explicitly responds to it, and thus involves a reference to the self of the individual making it. The gesture in general, and the vocal gesture in particular, indicates some object or other within the field of social behavior, an object of common interest to all the individuals involved in the given social act thus directed toward or upon that object. The function of the gesture is to make adjustment possible among the individuals implicated in any given social act with reference to the object or objects with which that act is concerned; and the significant gesture or significant symbol affords far greater facilities for such adjustment and readjustment than does the non-significant gesture, because it calls out in the individual making it the same attitude toward it (or toward its meaning) that it calls out in the other individuals participating with him in the given social act. Thus it makes him conscious of their attitude toward it (as a component of his behavior) and enables him to adjust his subsequent behavior to theirs in the light of that attitude. In short, the conscious or significant conversation of gestures is a much more adequate and effective mechanism of mutual adjustment within the social act—involving, as it does, the taking, by each of the individuals carrying it on, of the attitudes of the others toward himself—than is the unconscious or non-significant conversation of gestures.

. . . Only in terms of gestures as significant symbols is the existence of mind or intelligence possible; for only in terms of gestures which are significant symbols can thinking—which is simply an internalized or implicit conversation of the individual with himself by means of such gestures—take place. The internalization in our experience of the external conversation of gestures which we carry on with other individuals in the social process is the essence of thinking; and the gestures thus internalized are significant symbols because they have the same meanings for all individual members of the given society or social group, that is, they respectively arouse the same attitudes in the individuals making them that they arouse in the individuals responding to them. Otherwise the individual could not internalize them or be conscious of them and their meanings.

Mead's mixed behavioral and mentalistic analysis of communication was overshadowed during the 1930s and 1940s by attempts to solve within a consistently behavioral framework the difficulties encountered by direct-response theories, in particular, the problem of identifying a response directly caused by the sign stimulus. To Charles Morris we owe an alternative that was to have considerable influence. Morris's theory preserves the inclusive framework of the earlier theories, with responses to environmental stimuli and linguistic utterances used in defining both the sign and its significance. What is novel is the definition of a sign as a "prepatory stimulus" that rather than evoking a direct response, causes a disposition to respond later to a subsequent stimulus. The extended passage that follows, from *Signs, Language and Behavior,* sets forth this definition after criticizing earlier theories in which the sign is defined as a "substitute stimulus." In the passage, Morris attempts to equate this substitute stimulus with the natural signs of the classical tradition—e.g., clouds as a sign of rain. In fact, Morris's preparatory stimulus and the classical evidential sign of Aristotle and Augustine are interpreted in very different ways. A buzzer is interpreted by the dog in a direct, unmediated way as a sign of food. In contrast, clouds are interpreted as a sign of rain through the mediation of a linguistic generalization such as 'Clouds cause rain', for it is on the basis of a belief in such a generalization that the interpreter predicts the rain on seeing the clouds. This feature of the interpretation of the classical natural signs correctly lead the Stoics, as we saw in 2.2.1, to regard the sign as a proposition that is a singular premiss in an inference. Far from being the primitive evolutionary precursor of linguistic signs being defined by Morris, the classical natural sign presupposed for its interpretation the use of discursive language.

5.2.2 Charles Morris[6]

There is wide disagreement as to when something is a sign. Some persons would unhesitatingly say that blushing is a sign, others would not. There are mechanical dogs which will come out of their kennels if one claps one's hands loudly in their presence. Is such clapping a sign? Are clothes signs of the personality of those who wear them? Is music a sign of anything? Is a word such as 'Go!' a sign in the same sense as is a green light on a street intersection? Are punctuation marks signs? Are dreams signs? Is the Parthenon a sign of Greek culture? Disagreements are widespread; they show that the term 'sign' is both vague and ambiguous.

6. Charles Morris, *Signs, Language and Behavior* (New York: Braziller, 1946), pp. 3–11.

This disagreement extends to many other terms which are commonly used in describing sign-processes. The terms 'express', 'understand', 're-fer', 'meaning' would provide many instances. So would 'communication' and 'language'. Do animals communicate? If so, do they have a language? Or do only men have language? Yes, run some answers; no, run others. We find the same diversity of replies if we ask whether thought or mind or consciousness is involved in a sign-process; whether a poem "refers" to what it "expresses"; whether men can signify what cannot be experienced; whether mathematical terms signify anything; whether language signs are preceded genetically by non-language signs; whether the elements in an undeciphered "dead" language are signs.

In the face of such disagreements, it is not easy to find a starting point. If we are to seek for a formulation of the word 'sign' in biological terms, the task is to isolate some distinctive kind of behavior which agrees fairly well with frequent usages of the term 'sign'. Since usage of the term is, however, not consistent, it cannot be demanded that the chosen behavioral formulation agree with all the various usages which are actually current. At some point the semiotician must say: "Henceforth we will recognize that anything which fulfills certain conditions is a sign. These conditions are selected in the light of current usages of the term 'sign', but they may not fit in with all such usages. They do not therefore claim to be a statement of the way the term 'sign' is always used, but a statement of the conditions under which we will henceforth admit within semiotic that something is a sign."

Then from such a starting point a behavioral theory of signs will build up step by step a set of terms to talk about signs (taking account of current distinctions but attempting to reduce for scientific purposes their vagueness and ambiguity), and will endeavor to explain and predict sign phenomena on the basis of the general principles of behavior which underlie all behavior, and hence sign-behavior. The aim is to take account of the distinctions and analyses which former investigators have made, but to ground these results whenever possible upon general behavior theory. In the nature of the case such a scientific semiotic will often deviate from current terminology, and can only be developed slowly and laboriously. It will often seem pedantic and less illuminating for many purposes than less scientific approaches—which therefore are to be encouraged in the light of the many problems and purposes which a treatment of signs aims to fulfill. It is not to be expected that all discussions of literary, religious, and logical signs can be translated at once with profit into a behavioral formulation. The present approach does not therefore wish to exclude other approaches to semiotic. But it does proceed upon the belief that basic progress in this complex field rests finally upon the development of a genuine science of signs, and that this development can be most profitably carried on by a biological orientation which places signs within the context of behavior.

Preliminary Isolation of Sign Behavior

We shall begin by taking two examples of behavior to which the term 'sign' is often applied both in common usage and in the writings of semioticians. Then a superficial analysis of these examples will disclose the features which a more technical formulation of the nature of a sign must embody. If both situations reveal certain common elements, then both may be called sign-behavior; the differences in the two situations would then suggest differences between kinds of signs. If analysis shows too great differences, then the alternative would be to choose different terms to describe the two situations, and to adopt a narrower definition of 'sign': in either case we would then be in a position to consider whether any additional phenomena are to be called signs, that is, whether the characterization of signs based upon the two examples in question is to be held as a basis for determining when something is a sign or whether it is to be expanded to include situations of a widely different sort.

The first example is drawn from experiments on dogs. If a hungry dog that goes to a certain place to obtain food when the food is seen or smelled, is trained in a certain way, it will learn to go to this place for food when a buzzer is sounded even though the food is not observed. In this case the dog is attentive to the buzzer but does not normally go to the buzzer itself; and if the food is not made available until some time after the buzzer has sounded, the dog may not go to the place in question until the time interval has elapsed. Many persons would say in such a situation that the buzzer sound is to the dog a sign of food at the given place, and in particular, a non-language sign. If we abstract from the experimenter and his purposes in this example, and consider only the dog, the example approximates what have often been called "natural signs," as when a dark cloud is a sign of rain. It is in this way that we wish the experiment to be considered.

The second example is drawn from human behavior. A person on the way to a certain town is driving along a road; he is stopped by another person who says that the road is blocked some distance away by a land-slide. The person who hears the sounds which are uttered does not continue to the point in question, but turns off on a side-road and takes another route to his destination. It would be commonly said that the sounds made by the one person and heard by the other (and indeed by the utterer also) were signs to both of them of the obstacle on the road, and in particular were language signs, even though the actual responses of the two persons are very different.

Common to these two situations is the fact that both the dog and the person addressed behave in a way which satisfies a need—hunger in the one case, arrival at a certain town in the other. In each case the organisms have various ways of attaining their goals: when food is smelled the dog reacts differently than when the buzzer is sounded; when the obstacle is encountered the man reacts differently than when spoken to at a distance from the obstacle. Further, the buzzer is not responded to as food nor the spoken words as an obstacle; the dog may wait awhile before going for food and the man may continue to drive for a time down the blocked road before turning off to another road. And yet in some sense both the buzzer and the words control or direct the course of behavior toward a goal in a way similar to (though not identical with) the control which would be exercised by the food or the obstacle if these were present as stimuli: the buzzer determines the dog's behavior to be that of seeking food in a certain place at a certain time; the words determine the man's behavior to be that of getting to a certain town by avoiding a certain obstacle at a given place on a given road. The buzzer and the words are in some sense "substitutes" in the control of behavior for the control over behavior which would be exercised by what they signify if this was itself observed. The differences between non-language and language signs remain for subsequent discussion.

It is clear at once that the formulation of 'sign' frequent in early behavior theory is too simple: namely, it cannot be simply said that a sign is a substitute stimulus which calls out to itself the same response which would have been called out be something else had it been present. For the response to food is to food itself, while the response to the buzzer is not to it as if it were food; and the actual response to the situation in which the sign appears may be greatly different from the response to a situation where what is signified, and not the sign, is present. The dog, for instance, may salivate when the buzzer is sounded but it cannot actually eat unless food is present; the man may feel anxiety when he is addressed, but his turning off the road before reaching the obstacle is a very different response from that which he would make if he had gone directly to the place of blockage itself (and even more different from the behavior of the person who told him of the obstacle).

Nor can the difficulties in the earlier attempts to identify signs with any and all substitute stimuli be avoided by attempting to say that whatever influences a response with respect to what is not at the moment a stimulus is a sign. For example, a drug will influence the way an organism will respond to stimuli which later affect it, and yet it would be too great a departure from common usage to call such a drug a sign.

The difficulties in these formulations may perhaps be avoided if, as our examples suggest, signs are identified within goal-seeking behavior. So in the light of our analysis of what the two examples chosen as a point of reference have in common (and neglecting for the time being their differences) we arrive at the following preliminary formulation of at least one set of conditions under which something may be called a sign: *If something, A, controls behavior towards a goal in a way similar to (but not necessarily identical with) the way something else, B, would control behavior with respect to that goal in a situation in which it were observed, then A is a sign.*

The buzzer and the spoken sounds are then signs of food and obstacle because they control the course of behavior with respect to the goals of getting food and getting to a certain place in a way similar to the control which food and obstacle would exercise if they were observed. Whatever exercises this type of control in goal-seeking behavior is a sign. And goal-seeking behavior in which signs exercise control may be called *sign-behavior*.

Toward Precision in the Identification of Sign-Behavior

For many purposes the preceding account of a sign is adequate; it at least suggests a behavioral way of formulating what is commonly meant in saying that a sign "stands for" or "represents" something other than itself. But for more strictly scientific purposes a more exact formulation is required in order to clarify the notions of similarity of behavior and goal-seeking behavior. We might at this point simply leave it to the scientists in their field to state further refinements, and indeed anything we add is in the nature of the case tentative. But since our concern is to push semiotic as rapidly as possible in the direction of a natural science, the following suggestions are made.

Implicit in the preceding account are four concepts which need further clarifications: preparatory-stimulus, disposition to respond, response-sequence, and behavior-family. When these notions are elucidated a more precise statement of a set of conditions sufficient for something to be called a sign can be given.

A *preparatory-stimulus* is any stimulus which influences a response to some other stimulus. Thus it has been found by O. H. Mowrer that the magnitude of the jump of a rat to a shock stimulus is increased if a tone sound before the shock stimulus is encountered. Such a stimulus differs from other stimuli, say the shock, in that as a preparatory-stimulus it influences a response to something other than itself rather than causing a response to itself (it may of course also cause a response to itself, that is, not be merely or solely a preparatory-stimulus). By a *stimulus* is meant, following Clark L. Hull, any physical energy which acts upon a receptor of a living organism; the source of this energy will be called the *stimulus-object*. By a *response* is meant any action of a muscle or gland; hence there are reactions of an organism which are not necessarily responses. A preparatory-stimulus affects or causes a reaction in an organism, but, as Mowrer makes clear, it need not call out a response to itself, but only to some other stimulus. In the account toward which we are moving it is not held that all preparatory-stimuli are signs, but only that preparatory-stimuli which meet certain additional requirements are signs. That a preparatory-stimulus need not when presented call out a response makes intelligible the fact that a command to turn right at a certain place may produce at the time of utterance no overt, or as far as we know, "implicit" response of turning right, and yet may determine that the person commanded turns right when he reaches the place in question. A preparatory-stimulus does however cause some reaction in an organism, affects it in some way, and this leads to the introduction of the term 'disposition to respond'.

A *disposition to respond* to something in a certain way is a state of an organism at a given time which is such that under certain additional conditions the response in question takes place. These additional conditions may be very complex. An animal disposed to go to a certain place to obtain food may not go there even if food is observed—he may not be willing or able to swim across an intervening water barrier or to move if certain other animals are present as stimulus-objects. The complex of conditions also includes other states of the organism. The person commanded to turn at a certain corner may not turn even when the corner is reached: as he walked to the corner he may have come to believe that his informant was deliberately trying to misdirect him, so that confidence in one's informant may be at times a necessary condition for making a response to which one is disposed because of signs.

There may be dispositions to respond which are not caused by preparatory-stimuli, but every preparatory-stimulus causes a disposition to respond in a certain way to something else. Logically, therefore, 'disposition to respond' is the more basic notion, and a preparatory-stimulus is a stimulus which causes a disposition to respond in a certain way to something else. And since not all preparatory-stimuli would normally be called signs, and not all dispositions to response which are caused by preparatory-stimuli are relevant to the delimitation of sign-processes, additional criteria are involved; and to be in accord with our own preliminary formulation of sign-behavior, these criteria must introduce the notion of behavior toward a goal.

A *response-sequence* is any sequence of consecutive responses whose first member is initiated by a stimulus-object and whose last member is a response to this stimulus-object as a goal-object, that is, to an object which partially or completely removes the state of the organism (the "need") which motivates the sequence of responses. Thus the series of responses of a hungry dog which sees a rabbit, runs after it, kills it, and so obtains food is a response-sequence. For the sight of the rabbit starts a series of responses to the rabbit in terms of which the rabbit is finally obtained as food. The intervening responses in the sequence can occur only if the environment provides the necessary stimuli for their release, and such sources of stimuli may be called *supporting stimulus-objects*. The terrain over which the dog runs in this case provides the support necessary for the responses of following the rabbit and tracking it down, while the rabbit provides the stimuli initiating and terminating the series of responses.

A *behavior-family* is any set of response-sequences which are initiated by similar stimulus-objects and which terminate in these objects as similar goal-objects for similar needs. Hence all the response-sequences which start from rabbits and eventuate in securing rabbits as food would constitute the rabbit-food behavior-family. A behavior-family may in an extreme case have only one member; no limit is set to the number of possible members. Behavior-families have various degrees of inclusiveness. All the objects which a dog eats would, for instance, determine an extensive "object- food" behavior-family which would include the rabbit-food behavior-family as a subordinate behavior-family.

In these terms it is possible to formulate more precisely a set of conditions sufficient for something to be a sign: *If anything, A, is a preparatory-stimulus which in the absence of stimulus-objects initiating response-sequences of a certain behavior-family causes a disposition in some organism to respond under certain condition by response-sequences of this behavior-family, then A is a sign.*

According to these conditions, the buzzer is a sign to the dog since it disposes the animal to seek food in a certain place in the absence of direct stimulation from food objects at this place, and similarly, the spoken words are signs to the driver since they dispose him to response-sequences of avoiding an obstacle at a certain point on a certain road although the obstacle is not itself at the time of hearing the sounds a stimulus-object.

The merit of this formulation is that it does not require that the dog or the driver respond to the sign itself, the sign serving merely as a preparatory- stimulus for response to something else. Nor does it require that the dog or the driver finally respond overtly as they would if food or an obstacle had been stimulus-objects; it merely requires that if the animal makes the response-sequences which it is disposed to make when certain additional conditions are met (conditions of need and of supporting stimulus-objects) these response-sequences will be of the same behavior-family as those which the food or obstacle would have initiated. In this way the difficulties which earlier behavioral formulations of signs encountered are avoided. And yet objective behavioral criteria are furnished for determining whether something is or is not a sign. It is further believed that these criteria do not deviate from those which underlie certain common usages of the term 'sign'.

5.3 Carnap and Quine's Revisions

Morris's theory avoids some difficulties only to raise many others. What exactly is a response-sequence? How do we identify one? How do we distinguish the "last member" of the sequence as the "goal object" (e.g., the eating of food) from earlier stages of the sequence (e.g., searching for food)? Someone says to me 'It is raining', and I nod in acknowledgment. Is this nod the response-sequence, and if so, how does this aid in determining the meaning of the sentence?

In an effort to specify a clearly identifiable subsequent stimulus and to make the theory applicable to language, Rudolph Carnap and W. V. O. Quine proposed similar refinements. With Carnap, the attempt to construct a framework inclusive of linguistic and nonlinguistic signs is abandoned. In its place is established the more limited goal of specifying, in the behavioral terms of a science of "pragmatics," both the extension and intension of a linguistic term. The extension of a term in a language becomes defined as those objects to which a native speaker of this language would apply it. Thus, the extension of the German term 'hund' is the class of dogs. A term's intension is determined by identifying those common properties of objects evoking this response. Carnap recognizes the problem of identifying such properties. His attempted solution is to introduce the nonempirical concept of possibility and to claim that in certain cases appeal can be made to descriptions or even pictures of objects.

5.3.1 Rudolph Carnap[7]

The Determination of Extensions

We take as example the German language. We imagine that a linguist who does not know anything about this language sets out to study it by observing the linguistic behavior of German-speaking people. More specifically, he studies the German language as used by a given person Karl at a given time. For simplicity, we restrict the discussion in this paper mainly to predicates applicable to observable things, like 'blau' and 'Hund'. It is generally agreed that, on the basis of spontaneous or elicited utterances of a person, the linguist can ascertain whether or not the person is willing to apply a given predicate to a given thing, in other words, whether the predicate denotes the given thing for the person. By collecting results of this kind, the linguist can determine first, the extension of the predicate 'Hund' within a given region for Karl, that is, the class of the things to which Karl is willing to apply the predicate, second, the extension of the contradictory, that is, the class of those things for which Karl denies the application of 'Hund', and, third, the intermediate class of those things for which Karl is not willing either to affirm or to deny the predicate. The size of the third class indicates the degree of vagueness of the predicate 'Hund', if we disregard for simplicity the effect of Karl's ignorance about relevant facts. For certain predicates, e.g., 'Mensch', this third class is relatively very small; the degree of their extensional vagueness is low. On the basis of the determination of the three classes for the predicate 'Hund' within the investigated region, the linguist may make a hypothesis concerning the responses of Karl to things outside of that region, and maybe even a hypothesis concerning the total extension in the universe. The latter hypothesis cannot, of course, be completely verified, but every single instance of it can in principle be tested. On the other hand, it is also generally agreed that this determination of extension involves uncertainty and possible error. But since this holds for all concepts of empirical science, nobody regards this fact as a sufficient reason for rejecting the concepts of the theory of extension. The sources of uncertainty are chiefly the following: first, the linguist's acceptance of the result that a given thing is denoted by 'Hund' for Karl may be erroneous, e.g., due to a misunderstanding or a factual error of Karl's; and, second, the generaliza-

---

7. Rudolph Carnap, "Meaning and Synonymy in Natural Languages," Appendix D of *Meaning and Necessity* (Chicago: University of Chicago Press, 1947), pp. 234–238.

tion to things which he has not tested suffers, of course, from the uncertainty of all inductive inference.

The Determination of Intensions

The purpose of this paper is to defend the thesis that the analysis of intension for a natural language is a scientific procedure, methodologically just as sound as the analysis of extension. To many linguists and philosophers this thesis will appear as a truism. However, some contemporary philosophers, especially Quine and White, believe that the pragmatical intension concepts are foggy, mysterious, and not really understandable, and that so far no explications for them have been given. They believe further that, if an explication for one of these concepts is found, it will at best be in the form of a concept of degree. They acknowledge the good scientific status of the pragmatical concepts of the theory of extension. They emphasize that their objection against the intension concepts is based on a point of principle and not on the generally recognized facts of the technical difficulty of linguistic investigations, the inductive uncertainty, and the vagueness of the words of ordinary language. I shall therefore leave aside in my discussion these difficulties, especially the two mentioned at the end of the last section. Thus the question is this: *granted that the linguist can determine the extension of a given predicate, how can he go beyond this and determine also its intension?*

The technical term 'intension', which I use here instead of the ambiguous word 'meaning', is meant to apply only to the cognitive or designative meaning component. I shall not try to define this component. It was mentioned earlier that determination of truth presupposes knowledge of meaning (in addition to knowledge of facts); now, cognitive meaning may be roughly characterized as that meaning component which is relevant for the determination of truth. The non-cognitive meaning components, although irrelevant for questions of truth and logic, may still be very important for the psychological effect of a sentence on a listener, e.g., by emphasis, emotional associations, motivational effects.

It must certainly be admitted that the pragmatical determination of intensions involves a new step and therefore a new methodological problem. Let us assume that two linguists, investigating the language of Karl, have reached complete agreement in the determination of the extension of a given predicate in a given region. This means that they agree for every thing in this region, whether or not the predicate in question denotes it for Karl. As long as only these results are given, no matter how large the region is—you may take it, fictitiously, as the whole world, if you like—it is still possible for the linguists to ascribe to the predicate different intensions. For there are more than one and possibly infinitely many properties whose extension within the given region is just the extension determined for the predicate.

Here we come to the core of the controversy. It concerns the nature of a linguist's assignment of one of these properties to the predicate as its intension. This assignment may be made explicit by an entry in the German-English dictionary, conjoining the German predicate with an English phrase. The linguist declares hereby the German predicate to be synonymous with the English phrase. *The intensionalist thesis* in pragmatics, which I am defending, says that the assignment of an intension is an empirical hypothesis which, like any other hypothesis in linguistics, can be tested by observations of language behavior. On the other hand, *the extensionalist thesis* asserts that the assignment of an intension, on the basis of the previously determined extension, is not a question of fact but merely a matter of choice. The thesis holds that the linguist is free to choose any of those properties which fit to the given extension; he may be guided in his choice by a consideration of simplicity, but there is no question of right or wrong. Quine seems to maintain this thesis; he says: "The finished lexicon is a case evidently of *ex pede Herculem*. But there is a difference. In projecting Hercules from the foot we risk error but we may derive comfort from the fact that there is something to be wrong about. In the case of the lexicon, pending some definition of synonymy, we have not stating of the problem; we have nothing for the lexicographer to be right or wrong about."

I shall now plead for the intensionalist thesis. Suppose, for example, that one linguist, after an investigation of Karl's speaking behavior, writes into his dictionary the following:

(1)   Pferd, horse,

while another linguist writes:

(2)   Pferd, horse or unicorn.

Since there are no unicorns, the two intensions ascribed to the word 'Pferd' by the two linguists, although different, have the same extension. If the extensionalist thesis were right, there would be no way for empirically deciding between (1) and (2). Since the extension is the same, no response by Karl, affirmative or negative, with respect to any actual thing can make a difference between (1) and (2). But what else is there to investigate for the linguist beyond Karl's responses concerning the application of the predicate to all the cases that can be found? The answer is, he must take into account not only the actual cases, but also possible cases. The most direct way of doing this would be for the linguist to use, in the German questions directed to Karl, modal expressions corresponding to "possible case" or the like. To be sure, these expressions are usually rather ambiguous; but this difficulty can be overcome by giving suitable explanations and examples. I do not think that there is any objection of principle against the use of modal terms. On the other hand, I think that their use is not necessary. The linguist could simply describe for Karl cases, which he knows to be possible, and leave it open whether there is anything satisfying those descriptions or not. He may, for example, describe a unicorn (in German) by something corresponding to the English formulation: "a thing similar to a horse, but having only one horn in the middle of the forehead." Or he may point toward a thing and the describe the intended modification in words, e.g.: "a thing like this one but having one horn in the middle of the forehead." Or, finally , he might just point to a picture representing a unicorn. Then he asks Karl whether he is willing to apply the word 'Pferd' to a thing of this kind. An affirmative or a negative answer will constitute a confirming instance for (2) or (1) respectively. This shows that (1) and (2) are different empirical hypotheses.

Quine's alternative is stated by conceiving of an English-speaking linguist entering a community with an entirely unknown language and having no bilingual informants. His problem is that of translating expressions of this alien language into English on the sole basis of native speakers' verbal behavior triggered by environmental stimuli and questioning. Suppose, for example, a rabbit is in view, and the native informant says the single-word sentence 'Gavagai'. Then the linguist might frame the initial hypothesis that 'Gavagai' is synonymous with the English sentence 'Rabbit'. The hypothesis can be tested by his asking 'Gavagai?' in the presence of a variety of objects having various attributes. If the native responds affirmatively in the presence of rabbits in varying states and negatively in their absence, then the ocular stimuli impinging on the native's retina is for Quine the "affirmative stimulus meaning" of 'Gavagai', and the absence of this pattern of stimulation is the "negative stimulus meaning" of the expression.

5.3.2 W. V. O. Quine[8]

Certain sentences of the type of 'Gavagai' are the sentences with which our jungle linguist must begin, and for these we now have before us the makings of a crude concept of empirical meaning. For meaning,

8. W. V. O. Quine, *Word and Object* (Cambridge: M.I.T. Press, 1960), p. 32.

supposedly, is what a sentence shares with its translation; and translation at the present stage turns solely on correlations with non-verbal stimulation.

Let us make this concept of meaning more explicit and give it a neutrally technical name. We may begin by defining the *affirmative stimulus meaning* of a sentence such as 'Gavagai', for a given speaker, as the class of all the stimulations (hence evolving ocular irradiation patterns between properly timed blindfoldings) that would prompt his assent. . . .We may define the *negative* stimulus meaning similarly with 'assent' and 'dissent' interchanged, and then define the *stimulus meaning* as the ordered pair of the two. We could refine the notion of stimulus meaning by distinguishing degrees of doubtfulness of assent and dissent, say by reaction time; but for the sake of fluent exposition let us forbear. The imagined equating of 'Gavagai' and 'Rabbit' can now be stated thus: they have the same stimulus meaning.

The reader will note how different Carnap and Quine's translation procedures are from the procedure advocated by Gérando for coming to understand the expressions of an alien language through a shared "language of gestures" in 3.3.1. For Gérando, this understanding requires becoming a user of the language and participating in communication with the people being studied. This communication will start with primitive gestures as a kind of "natural language" common to all. To understand the meaning of an expression is to be able to use it as they do, and such understanding makes translation possible. In contrast, Carnap and Quine advocate a method restricted to observation of objectified linguistic behavior.

The project of behavioral semiotic can be characterized as that of "reductionism," the elimination of psychological terms such as 'believe', 'expect', and 'perceive' in order to replace them with terms describing physical states and events. That such a replacement is impossible because of irreducibly intentional features of the psychological is argued by Roderick Chisholm. The criticisms in the following passage are aimed at Morris, but can also be extended to Carnap and Quine.

5.3.3 Roderick Chisholm[9]

Franz Brentano wrote, in a well-known passage, that *intentionality* is peculiar to psychical phenomena. No *physical* phenomenon, he said,

---

9. Roderick Chisholm, "Intentionality and the Theory of Signs," *Philosophical Studies* 3 (1952): 56–63; the passage is from the Introduction and Section II.

shows anything like it; hence intentionality affords us a criterion of the mental or psychical. Let us refer to this view as "Brentano's thesis." Among the phenomena which he would have called "intentional" is the interpretation of *signs*. One may ask, is it possible to provide an adequate theory of signs which will show Brentano's thesis to be mistaken? . . .

We cannot be satisfied with the traditional analyses of sign situations since these, almost invariably, define such terms as 'sign' by means of other intentional concepts. That is, we cannot say merely that an object is a sign if it causes someone to *believe*, or *expect*, or *think of* something, since 'believe', 'expect', and 'think of' are clearly intentional terms. Nor can we say merely that an object is a sign if it causes someone to be *set* for, or to be *ready for*, or to *behave appropriately* to something, for these terms, despite their behavioristic overtones, are also intentional. Moreover, if we are to *show* that Brentano is mistaken, then we must not introduce any new technical terms into our analysis of sign behavior unless we can show that these terms apply also to nonpsychological situations. If we take our cue from previous investigations, we will find that two rather different nonintentional conceptions of *sign* are at hand. According to the one, a sign is essentially a *substitute* stimulus; according to the other, it is a *preparatory* stimulus. The second of these conceptions, I believe, is somewhat more promising than the first.

If we use the term 'referent' as short for 'what is signified', we may say that, according to the first view, the sign is a substitute for the referent. It is a substitute in the sense that, as a stimulus, it causes effects upon the organism similar to those which the referent would have caused. According to this conception, something S may be said to be a sign of something E for an organism O, if and only if S affects O in a manner similar to that in which E would have affected O. Hence the bell may be said to be a sign of food to the dog, since it affects the dog's responses, or dispositions to respond, in a manner similar to that in which the food would have affected them.

This type of definition involves many difficulties of detail, but we shall concern ourselves with only one, viz., that of specifying the respect or degree of similarity which must obtain between the effects caused by the sign and the effects which the referent would have caused. Shall we say that S is a sign of E provided merely that S has *some* of the effects which E would have had? This would have the unacceptable consequence that all stimuli signify each other, since any two stimuli have at least some effects in common. Every stimulus causes neural activity, for example; hence, to that extent at least, any two stimuli will have similar effects. Shall we say that S is a sign of E provided that S has the effects which *only* E would have had? If the sign has effects which only the referent can have, then the sign *is* the referent and only food can be a sign of food. The other methods of specifying the degree or respect of similarity required by the substitute stimulus theory, so far as I can see, have equally unacceptable consequences. Let us turn, therefore, to the preparatory-stimulus theory.

According to the preparatory-stimulus theory, the sign is to be viewed as affecting the organism's responses, or dispositions to respond, to the referent. As a result of being stimulated by the sign, the organism will respond differently, if subsequently stimulated by the referent, than it otherwise would have done. In order to formulate a paradigm for this type of definition, let us borrow Husserl's terms 'fulfill' and 'disrupt' (or 'disappoint'). We may say, then: S is a sign of E for O, if and only if S occasions in O a disposition which would be *fulfilled* if E were to occur, or which would be *disrupted* if E were not to occur. Our problem now becomes that of finding appropriate meanings for the terms 'fulfill' and 'disrupt'.

Russell's terms, 'yes feeling' (or 'quite-so feeling') and 'surprise', may be suggestive in this context. Thus we might say that, as a result of being stimulated by the bell, the dog would have a yes-feeling if food were provided and would be surprised if it were not. Let us assume that we can provide causal nonintentional accounts of *yes-feeling* and *surprises*; possibly they can be defined by means of such terms as 'reinforcement', 'disequilibration', and 'shock'.

It may well be that, with these concepts, we can provide an account of the dog and the bell which will show that this elementary sign situation is not intentional. It is possible that the dog, in virtue of the sound of the bell, is put into a bodily state such that he will be shocked or surprised if he does not receive food within the moment. And it may be that this bodily state which would lead to the shock or surprise can be specified in physiological terms, independently of the stimulus and of the shock. Whether this is so, of course is a psychological question. But if it is so, then we must conclude that some sign situations are not intentional. Nevertheless, difficulties in principle seem to be involved when we attempt to extend the preparatory-stimulus theory to human behavior.

These difficulties concern the specification of the occasions upon which the appropriate fulfillments or disruptions must occur. According to our paradigm, these must be caused by the occurrence, or nonoccurrence, of the referent. But it is easy to think of elementary human sign situations where the appropriate events do not occur in the manner required. And to accommodate our definition to such cases, we seem required to make qualification which reintroduce the intentional concepts we are trying to eliminate.

An example will clarify this point. Jones, let us suppose, interprets certain words or noises as a sign that his aunt is waiting at the railroad station. Our definition, in application to this situation, gives us: "As a result of being stimulated by the words, Jones would experience a yes-feeling if his aunt were at the station, or would experience surprise if she were not." If Jones avoids the station, however, the requisite fulfillment or disruption may not occur. Shall we add, then, the qualification ". . . provided Jones visits the station"?

If his visit to the station is brief and if he is not concerned about his aunt, the requisite experiences may still fail to occur. Shall we add: " . . provided he looks for his aunt"? But now we have an intentional term again. And even if we allow him to look for her, the experiences may not occur if some diversion happens to interrupt his search.

Moreover, even after we have made the necessary qualifications, we must still add something about what Jones would perceive; for example, ". . . if Jones were to perceive that his aunt is there (or isn't there)." We cannot, at this point, interpret the term 'perceive' nonintentionally, construing it merely in terms of light waves, sensible stimulation, etc. For if Jones were to meet his aunt and if she were to serve as visual stimulus object, etc., he might yet take her to be someone else; or he might meet and be visually stimulated by someone else and yet take her to be his aunt. In such cases, the surprises and yes-feeling would not occur in the manner required by our definition.

Moreover, even if we allow ourselves the intentional terms 'look for' and 'perceive', our definition will still be inadequate. If Jones visits the bus terminal, believing it to be the railroad station, or if he visits the railroad station, believing it to be the bus terminal, the conditions prescribed by the definition may well fail to occur. Hence we must add to our other intentional qualifications further qualifications about what Jones must believe, or not believe. And so on.

The difficulties which we have encountered in connection with this example are of the following sorts: We have found it necessary to add that the organism, rather than be merely stimulated by the referent, must perceive it, or recognize it, or have it manifested to him, or take something to be it, or else we must add that these intentional events do not occur. We have seen that it may be necessary to add that the organism must look for the referent. And we have seen that it is necessary to add that the organism must have certain beliefs concerning the nature of the conditions under which he perceives, or fails to perceive, the referent. Similar difficulties can readily be seen to apply to any example which may come to mind.

The analysis of signs, then, seems to lead us back to the intentional concepts with which we began. We noted, however, that there may be simple sign situations, involving the behavior of animals, which can be described nonintentionally. Possibly infants are involved in such situations. And possibly as Ogden and Richards intimated ordinary sign situations may be shown somehow to be "theoretically analyzable" into such simple situations. But to show how this might be done is a program or project for the science of semiotics; it is certainly not yet one of its accomplishments. And until this is shown, we can say, I think, that the presumption lies with the thesis of Brentano.

5.4 Instrumental Learning and Language Acquisition

The early conditioned-reflex models of animal learning provided the basis for the behavioral theories just discussed, with difficulties in identifying relevant responses leading finally to exclusive attention to language and the abandonment of the attempt to construct a theory comprehensive of both primitive responses to environmental stimuli and human responses to verbal utterances. A very different model of learning called the "instrumental" model, proposed by B. F. Skinner, provided the basis for another comprehensive semiotic theory. The paradigm applications are to examples of spontaneous behavior such as that of a rat randomly pressing a bar, which begins to exhibit regularity when followed by a schedule of reinforcements, e.g., the reward of food pellets. Such behavior is called operant behavior. It may be a response to a "controlling stimulus" (e.g., the sounding of a buzzer) that the animal learns to discriminate from other environmental stimuli. Thus, if the pellet is produced only when the bar is pressed after the buzzer sounds, the sound becomes the occasion for a discriminated operant of bar pressing only after buzzer sound. In this way, reinforcements satisfying animal drives such as hunger and environmental stimuli come to "shape" behavior.

Skinner applies this model to two types of verbal behavior. The first is the production of utterances of prescriptive expressions called "mands," expressions such as the commands 'Wait!' and 'Silence!'. Reinforcement comes for the speaker in the form of compliance with the commands, and it is because of such a reward that a child in the early stages of language acquisition learns to produce utterances of them.

5.4.1 B. F. Skinner (1)[10]

In a given verbal community, certain responses are characteristically followed by certain consequences. *Wait!* is followed by someone's waiting and *Sh-h!* by silence. Much of the verbal behavior of young children is of this sort. *Candy!* is characteristically followed by the receipt of candy and *Out!* by the opening of a door. These effects are not inevitable, but we can usually find one consequence of each response which is commoner than any other. There are nonverbal parallels. *Out!*, as we have seen, has the same ultimate effect as turning a knob and pushing against a door. Both forms of behavior become part of the repertoire of the organism through operant conditioning. When a response is characteristically reinforced in a given way, its likelihood of appearing in the behavior of the speaker is a function of the deprivation associated with that reinforcement. The response *Candy!* will be more likely to occur after a period of candy deprivation, and least likely after candy satiation. The response *Quiet!* is reinforced through the reduction of an aversive condition, and we can increase the probability of its occurrence by creating such a condition—that is, by making a noise.

It will be convenient to have a name for the type of verbal operant in which a response of given form is characteristically followed by a given consequence in a verbal community. The basic relationship has been recognized in syntactic and grammatical analyses (expressions such as the 'imperative mood' and 'commands and entreaties' suggest themselves), but no traditional term can safely be used here. The term 'mand' has a certain mnemonic value derived from 'command', 'demand', 'countermand', and so on, and is conveniently brief. A 'mand', then, may be defined as a verbal operant in which the response is reinforced by a characteristic consequence and is therefore under the functional control of relevant conditions of deprivation or aversive stimulation. Adjectival and verbal uses of the term are self-explanatory. In particular, and in contrast with other types of verbal operants to be discussed later, the response has no specified relation to a prior stimulus.

A mand is characterized by the unique relationship between the form of the response and the reinforcement characteristically received in a given verbal community. It is sometimes convenient to refer to this relation by saying that a mand "specifies" its reinforcement. *Listen!, Look!, Run!, Stop!,* and *Say yes!* specify the behavior of a listener; but when a

10. B. F. Skinner, *Verbal Behavior* (New York: Appleton-Century-Croft, 1957), ch. 3, pp. 35–37.

hungry diner calls *Bread!*, or *More soup!*, he is specifying the ultimate reinforcement. Frequently both the behavior of the listener and the ultimate reinforcement are specified. The mand *Pass the salt!* specifies an action (*pass*) and an ultimate reinforcement (*the salt*).

A mand is a type of verbal operant singled out by its controlling variables. It is not a formal unit of analysis. No response can be said to be a mand from its form alone. As a general rule, in order to identify any type of verbal operant we need to know the kind of variable of which the response is a function. In a given verbal community, however, certain formal properties may be so closely associated with specific kinds of variables that the latter may often be safely inferred. In the present case, we may say that some responses, simply because of formal properties, are very probably mands.

The pattern of response which characteristically achieves the given reinforcement depends of course, upon the "language"—that is, upon the reinforcing practices of the verbal community. But we have to explain not only the relationships between patterns of response and reinforcements, but the maintenance of the behavior of the listener. When we come to consider other types of verbal operants, we shall find that the behavior functions mainly for the benefit of the listener, and in that case his behavior is not difficult to explain. The mand, however, works primarily for the benefit of the speaker; why should the listener perform the necessary mediation of reinforcement?

What needs to be explained, in other words, is the total speech episode. This can be done by listing all relevant events in the behavior of both speaker and listener in their proper temporal order. The deprivation or aversive stimulation responsible for the strength of each must be specified, and the reinforcing contingencies must explain the origin and continued maintenance of the behavior. Several interchanges between the two organisms frequently occur.

The "tact," in contrast, is a verbal operant differentially produced as a response not simply to a schedule of reinforcements but also to a controlling stimulus in a manner analogous to the way the sounding of a buzzer controls the rat's pressing the bar.

5.4.2 B. F. Skinner (2)[11]

In all verbal behavior under stimulus control there are three important events to be taken into account: a stimulus, a response, and a rein-

---

11. Skinner, *Verbal Behavior*, ch. 5, pp. 81–84.

forcement. These are contingent upon each other, as we have seen, in the following way: the stimulus, acting prior to the emission of the response, sets the occasion upon which the response is likely to be reinforced. Under this contingency, through a process of operant discrimination, the stimulus becomes the occasion upon which the response is likely to be emitted.

In echoic, textual, and intraverbal operants the proper stimulus is verbal. There are two important types of controlling stimuli which are usually nonverbal. One of these has already been mentioned: an audience characteristically controls a large group of responses through a process to be discussed in detail. The other is nothing less than the whole of the physical environment—the world of things and events which a speaker is said to "talk about." Verbal behavior under the control of such stimuli is so important that it is often dealt with exclusively in the study of language and in theories of meaning.

The three-term contingency in this type of operant is exemplified when, in the presence of a doll, a child frequently achieve some sort of generalized reinforcement by saying *doll;* or when a teleost fish, or picture thereof, is the occasion upon which the student of zoology is reinforced when he says *teleost fish.* There is no suitable term of this type of operant. 'Sign', 'symbol', and more technical terms from logic and semantics commit us to special schemes of reference and stress the verbal response itself rather than the controlling relationship. The invented term 'tact' will be used here. The term carries a mnemonic suggestion of behavior which "makes contact with" the physical world. A tact may be defined as a verbal operant in which a response of given form is evoked (or at least strengthened) by a particular object or event or property of an object or event We account for the strength by showing that in the presence of the object or event a response of that form is characteristically reinforced in a given verbal community. . . .

It serves no useful purpose, and may be misleading, to call a tact an "announcement," "declaration," or "proposition," or to say that it "states," "asserts," or "denotes" something, or that it "makes known" or "communicates" a condition of the stimulus. If these terms have any scientific meaning at all, beyond a paraphrase of the present relation, they refer to certain additional processes to be considered. . . . We shall see, for example, that the tact is more likely to be "asserted" than any other type of operant but, taken by itself, is not for that reason an assertion.

The Controlling Relation

The tact emerges as the most important of verbal operants because of the unique control exerted by the prior stimulus. This control is established by the reinforcing community for reasons to be noted in a moment. It contrasts sharply with the controlling relations in the mand, where the most efficient results are obtained by breaking down any connection with prior stimuli, thus leaving deprivation or aversive stimulation in control of the response. Either explicitly or as the effect of common contingencies, a response is reinforced in a single way under many different stimulating circumstances. The response then comes to "specify" its characteristic consequences regardless of the condition under which it occurs. In the tact, however, (as well as in echoic, textual, and intraverbal behavior) we weaken the relation to any specific deprivation or aversive stimulation and set up a unique relation to a discriminative stimulus. We do this by reinforcing the response as consistently as possible in the presence of one stimulus with many different reinforcers or with a generalized reinforcer. The resulting control is through the stimulus. A given response "specifies" a given stimulus property. This is the "reference" of semantic theory. Roughly speaking, the mand permits the listener to infer something about the condition of the speaker regardless of external circumstances, while the tact permits him to infer something about the circumstances regardless of the condition of the speaker. These "inferences" need to be more sharply represented by analyzing the reinforcing practices of the community which maintain mands and tacts in strength.

A tact which is established with a completely generalized reinforcement might be called "pure" or "objective." Whether the response is emitted at all may depend upon other variables; but whenever it is emitted, its form is determined solely by a specific feature of the stimulating environment. A truly generalized reinforcement is, however, rare . . . and pure objectivity in this sense is probably never achieved. Verbal behavior in which the reinforcement is thoroughly generalized, and the control of which therefore rests almost exclusively with the environment, is developed by the methods of science. The reinforcing practices of the scientific community thoroughly suppress the special interests of the speaker. This is not necessarily a sign of superior ethics in scientists; it is merely an evolved practice which has proved to be particularly valuable. It is responsible for much of the power of the scientific method.

This theory is the object of Noam Chomsky's criticisms, though some aspects of them can be (and have been by Chomsky) applied to the whole program of program of behavioral semiotic. Chomsky concedes the scientific value of stimulus-response analyses of animal behavior but denies the possibility of extending them to what he regards as the radically different features of human linguistic behavior and language acquisition.

5.4.3 Noam Chomsky[12]

Skinner's thesis is that external factors consisting of present stimulation and the history of reinforcement (in particular the frequency, arrangement, and withholding of reinforcing stimuli) are of overwhelming importance, and that the general principles revealed in laboratory studies of these phenomena provide the basis for understanding the complexities of verbal behavior. He confidently and repeatedly voices his claim to have demonstrated that the contribution of the speaker is quite trivial and elementary, and that precise prediction of verbal behavior involves only specification of the few external factors that he has isolated experimentally with lower organisms.

Careful study of the book [*Verbal Behavior*] (and of the research on which it draws) reveals, however, that these astonishing claims are far from justified. It indicates, furthermore, that the insights that have been achieved in the laboratories of the reinforcement theorist, though quite genuine, can be applied to complex human behavior only in the most gross and superficial way, and that speculative attempts to discuss linguistic behavior in these terms alone omit from consideration factors of fundamental importance that are, no doubt, amenable to scientific study, although their specific character cannot at present be precisely formulated. Since Skinner's work is the most extensive attempt to accommodate human behavior involving higher mental faculties within a strict behaviorist schema of the type that has attracted many linguists and philosophers, as well as psychologists, a detailed documentation is of independent interest. The magnitude of the failure of this attempt to account for verbal behavior serves as a kind of measure of the importance of the factors omitted from consideration, and an indication of how little is really known about this remarkably complex phenomenon. . . .

Although this book makes no direct reference to experimental work, it can be understood only in terms of the general framework that Skinner has developed for the description of behavior. Skinner divides the responses of the animal into two main categories. *Respondents* are purely reflex responses elicited by particular stimuli. *Operants* are emitted responses, for which no obvious stimulus can be discovered. Skinner has been concerned primarily with operant behavior. The experimental arrangement that he introduced consists basically of a box with a bar

12. Noam Chomsky, "Review of B. F. Skinner's *Verbal Behavior*," *Language* 35 (1959): 25–58. The excerpt is from pp. 27–36. I have deleted Chomsky's page references to *Verbal Behavior*.

attached to one wall in such a way that when the bar is pressed, a food pellet is dropped into a tray (and the bar press is recorded). A rat placed in the box will soon press the bar, releasing a pellet into the tray. This state of affairs, resulting from the bar press, increases the *strength* of the bar-pressing operant. The food pellet is called a *reinforcer;* the event, a reinforcing event. The strength of an operant is defined by Skinner in terms of the rate of response during extinction (i.e., after the last reinforcement and before return to the preconditioning rate).

Suppose that release of the pellet is conditional on the flashing of a light. Then the rat will come to press the bar only when the light flashes. This is called *stimulus discrimination*. The response is called a *discriminated operant* and the light is called the *occasion* for its emission; this is to be distinguished from elicitation of a response by a stimulus in the case of the respondent. Suppose that the apparatus is so arranged that bar-pressing of only a certain character (e.g., duration) will release the pellet. The rat will then come to press the bar in the required way. This process is called response differentiation. By successive slight changes in the conditions under which the response will be reinforced it is possible to shape the response of a rat of a pigeon in very surprising ways in a very short time, so that rather complex behavior can be produced by a process of successive approximation.

A stimulus can become reinforcing by repeated association with an already reinforcing stimulus. Such a stimulus is called a secondary reinforcer. Like many contemporary behaviorists, Skinner considers money, approval, and the like to be secondary reinforcers which have become reinforcing because of their association with food etc. Secondary reinforcers can be *generalized* by associating them with a variety of different primary reinforcers.

Another variable that can affect the rate of the bar-pressing operant is drive, which Skinner defines operationally in terms of hours of deprivation. His major scientific book, *Behavior of Organisms,* is a study of the effects of food-deprivation and conditioning on the strength of the bar-pressing response of healthy mature rats. Probably Skinner's most original contribution of animal behavior studies has been his investigation of the effects of intermittent reinforcement, arranged in various different ways, presented in *Behavior of Organisms* and extended (with pecking of pigeons as the operant under investigation) in the recent *Schedules of Reinforcement* by Ferster and Skinner. It is apparently these studies that Skinner has in mind when he refers to the recent advances in the study of animal behavior.

The notions 'stimulus', 'response', 'reinforcement' are relatively well defined with respect to the bar-pressing experiments and others similarly restricted. Before we can extend them to real-life behavior, however, certain difficulties must be faced. We must decide, first of all, whether any physical event to which the organism is capable of reacting is to be called a stimulus on a given occasion, or only one to which the organism in fact reacts; and correspondingly, we must decide whether any part of behavior is to be called a response, or only one connected with stimuli in lawful ways. Questions of this sort pose something of a dilemma for the experimental psychologist. If he accepts the broad definitions, characterizing any physical event impinging on the organism as a stimulus and any part of the organism's behavior as a response, he must conclude that behavior has not been demonstrated to be lawful. In the present state of our knowledge, we must attribute an overwhelming influence on actual behavior to ill-defined factors of attention, set, volition, and caprice. If we accept the narrower definitions, then behavior is lawful by definition (if it consists of responses); but this fact is of limited significance, since most of what the animal does will simply not be considered behavior. Hence the psychologist either must admit that behavior is not lawful (or that he cannot at present show that it is—not at all a damaging admission for a developing science), or must restrict his attention to those highly limited areas in which it is lawful (e.g., with adequate controls, bar-pressing in rats; lawfulness of the observed behavior provides, for Skinner, an implicit definition of a good experiment).

Skinner does not consistently adopt either course. He utilizes the experimental results as evidence for the scientific character of his system of behavior, and analogic guesses (formulated in terms of a metaphoric extension of the technical vocabulary of the laboratory) as evidence for its scope. This creates the illusion of a rigorous scientific theory with a very broad scope, although in fact the terms used in the description of real-life and of laboratory behavior may be mere homonyms, with at most a vague similarity of meaning. To substantiate this evaluation, a critical account of his book must show that with a literal reading (where the terms of the descriptive system have something like the technical meanings given in Skinner's definitions) the book covers almost no aspect of linguistic behavior, and that with a metaphoric reading, it is no more scientific than the traditional approaches to this subject matter, and rarely as clear and careful.

Consider first Skinner's use of the notions 'stimulus' and 'response'. In *Behavior of Organisms* he commits himself to the narrow definitions for these terms. A part of the environment and a part of behavior are called stimulus (eliciting, discriminated, or reinforcing) and response, respectively, only if they are lawfully related; that is, if the "dynamic laws" relating them show smooth and reproducible curves. Evidently stimuli and responses, so defined, have not been shown to figure very widely in ordinary human behavior. We can, in the face of presently available evidence, continue to maintain the lawfulness of the relation between stimulus and response only by depriving them of their objective character. A typical example of "stimulus control" for Skinner would be the response to a piece of music with the utterance *Mozart* or to a painting with the response *Dutch*. These responses are asserted to be "under the control of extremely subtle properties" of the physical object or event. Suppose instead of saying *Dutch* we had said *Clashes with the wallpaper, I thought you liked abstract work, Never saw it before, Tilted, Hanging too low, Beautiful, Hideous, Remember our camping trip last summer?*, or whatever else might come into our minds when looking at a picture (in Skinnerian translation, whatever other responses exist in sufficient strength). Skinner could only say that each of these responses is under the control of some other stimulus property of the physical object. If we look at a red chair and say *red*, the response is under the control of the stimulus 'redness'; if we say *chair*, it is under the control of the collection of properties (for Skinner, the object) 'chairness', and similarly for any other response. This device is as simple as it is empty. Since properties are free for the asking (we have as many of them as we have nonsynonymous descriptive expressions in our language, whatever this means exactly), we can account for a wide class of responses in terms of Skinnerian functional analysis by identifying the "controlling stimuli." But the word 'stimulus' has lost all objectivity in this usage. Stimuli are no longer part of the outside physical world; they are driven back into the organism. We identify the stimulus when we hear the response. It is clear from such examples, which abound, that the talk of "stimulus control" simply disguises a complete retreat to mentalistic psychology. We cannot predict verbal behavior in terms of the stimuli in the speaker's environment, since we do not know what the current stimuli are until he responds. Furthermore, since we cannot control the property of a physical object to which an individual will respond, except in highly artificial cases, Skinner's claim that his system, as opposed to the traditional one, permits the practical control of verbal behavior is quite false.

Other examples of "stimulus control" merely add to the general mystification. Thus a proper noun is held to be a response "under the control of a specific person or thing" (as controlling stimulus). I have often used the words *Eisenhower* and *Moscow*, which I presume are proper nouns if any thing is, but have never been "stimulated" by the corresponding objects. How can this fact be made compatible with this definition? Suppose that I use the name of a friend who is not present. Is this an instance of a proper noun under the control of the friend as stimulus? Elsewhere it is asserted that a stimulus controls a response in the sense that presence of the stimulus increases the probability of the response. But it is obviously untrue that the probability that a speaker will produce a full name is increased when its bearer faces the speaker. Furthermore, how can one's own name be a proper noun in this sense? A multitude of similar questions arise immediately. It appears that the word 'control' here is merely a misleading paraphrase for the traditional 'denote' or 'refer'. The assertion that so far as the speaker is concerned, the relation of reference is "simply the probability that the speaker will emit a response of a given form in the presence of a stimulus having specified properties" is surely incorrect if we take the words 'presence', 'stimulus', and 'probability' in their literal sense. That they are not intended to be taken literally is indicated by many examples, as when a response is said to be "controlled" by a situation or state of affairs as "stimulus." Thus, the expression *a needle in a haystack* "may be controlled as a unit by a particular type of situation"; the words in a single part of speech, e.g., all adjectives, are under the control of a single set of subtle properties of stimuli; "the sentence *The boy runs a store* is under the control of an extremely complex stimulus situation"; "*He is not at all well* may function as a standard response under the control of a state of affair which might also control *He is ailing*"; when an envoy observes events in a foreign country and reports upon his return, his report is under "remote stimulus control"; the statement *This is war* may be a response to a "confusing international situation"; the suffix *-ed* is controlled by that "subtle property of stimuli which we speak of as action-in-the-past" just as the *-s* in *The boy runs* is under the control of such specific features of the situation as its "currency." No characterization of the notion "stimulus control" that is remotely related to the bar-pressing experiment (or that preserves the faintest objectivity) can be made to cover a set of examples like these, in which, for example, the "controlling stimulus" need not even impinge on the responding organism.

Consider now Skinner's use of the notion 'response'. The problem of identifying units in verbal behavior has of course been a primary concern of linguists, and it seems very likely that experimental psychologists should be able to provide much-needed assistance in clearing up the many remaining difficulties in systematic identification. Skinner recognizes the fundamental character of the problem of identification of a unit of verbal behavior, but is satisfied with an answer so vague and subjective that it does not really contribute to its solution. The unit of verbal behavior—the verbal operant—is defined as a class of responses of identifiable form functionally related to one or more controlling variables. No method is suggested for determining in a particular instance what are the controlling variables, how many such units have occurred, or where their boundaries are in the total response. Nor is any attempt made to specify how much or what kind of similarity in form or "control" is required for two physical events to be considered instances of the same operant. In short, no answers are suggested for the most elementary questions that must be asked of anyone proposing a method for description of behavior. Skinner is content with what he calls an "extrapolation" of the concept of operant developed in the laboratory to the verbal field. In the typical Skinnerian experiment, the problem of identifying the unit of behavior is not too crucial. It is defined, by fiat, as a recorded peck or bar-press, and systematic variations in the rate of this operant and its resistance to extinction are studied as a function of deprivation and scheduling of reinforcement (pellets). The operant is thus defined with respect to a particular experimental procedure. This is perfectly reasonable, and has led to many interesting results. It is, however, completely meaningless to speak of extrapolating this concept of operant to ordinary verbal behavior. Such "extrapolation" leaves us with no way of justifying one or another decision about the units in the "verbal repertoire."

Skinner specifies "response strength" as the basic datum, the basic dependent variable in his functional analysis. In the bar-pressing experiment, response strength is defined in terms of rate of emission during extinction. Skinner has argued that this is "the only datum that varies significantly and in the expected direction under conditions which are relevant to the 'learning process'." In the book under review, response strength is defined as "probability of emission." This definition provides a comforting impression of objectivity, which, however, is quickly dispelled when we look into the matter more closely. The term 'probability' has some rather obscure meaning for Skinner in this book. We are told, on the one hand, that "our evidence for the contribution of each variable [to response strength] is based on observation of frequencies alone." At the same time, it appears that frequency is a very misleading measure of strength, since, for example, the frequency of a response may be "primarily attributable to the frequency of occurrence of controlling variables." It is not clear how the frequency of a response can be attributable to anything *but* the frequency of occurrence of its controlling variables if we accept Skinner's view that the behavior occurring in a given situation is "fully determined" by the relevant controlling variables. Furthermore, although the evidence for the contribution of each variable to response strength is based on observation of frequencies alone, it turns out that "we base the notion of strength upon several kinds of evidence," in particular: emission of the response (particularly in unusual circumstances), energy level (stress), pitch level, speed and delay of emission, size of letters etc. In writing, immediate repetition, and—a final factor, relevant but misleading—over-all frequency.

Of course, Skinner recognizes that these measures do not co-vary, because (among other reasons) pitch, stress, quantity, and reduplication may have internal linguistic functions. However, he does not hold these conflicts to be very important, since the proposed factors indicative of strength are "fully understood by everyone" in the culture. For example, "if we are shown a prized work of art and exclaim *Beautiful!*, the speed and energy of the response will not be lost on the owner." It does not appear totally obvious that in this case the way to impress the owner is to shriek *Beautiful* in a loud, high-pitched voice, repeatedly, and with no delay (high response strength). It may be equally effective to look at the picture silently (long delay), and then to murmur *Beautiful* in a soft, low-pitched voice (by definition, very low response strength).

It is not unfair, I believe, to conclude from Skinner's discussion of response strength, the "basic datum" in functional analysis, that his "extrapolation" of the notion of probability can best be interpreted as, in effect, nothing more than a decision to use the word 'probability', with its favorable connotations of objectivity, as a cover term to paraphrase such low-status words as 'interest', 'intention', 'belief', and the like. This interpretation is fully justified by the way in which Skinner uses the terms 'probability' and 'strength'. To cite just one example, Skinner defines the process of confirming an assertion in science as one of "generating additional variables to increase its probability," and more generally, its strength. If we take this suggestion quite literally, the degree of confirmation of a scientific assertion can be measured as a simple function of the loudness, pitch, and frequency with which it is proclaimed, and a general procedure for increasing its degree of confirmation would be, for instance, to train machine guns on large crowds of people who have been instructed to shout it. A better indication of what Skinner probably has in mind here is given by his description of how the theory of evolution, as an example, is confirmed. This "single set of verbal responses . . . is made more plausible—is strengthened—by several types of construction based upon verbal responses in geology, paleontology, genetics, and so on." We are no doubt to interpret the terms 'strength' and 'probability' in this context as paraphrases of more familiar locutions such as 'justified belief' or 'warranted assertability', or something of the sort. Similar latitude of interpretation is presumably expected when we read that "frequency of effective action accounts in turn for what we may call the listener's 'belief'" or that "our belief in what someone tells us is similarly a function of, or identical with, our tendency to act upon the verbal stimuli which he provides." . . .

I think it is evident, then, that Skinner's use of the terms 'stimulus', 'control', 'response', and 'strength' justify the general conclusion stated . . . above. The way in which these terms are brought to bear on the actual data indicates that we must interpret them as mere paraphrases for the popular vocabulary commonly used to describe behavior, and as having no particular connection with the homonymous expressions used in the description of laboratory experiments. Naturally, this terminological revision adds no objectivity to the familiar "mentalistic" mode of description.

The preceding discussion covers all the major notions that Skinner introduces in his descriptive system. My purpose in discussing the concepts one by one was to show that in each case, if we take his terms in their literal meaning, the description covers almost no aspect of verbal behavior, and if we take them metaphorically, the description offers no improvement over various traditional formulations. The terms borrowed from experimental psychology simply lose their objective meaning with this extension, and take over the full vagueness of ordinary language. Since Skinner limits himself to such a small set of terms for paraphrase, many important distinctions are obscured. I think that this analysis supports the view expressed above, that elimination of the independent contribution of the speaker and learner (a result which Skinner considers of great importance) can be achieved only at the cost of eliminating all significance from the descriptive system, which then operates at a level so gross and crude that no answers are suggested to the most elementary questions. The questions to which Skinner has addressed his speculations are hopelessly premature. It is futile to inquire into the causation of verbal behavior until much more is known about the specific character of this behavior; and there is little point in speculating about the process of acquisition without much better understanding of what is acquired.

Chomsky's criticisms have been instrumental in leading to the virtual abandonment of behavioral models of language acquisition and use. In their place have been substituted models of "sentential processing" as formulated within the general field of "cognitive science" developed in the past two decades. The effect has been to establish a sharp distinction between the use and interpretation of primitive signs by lower animals and the use and interpretation of language by humans. The former continues to be studied by behavioral methods of the kind developed by Skinner; the latter is the topic of cognitive science. Such a division is, of course, antithetical to Morris's project of developing an empirical science comprehending all signs.

CHAPTER SIX

Semiology and Semiotics

6.1 Saussure's Program

Saussure's outline of a science of signs to be called semiology is very brief and fragmentary. Semiology is to study all systems of signs used in human communication, including, in addition to language, nonverbal codes, systems of gestures, and other forms of communication. Though linguistics studies the most important means of communication, it is assigned by Saussure the role of a subbranch within the wider domain of semiology.

6.1.1 Ferdinand de Saussure[1]

Place of Language in Human Facts: Semiology

The foregoing characteristics of language reveal an even more important characteristic. Language, once its boundaries have been marked off within the speech data, can be classified among human phenomena, whereas speech cannot.

We have just seen that language is a social institution; but several features set it apart from other political, legal, etc. institutions. We must call in a new type of facts in order to illuminate the special nature of language.

Language is a system of signs that express ideas, and is therefore comparable to a system of writing, the alphabet of deaf-mutes, symbolic rites, polite formulas, military signals, etc. But it is the most important of all these systems.

A science that studies the life of signs within society is conceivable; it would be a part of social psychology and consequently of general psychology; I shall call it *semiology* (from Greek *semeion* 'sign'). Semiology would show what constitutes signs, what laws govern them. Since the science does not yet exist, no one can say what it would be; but it has a right to existence, a place staked out in advance. Linguistics is only a part

1. Ferdinand de Saussure, *Course in General Linguistics* (1915), ed. C. Bally and A. Sechehtrans with A. Riedlinger, trans. W. Baskin (New York: Philosophical Library, 1959), p. 16.

of the general science of semiology; the laws discovered by semiology will be applicable to linguistics, and the latter will circumscribe a well-defined area within the mass of anthropological facts.

To determine the exact place of semiology is the task of the psychologist. The task of the linguist is to find out what makes language a special system within the mass of semiological data. This issue will be taken up again later; here I wish merely to call attention to one thing; if I have succeeded in assigning linguistics a place among the sciences, it is because I have related it to semiology.

Why has semiology not yet been recognized as an independent science with its own object like all the other sciences? Linguists have been going around in circles: language, better than anything else, offers a basis for understanding the semiological problem; but language must, to put it correctly, be studied in itself; heretofore language has almost always been studied in connection with something else, from other viewpoints.

There is first of all the superficial notion of the general public: people see nothing more than a name-giving system in language thereby prohibiting any research into its true nature.

Then there is the viewpoint of the psychologist, who studies the sign-mechanism in the individual; this is the easiest method, but it does not lead beyond individual execution and does not reach the sign, which is social.

Or even when signs are studied from a social viewpoint, only the traits that attach language to the other social institutions—those that are more or less voluntary—are emphasized; as a result, the goal is by-passed and the specific characteristics of semiological systems in general and of language in particular are completely ignored. For the distinguishing characteristic of the sign—but the one that is least apparent at first sight—is that in some way it always eludes the individual or social will.

In short, the characteristic that distinguishes semiological systems from all other institutions shows up clearly only in language where it manifests itself in the things which are studied least, and the necessity or specific value of a semiological science is therefore not clearly recognized. But to me the language problem is mainly semiological, and all developments derive their significance from that important fact. If we are to discover the true nature of language we must learn what it has in common with all other semiological systems; linguistic forces that seem very important at first glance (e.g., the role of the vocal apparatus) will receive only secondary consideration if they serve only to set language apart from the other systems. This procedure will do more than to clarify the linguistic problem. By studying rites, customs, etc. as signs, I believe that we shall throw new light on the facts and point up the need for including them in a science of semiology and explaining them by its laws.

Excluded from semiology are the classical natural signs and subhuman signaling systems. Its orientation is exclusively anthropocentric. Among Continental writers, only Karl Buhler seems to have been concerned with comparisons between language and communication systems used by lower animals. The following passage expresses Buhler's interest in such comparisons.

6.1.2 Karl Buhler[2]

That every language is a system of signs, that the sounds of language arises as the mediator between individuals in the exchange of signs—in this or some similar way we can begin to speak about language. In any case, the first thing needed logically in order to define it is a general term such as sign (*sema, signum, seign*). What are signs?

In the domain of the Indo-Germanic languages and, within this group, especially in Greek, Latin, and German, as the languages in which Western thought grew, the roots of the two chief groups of words denoting signs point to the realm of what is visible. The two originally grasped moments are, then, "brightness, visible" or "to make bright and visible," and on the other hand, "to place before the eyes"; the "lighting up" directs attention to itself, that which has been "put before the eyes" enters in this fashion into the field of perception. It is, to put it briefly, the [notions of] making present and disclosing things or [the] pointing to things that, as a rule, characterize the multistemmed [*Mehrstammige*] kinship of the Indo-European words for signs.

Basically, the same explanation of the sign function is arrived at if we go farther and, with the help of the comparative psychologist, investigate *the means of guidance in the social life* of animals and men. We can reduce to an extremely simple formula the multiform complex of facts that belong to it, a formula that I recommended in the *Crisis of Psychology* and justified in detail. It is apparent that the biological point of origin of the production of signs is universally to be found in the higher social life of animals only where a cooperation adapted to specific situations demands from individuals the widening of the common perceptual horizon.

2. Karl Buhler, "The Axiomatization of the Language Sciences" (1933), in R. E. Innis, *Karl Buhler* (New York: Plenum Press, 1982), pp. 91–93.

If *one* of the individuals participating in the cooperative life is in possession of more information relevant to the perception or remembering of important aspects of the situation, this constitutes the cognitional surplus that becomes the content of the communication.

If we imagine what must be described here using human words, which are only partially adequate, and if we imagine it in a primitive way for the complicated cases of refined human social life, then the formula touches without remainder on everything that comparative psychology has found out about the sign-constituted means of communication possessed by animals. It also touches on, above all, the most conclusive cases for the question of origin, where we can observe newly appearing signs. For example, those who drive trucks on our bustling streets some years ago invented their well-known traffic signals and introduced them precisely for the situations that our formula describes, and only for them. The directing of the trucks in the busy traffic is successful without the aid of signs as long as and insofar as the indispensable attention that one person must pay to another can be *directly* determined from a personal perception of what is going on. If someone decides to stop suddenly or to veer off from the direction he is driving in, in each case, and only then, he has to give a sign. Why? Because the behavior of the traffic partners has to be determined before the event. What still lies in the bosom of the future—imperceptible to the partners, but known to one acting—must be incorporated into something that can be commonly perceived. The sign offers a supplementary stimulus to the given perceptual data, which no longer suffice alone.

Or take an example from the animal realm: if an individual in a herd of animals, by reason of his position or heightened attentiveness, is the only one who detects an ominous smell or catches sight of a danger and reacts, in addition to fleeing, with a "cry of fright" [*Schreckruf*], the behavior of his fellow members of the herd, which we can thereby observe is the same as if they all themselves had had the same original impression of danger. It is "as if" their own perceptual horizon had been widened. The supplementary stimulus of the cry of fright, which breaks into their field of perception, fulfills the function of a communication that is of significance to life itself. This is not the place to address other analyses of the "as if" formula.

Only one point remains to be noted: etymologies of the words for signs, which refer back to the indicating of "things" or the steering of a fellow observer in the direction of "things," presuppose altogether something specifically human. The authentic finger gesture of man is frequently already characterized as beyond the animal realm; it appears conspicuously in the etymologies of the Indo-European words for signs, and only a single case is still disputed, namely, in the Greek word *em-nueion*. However, it remains true that the factor of thing constancy in the field of application of signs, which is contained implicitly in the aforementioned etymologies, has not been able to be proved up to the present day for any of the animal means of communication.

Exactly how human nonverbal systems of communication are to be investigated was left unclear by Saussure, though he indicated that this new science was to be modeled on linguistics. A suggestive guide to the way linguistics could provide the model was later to be given by the linguist Louis Hjelmslev through his abstract characterization of language as a system of signs. The goal of a semantic theory for language, according to Hjelmslev, is to identify minimal sign-expressions bearing meaning. These elements, the morphemes of linguistics, are combined to form more complex sign-expressions with content or meaning. The function of a sign is determined both by its form as expression, its syntactic aspect, and by its content, its semantic aspect. This formulation was abstract enough to suggest applications to nonlinguistic forms of communication in which minimal meaningful sign elements could be isolated and their rules of combination specified.

6.1.3 Louis Hjelmslev[3]

That a language is a system of signs seems *a priori* an evident and fundamental proposition, which linguistic theory will have to take into account at an early stage. Linguistic theory must be able to tell us what meaning can be attributed to this proposition, and especially to the word *sign*. For the present we shall have to be content with the vague conception bequeathed by tradition. According to this conception a "sign" (or, as we shall say, in anticipation of a terminological refinement to be introduced later a *sign-expression*) is characterized first and foremost by being a sign *for* something else—a peculiarity that is likely to arouse our interest, since this seems to indicate that a "sign" is defined by a function. A "sign" functions designates, denotes; a "sign," in contradistinction to a non-sign, is the bearer of a meaning.

3. Louis Hjelmslev, *Prolegomena to a Theory of Language* (1943), trans. F. Whitfield (Madison: University of Wisconsin Press, 1963), pp. 43–49. See Paul Garvin, "Review of L. Hjelmslev, *Prolegomena*," *Language*, 30 (1954): 69–96, for a discussion of Hjelmslev's project of extending his analysis to nonlinguistic systems of communication.

We shall content ourself with this provisional conception and try on the basis of it to decide to what extent the proposition can be correct that a language is a system of "signs."

In its first stages, a certain tentative textual analysis might seem to give full support to this proposition. The entities commonly referred to as sentences, clauses, and words seem to fulfill the stated conditions: they are bearers of meanings, thus "signs," and the inventories established by an analysis following such traditional lines would lead us to recognize a sign system behind the sign process. Here as elsewhere it will be of interest to try to carry out the analysis as far as possible, in order to test for an exhaustive and maximally simple description. Words are not the ultimate, irreducible signs, as the centering of conventional linguistics around the word might lead us to think. Words can be analyzed into parts which, like words, are themselves bearers of meaning: roots, derivational elements, inflexional elements. Some languages go further in this respect than others. The Latin ending *-ibus* cannot be resolved into signs of smaller extension, but is in itself a simple sign that bears both case meaning and number meaning; the Hungarian ending for the dative plural in a word like *magyaroknak* (from *magyar* 'Hungarian') is a composite sign consisting of one sign *-ok*, bearing plural meaning, and another sign *-nak*, bearing dative meaning. Such an analysis is not affected by the existence of languages without derivational and inflexional elements, or by the fact that even in languages that have such elements words may occur consisting of a root alone. Once we have made the general observation that an entity can sometimes be of the same extension as an entity of a higher degree, and in that case will have to be transferred unanalyzed from operation to operation, this fact can no longer cause us difficulties. The analysis has, precisely for this reason, the same general form in this as in all other cases, and can be continued until it can be considered exhausted. When, for example, the analysis of an English word like *in-act-iv-ate-s* is carried through in this way, it can be shown to contain five distinguishable entities which each bear meaning and which are consequently five signs.

In suggesting so far-reaching an analysis on a conventional basis, we should perhaps draw attention to the fact that the "meaning" which each such minimal entity can be said to bear must be understood as being a purely contextual meaning. None of the minimal entities, nor the roots, have such an "independent" existence that they can be assigned a lexical meaning. But from the basic point of view we have assumed—the continued analysis on the basis of functions in the text—there exist no other perceivable meanings than contextual meanings; any entity, and thus also any sign, is defined relatively, not absolutely, and only by its place in the context. From this point of view it is meaningless to distinguish between meanings that appear only in the context and meanings that might be assumed to have an independent existence, or—with the old Chinese grammarians—between "empty" and "full" words. The so-called lexical meanings in certain signs are nothing but artificially isolated contextual meanings, or artificial paraphrases of them. In absolute isolation no sign has any meaning; any sign-meaning arises in a context, by which we mean a situational context or explicit context, it matters not which, since in an unlimited or productive text (a living language) we can always transform a situational into an explicit context. Thus we must not imagine, for example, that a substantive is more meaningful than a preposition, or a word more meaningful than a preposition, or a word more meaningful than a derivational or inflexional ending. When comparing one entity with another we may speak not merely of a difference in meaning but also of different kinds of meaning, but concerning all such entities we may speak of meaning with precisely the same relative right. This is not changed by the fact that meaning in the traditional sense is a vague concept that we shall not retain in the long run without closer analysis.

But when we attempt to analyze sign-expressions in the manner suggested, inductive experience shows that in all hitherto observed languages there comes a stage in the analysis of the expression when the entities yielded can no longer be said to be bearers of meaning and thus no longer are sign-expressions. Syllables and phonemes are not sign-expressions, but only parts of sign-expressions. That a sign-expression, for example a word or an ending, can consist of one syllable and can consist of one phoneme does not mean that the syllable is a sign-expression or that the phoneme is a sign-expression. From one point of view the *s* in *in-act-iv-ate-s* is a sign-expression, from another point of view a phoneme. The two points of view lead to the recognition of two different objects. We can very well preserve the formulation the the sign-expression *s* includes one, and only one, phoneme, but this is not the same as identifying the sign-expression with that phoneme; the phoneme enters into other combinations where it is not a sign-expression (e.g., in the word *sell*).

Such considerations lead us to abandon the attempt to analyze into "signs," and we are led to recognize that a description in accordance with our principles must analyze content and expression separately, with each of the two analyses eventually yielding a restricted number of entities, which are not necessarily susceptible of one-to-one matching with entities in the opposite plane.

The relative economy between inventory lists for signs and for non-signs corresponds entirely to what is presumably the aim of language. A language is be its aim first and foremost a sign system; in order to be fully adequate it must always be ready to form new signs, new words or new roots. But, with all its limitless abundance, in order to be fully adequate, a language must likewise be easy to manage, practical in acquisition and use. Under the requirement of an unrestricted number of signs, this can be achieved by all the signs being constructed of non-signs whose number is restricted, and, preferably, severely restricted. Such non-signs as enter into a sign system as parts of signs we shall here call *figurae*; this is a purely operative term, introduced simply for convenience. Thus, a language is so ordered that with the help of a handful of figurae and through ever new arrangements of them a legion of signs can be constructed. If a language were not so ordered it would be a tool unusable for its purpose. We thus have every reason to suppose that in this feature—the construction of the sign from a restricted number of figurae—we have found an essential basic feature in the structure of any language.

Languages, then, cannot be described as pure sign systems. By the aim usually attributed to them they are first and foremost sign systems; but by their internal structure they are first and foremost something different, namely systems of figurae that can be used to construct signs. The definition of a language as a sign system has thus shown itself, on closer analysis, to be unsatisfactory. It concerns only the external functions of a language, its relation to the non-linguistic factors that surround it, but not its proper, internal functions.

Expression and Content

Up to this point we have intentionally adhered to the old tradition according to which a sign is first and foremost a sign *for* something. In this we are certainly in agreement with the popular conception and, moreover, with a conception widely held by epistemologists and logicians. But it remains for us to show that their conception is linguistically untenable, and here we are in agreement with recent linguistic thinking.

While, according to the first view, the sign is an *expression* that points to a *content* outside the sign itself, according to the second view (which is put forth in particular by Saussure and, following him, by Weisgerber) the sign is an entity generated by the connexion between an expression and a content.

Which of these views shall be preferred is a question of appropriateness. In order to answer this question we shall for the moment avoid speaking about signs, which are precisely what we shall attempt to define. Instead, we shall speak of something whose existence we think we have established, namely the *sign function,* posited between two entities, and *expression* and a *content.* On this basis we shall be able to determine whether it is appropriate to consider the sign function as an external or an internal function of the entity that we shall call a *sign.*

We have here introduced *expression* and *content* as designations of the functives that contract the function in question, the sign function. This is a purely operative definition and a formal one in the sense that, in this context, no other meaning shall be attached to the terms *expression* and *content.*

There will always be solidarity between a function and (the class of) its functives: a function is inconceivable without its terminals, and the terminals are only end points for the function and are thus inconceivable without it. If one and the same entity contracts different functions in turn, and thus might apparently be said to be selected by them, it is a matter, in each case, not of one and same functive, but of different functives, different objects, depending on the point of view that is assumed, i.e., depending on the function from which the view is taken. This does not prevent us from speaking of the "same" entity from other points of view, for example from a consideration of the functions that enter into it (are contracted by its components) and establish it. If several sets of functives contract one and the same function, this means that there is solidarity between the function and the whole class of these functives, and that consequently each individual functive selects the function.

Thus there is also solidarity between the sign function and its two functives, expression and content. There will never be a sign function without the simultaneous presence of both these functives; and an expression and its content, or a content and its expression, will never appear together without the sign function's also being present between them.

The sign function is in itself a solidarity. Expression and content are solidary—they necessarily presuppose each other. An expression is expression only by virtue of being an expression of a content, and a content is content only by virtue of being a content of an expression. Therefore—except by an artificial isolation—there can be no content without an expression, or expressionless content; neither can there be an expression without a content, or content-less expression. If we think without speaking, the thought is not a linguistic content and not a functive for a sign function. If we speak without thinking, and in the form of series of sounds to which no content can be attached by any listener, such speech is an abracadabra, not a linguistic expression and not a functive for a sign function. Of course, lack of content must not be confused with lack of meaning: an expression may very well have a content which from some point of view (for example, that of normative logic or physicalism) may be characterized as meaningless, but it is a content.

The extension of this account beyond language to nonlinguistic signs is made by H. J. Uldall in cooperation with Hjelmslev in the form of a proposal for a science of "glossematics" formulating an abstract algebra with broad applications. This algebra consists of a set of combinatory recursive rules, or "operations," that when performed on elements generate successively more complex signs or "objects."

6.1.4 H. J. Uldall[4]

When the components of an object are heterogeneous, operations must be repeated as many times as may be necessary. This is the case, for example, when the object of the description is a language. The theory leads to the description of a text as composed of four separate but connected parts, or *strata,* viz. the two parts conventionally called *content* and *expression,* each of which consists of two strata which, in the terminology taken over from F. de Saussure, are called *form* and *substance.*

These four are certainly different in kind, from the common-sense point of view: the two central strata, content form and expression form, are "linguistic forms," i.e., abstractions, which have never been described in any other terms than functions, and which have often been denied any existence at all. The expression substance varies—it may be speech-sounds, which have been described both physiologically and physically, it may be writing of various kinds, dots and dashes, signal flags, buzzing noises, flashes of light, etc., even dancing; each of them can be described from some non-linguistic point of view. . . .

The algebra we have presented here . . . is universal, i.e., its application is not confined to materials of any kind, and it is thus not specifically linguistic, or even humanistic, in scope or character, though our main purpose in designing it has been to provide for the description of linguistic and other humanistic materials.

6.2 Barthes's Analysis of Nonverbal Communication

Roland Barthes is chiefly responsible for both renewed interest in Saussure's program of semiology and a direction it has taken that is

---

4. H. J. Uldall, *Outline of Glossematics* (Copenhagen: Nodisk Sprog-og Kulturforlag, 1957), pt. I, pp. 26, 86. This work is jointly authored by Hjelmslev and Uldall, with Part I titled "General Theory" by Uldall.

different in important respects from any Saussure anticipated. In the passage that follows from his *Elements of Semiology,* Barthes repeats Saussure's distinction between a language as a system of abstract rules by which all speakers are constrained and the actual manifestation of language in empirically identifiable utterances. He then goes on to extend this distinction to nonverbal systems of communication, with emphasis on such systems as those of clothing, food, cars, and furniture. These are among the means by which we convey to others our social status—the communication vehicles listed by Kant in 3.4.1. Influential in this extension is Hjelmslev's abstract characterization of a language as any system of signs in meaningful combinations. Barthes's goal is to survey systematically the various forms of nonlinguistic communication in order to analyze the basic features of their sign systems as nonverbal "languages."

6.2.1 Roland Barthes (1)[5]

In Saussure: The (dichotomic) concept of *language/speech* is central in Saussure and was certainly a great novelty in relation to earlier linguistics which sought to find the causes of historical changes in the evolution of pronunciation, spontaneous associations and the working of analogy, and was therefore a linguistics of the individual act. In working out this famous dichotomy, Saussure started from the "multiform and heterogeneous" nature of language, which appears at first sight as an unclassifiable reality the unity of which cannot be brought to light, since it partakes at the same time of the physical, the physiological, the mental, the individual and the social. Now this disorder disappears if, from the heterogeneous whole, is extracted a purely social object, the systematized set of conventions necessary to communication, indifferent to the *material* of the signals which compose it, and which is a *language (langue)*; as opposed to which *speech (parole)* covers the purely individual part of language (phonation, application of the rules and contingent combinations of signs).

The language (langue): A *language* is therefore, so to speak, language minus speech: it is at the same time a social institution and a system of values. As a social institution, it is by no means an act, and it is not subject to any premediation. It is the social part of language, the individual cannot by himself either create or modify it; it is essentially a collective contract which one must accept in its entirety if one wishes to communicate. Moreover, this social product is autonomous, like a game with its own

5. Roland Barthes, *Elements of Semiology* (1964), trans. A. Laverson and C. Smith (New York: Hill and Wang, 1968), pp. 13–16, 27–30.

rules, for it can be handled only after a period of learning., As a system of values, a language is made of a certain number of elements, each one of which is at the same time the equivalent of a given quantity of things and a term of a larger function, in which are found, in a differential order, other correlative values: from the point of view of the language the sign is like a coin which has the value of a certain amount of goods which it allows one to buy, but also has value in relation to other coins, in a greater or lesser degree. The institutional and the systematic aspect are of course connected: it is because a language is a system of contractual values (in part arbitrary, or more exactly, unmotivated) that it resists the modifications coming from a single individual, and is consequently a social institution.

Speech (parole): In contrast to the language, which is both institution and system, *speech* is essentially an individual act of selection and actualization; it is made in the first place of the "combination thanks to which the speaking subject can use the code of the language with a view to expressing his personal thought" (this extended speech could be called *discourse*), and secondly by the "psycho-physical mechanisms which allow him to exteriorize these combinations." It is certain that phonation, for instance, cannot be confused with the language; neither the institution not the system are altered if the individual who resorts to them speaks loudly or softly, with slow or rapid delivery, etc. The combinative aspect of speech is of course of capital importance, for it implies that speech is constituted by the recurrence of identical signs: it is because signs are repeated in successive discourses and within one and the same discourse (although they are combined in accordance with infinite diversity of various people's speech) that each sign becomes an element of language; and it is because speech is essentially a combinative activity that it corresponds to an individual act and not to a pure creation.

The dialectics of language and speech: Language and speech: each of these two terms of course achieves its full definition only in the dialectical process which unites one to the other: there is no language without speech, and no speech outside language: it is in this exchange that the real linguistic praxis is situated, as Merleau-Ponty has pointed out. And V. Brondal writes, "A language is a purely abstract entity, a norm which stands above individuals, a set of essential types, which speech actualizes in an infinite variety of ways." Language and speech are therefore in a relation of reciprocal comprehensiveness. On the one hand, the language is "the treasure deposited by the practice of speech, in the subject belonging to the same community" and since it is a collective summa of individual imprints, it must remain incomplete at the level of each isolated individual:

a language does not exist perfectly except in the "speaking mass"; one cannot handle speech except by drawing on the language. But conversely, a language is possible only starting from speech: historically, speech phenomena always precede language phenomena (it is speech which makes language evolve), and genetically, a language is constituted in the individual through his learning from the environmental speech (one does not teach grammar and vocabulary which are, broadly speaking, the language to babies). To sum, a language is at the same time the product and the instrument of speech: their relationship is therefore a genuinely dialectical one. It will be noticed (an important fact when we come to semiological prospects) that there could not possibly be (at least according to Saussure) a linguistics of speech, since any speech, as soon as it is grasped as a process of communication, is *already* part of the language: the latter only can be the object of a science. This disposes of two questions at the outset: it is useless to wonder whether speech must be studied *before* the language: the opposite is impossible: one can only study speech straight away inasmuch as it reflects the language (inasmuch as it is "glottic"). It is just as useless to wonder *at the outset* how to separate the language from speech: this is no preliminary operation, but on the contrary the very essence of linguistic and later semiological investigation: to separate the language from the speech means *ipso facto* constituting the problematics of the meaning.

. . . .

It can be seen from these brief indications how rich in extra- or metalinguistic developments the notion *language/speech* is. We shall therefore postulate that there exists a general category *language/speech*, which embraces all the systems of signs; since there are no better ones, we shall keep the terms *language* and *speech,* even when they are applied to communications whose substance is not verbal.

The garment system: We saw that the separation between the language and speech represented the essential feature of linguistic analysis; it would therefore be futile to propose to apply this separation straightaway to systems of objects, images or behavior patterns which have not yet been studied from a semantic point of view. We can merely, in the case of some of these hypothetical systems, foresee that certain classes of facts will belong to the category of the language and others to that of speech, and make it immediately clear that in the course of its application to semiology, Saussure's distinction is likely to undergo modifications which it will be precisely our task to note.

Let us take the garment system for instance; it is probably necessary to subdivide it into three different systems, according to which substance is used for communication.

In clothes as *written* about, that is to say described in a fashion magazine by means of articulated language, there is practically no "speech": the garment which is described never corresponds to an individual handling of the rules of fashion, it is a systematized set of signs and rules: it is a language in its pure state. According to the Saussurean schema, a language without speech would be impossible; what makes the fact acceptable here is, on the one hand, that the language of fashion does not emanate from the "speaking mass" but from a group which makes the decisions and deliberately elaborates the code, and on the other hand that the abstraction inherent in any language is here materialized as written language: fashion clothes (as written about) are the language at the level of vestilmentary communication and speech at the level of verbal communication.

In clothes as photographed (if we suppose, to simplify matters, that there is not duplication by verbal description), the language still issues from the fashion group, but it is no longer given in a wholly abstract form, for a photographed garment is always worn by an individual woman. What is given by the fashion photograph is a semi-formalized state of the garment system: for on the one hand, the language of fashion must here be inferred from a pseudo-real garment, and on the other, the wearer of the garment (the photographed model) is, so to speak, a normative individual, chosen for her canonic generality, and who consequently represents a "speech" which is fixed and devoid of all combinative freedom.

Finally in clothes as *worn* (or real clothes), as Trubetzkoy had suggested, we again find the classic distinction between language and speech. The language, in the garment system, is made i) by the oppositions of pieces, parts of garment and "details," the variation of which entails a change in meaning (to wear a beret or a bowler hat does not have the same meaning); ii) by the rules which govern the association of the pieces among themselves, either on the length of the body or in depth. Speech, in the garment system, comprises all the phenomena of anomic fabrication (few are still left in our society) or of individual ways of wearing (size of the garment, degree of cleanliness or wear, personal quirks, free association of pieces). As for the dialectic which unites here costume (the language) and clothing (speech), it does not resemble that of verbal language; true, clothing always draws on costume (except in the case of eccentricity, which, by the way, also has its signs), but costume, at least today, *precedes* clothing, since it comes from the ready-made industry, that is, from a minority group (although more anonymous than that of Haute Couture).

The food system: Let us now take another signifying system: food. We shall find there without difficulty Saussure's distinction. The alimentary language is made of i) rules of exclusion (alimentary taboos); ii) signifying oppositions of units, the type of which remains to be determined (for instance the type of *savoury/sweet*); iii) rules of association, either simultaneous (at the level of a dish) or successive (at the level of a menu); iv) rituals of use which function, perhaps as a kind of alimentary *rhetoric*. As for alimentary "speech," which is very rich, it comprises all the personal (or family) variations of preparation and association (one might consider cookery within one family, which is subject to a number of habits as an idiolect). The *menu*, for instance, illustrates very well this relationship between the language and speech: any menu is concocted with reference to a structure (which is both national—or regional—and social); but this structure is filled differently according to the days and the users, just as a linguistic "form" is filled by the free variations and combinations which a speaker needs for a particular message. The relationship between the language and speech would here be fairly similar to that which is found in verbal language: broadly, it is usage, that is to say, a sort of sedimentation of many people's speech, which makes up the alimentary language; however, phenomena of individual innovation can acquire an institutional value within it. What is missing, in any case, contrary to what happened in the garment system, is the action of a deciding group; the alimentary language is evolved only from a broadly collective usage, or from a purely individual speech.

The car system, the furniture system: To bring to a close, somewhat arbitrarily, this question of the prospects opened up by the *language/speech* distinction, we shall mention a few more suggestions concerning two systems of objects, very different, it is true, but which have in common a dependence in each case on a deciding and manufacturing group: cars and furniture.

In the car system, the language is made up by a whole set of forms and details, the structure of which is established differentially by comparing the prototypes to each other (independently of the number of their "copies"); the scope of "speech" is very narrow because, for a given status of buyer, freedom in choosing a model is very restricted: it can involve only two or three models, and within each model, color and fittings. But perhaps we should here exchange the notion of cars as *objects* for that of cars as sociological facts; we would then find in the *driving* of cars the variations in usage of the object which usually make up the plane of speech. For the user cannot in this instance have a direct action on the model and combine its units; his freedom of interpretation is found in the usage developed in time and within which "forms" issuing from the language must, in order to become actual, be relayed by certain practices.

Finally, the last system about which we should like to say a word, that of furniture, is also a semantic object: the "language" is formed both by the oppositions of functionally identical pieces (two types of wardrobe, two types of bed, etc), each of which, according to its "style," refers to a different meaning, and by the rules of association of the different units at the level of a room ("furnishing"); the "speech" is here formed either by the insignificant variations which the user can introduce into one unit (by tinkering with one element, for instance), or by freedom in associating pieces of furniture together.

6.3 From Semiology to Semiotics

Barthes's extension of linguistic concepts such as the language-speech distinction to systems of nonverbal communication is consistent with the original Saussure program of developing a science of communicative signs modeled on linguistics. But Barthes's view of the relationship between semiology and linguistics differs in an important respect from Saussure's. He denies any independent status for nonlinguistic systems of communication, claiming that all are interpreted relative to discourse frameworks and that it is only in terms of such frameworks that they have meaning for us. According to this view, semiology is a subbranch of linguistics dealing with "the great signifying unities of discourse." This reverses the ordering proposed by Saussure.

6.3.1 Roland Barthes (2)[6]

In his *Course in General Linguistics*, first published in 1916, Saussure postulated the existence of a general science of signs, or Semiology, of which linguistics would form only one part. Semiology aims to take in any system of signs, whatever their substance and limits; images, gestures, musical sound, objects, and the complex associations of all these, which form the content of ritual, convention or public entertainment: these constitute, if not *languages*, at least systems of signification. There is no doubt that the development of mass communications confers particular relevance today upon the vast field of signifying media, just when the success of disciplines such as linguistics, information theory, formal logic and structural anthropology provide semantic analysis with new instruments. There is at present a kind of demand for semiology, stemming not from the fads of a few scholars, but from the very history of the modern world.

6. Barthes, *Elements of Semiology*, pp. 9–11.

The fact remains that, although Saussure's ideas have made great headway, semiology remains a tentative science. The reason for this may well be simple. Saussure, followed in this by the main semiologists, thought that linguistics merely formed a part of the general science of signs. Now it is far from certain that in the social life of today there are to be found any extensive systems of signs outside human language. Semiology has so far concerned itself with codes of no more than slight interest, such as the Highway Code; the moment we go on to systems where the sociological significance is more than superficial, we are once more confronted with language. It is true that objects, images and patterns of behavior can signify, and do so on a large scale, but never autonomously; every semiological system has its linguistic admixture. Where there is a visual substance, for example, the meaning is confirmed by being duplicated in a linguistic message (which happens in the case of the cinema, advertising, comic strips, press photography, etc.) so that at least a part of the iconic message is, in terms of structural relationship, either redundant or taken up by the linguistic system. As for collections of objects (clothes, food), they enjoy the status of systems only in so far as they pass through the relay of language, which extracts their signifiers (in the form of nomenclature) and names their signifieds (in the forms of usages or reasons): we are, much more than in former times, and despite the spread of pictorial illustration, a civilization of the written word. Finally, and in more general terms, it appears increasingly more difficult to conceive a system of images and objects whose *signifieds* can exist independently of language: to perceive what a substance signifies is inevitably to fall back on the individuation of a language: there is no meaning which is not designated, and the world of signifieds is none other than that of language.

Thus, though working at the outset on nonlinguistic substances, semiology is required, sooner or later, to find language (in the ordinary sense of the term) in its path, not only as a model, but also as component, relay or signified. Even so, such language is not quite that of the linguist: it is a second-order language with its unities no longer monemes or phonemes, but larger fragments of discourse referring to objects or episodes whose meaning *underlies* language, but can never exist independently of it. Semiology is therefore perhaps destined to be absorbed into a *trans-linguistics*, the materials of which may be myth, narrative, journalism, or on the other hand objects of our civilization, in so far as they are *spoken* (through press, prospectus, interview, conversation and perhaps even the inner language, which is ruled by the laws of imagination). In fact, we must now face the possibility of inverting Saussure's declaration: linguistics is not a part of the general science of signs, even a privileged part, it is semiology which is a part of linguistics: to be precise, it is that part covering the *great signifying unities* of discourse. By this inversion we may expect to bring to light the unity of the research at present being done in anthropology, sociology, psycho-analysis and stylistics round the concept of signification.

Semiology has increasingly been regarded in recent years along the lines indicated by Barthes in the above passage. It is regarded as a discipline making explicit the linguistic contexts in terms of which nonverbal signs are interpreted rather than an extension of linguistics to these signs. There continue to be writers, however, who adhere more closely to Saussure's original conception. Pierre Guiraud, for example, defines semiology as the science of all signs used with communicative intent, excluding "natural indications" (the classical natural signs) but including even signs communicated by an "unconscious intention" of the sort interpreted by the psychiatrist.

6.3.2 Pierre Guiraud[7]

Signs and Signification

A sign is a stimulus—that is, a perceptible substance—the mental image of which is associated in our minds with that of another stimulus. The function of the former stimulus is to evoke the latter with a view to communication.

Communication

The foregoing definition excludes natural indications. Of course, in ordinary parlance one says that clouds are a sign of rain, smoke a sign of fire; but in such cases semiology withholds the status of sign because the cloud-laden sky has no intention of communication any more than has the wrongdoer or the hunted animal when they leave unwitting traces of their presence.

Such indications can, however, be used as signs: the clouds on television weather charts, or the description (in linguistic or other terms) of fingerprints sent out by the police. A sign is always marked by an intention of communicating something meaningful.

Nevertheless, there is a deep affinity between communication, de-

7. Pierre Guiraud, *Semiology* (1971), trans. G. Gross (London: Routledge and Kegan Paul, 1975), pp. 22–25.

fined in this way, and perception. Perception can rightly be thought of as a "communication" between energy-emitting sensory reality and our sense organs acting as receivers. It is worth while giving some thought to the curious terminology which uses one and the same term (i.e. *sens*) to designate both the *meaning* (sens) of the signs (or of things) and the *senses* (sens). This is so because from the point of view of archaic etymology *sentir*, "to direct," means "to put into line" (and hence into communication) the perceived object and the sense organs: the *sens* (physical capacity) for an acoustic sensation is hearing, and the *sens* (that which is perceived) of hearing is an acoustic sensation.

These, however, are merely natural indications, and we shall use the word sign as the mark of an intention to communicate a meaning.

This intention, however, may well be unconscious, a fact which considerably extends the range of semiology. In the visible world, ancient or "prelogical" cultures see messages from the beyond, from the gods, or from their ancestors; and much of their lore and their behaviour is founded upon the interpretation of such signs. Contemporary psychoanalysis stakes its claim in this vast domain. While it is true that medical "semiology" is purely a study of the natural indices of pathology, psychosomatics, by contrast, sees in such symptoms reactions which are destined to communicate information, desires which the subject is not able to express any other way. Psychoanalysis—particularly Lacan's school—considers the manifestations of the unconscious as a mode of communication and a language. Parapsychology, too, postulates the notion of subliminal messages which are not conscious. These notions have been taken up by literary criticism, the study of myth, the psychosociology of behaviour, propaganda, advertising, etc., under the heading of "depth psychology," and semiology must take this into account.

It is evident, however, that traffic signals and psychosomatics stem from profoundly different sign-systems and modes of communication. Nevertheless, in both cases we are faced with signs which, as is true of all signs, have two aspects: a signifier and a signified, to which we have to add a mode of signification or relation between the two.

Codification

The relation between signifier and signified is always conventional; it is the result of an agreement among those who use them. This is also true in the case of motivated signs ... or of natural indications used as signs. The convention may be implicit or explicit, and this is one of the (flexible) boundaries which separate technical codes from poetic codes.

This analysis has been developed by linguistics but it is true, mutatis mutandis, for all sign-systems. But the notion of convention—particularly that of implicit convention is relative. There are degrees of convention: it can be more or less strong, more or less unanimous, more or less constraining.

It is quasi-absolute in a highway code, in chemical or algebraic formulae, etc. It is strong in the rules of good manners, in the techniques of the theatre, in the more or less orthodox and explicit rules of rhetoric, etc. But the relation between signifier and signified may be much more intuitive, vague and subjective. Signification is more or less codified, and ultimately we are left with open systems which scarcely merit the designation "code" but are merely systems of hermeneutic interpretation. Here, too, we have the frontier between logics and poetics; though it is true that certain poetic systems are, as we shall see, highly codified. What is fundamental is the notion of a more or less codified sign or system of signs.

Codification, in fact, is an agreement among the users of a sign: they recognize the relation between the signifier and the signified and respect it in practice. Such agreement may be more or less inclusive and more or less precise. Thus a monosemic sign is more precise than a polysemic sign. Objective denotation is more precise than subjective connotation; an explicit sign is more precise than an implicit one, and a conscious sign more precise than an unconscious one.

The greater the imprecision of the convention, the more the value of the sign varies according to the different users.

The convention, furthermore, has a statistical character: it depends on the number of individuals in a given group who recognize and accept it. The more precise and widespread the convention, the more the sign is codified.

Codification, inasmuch as its origin is implicit, is a process: usage renders the sign more precise and extends the convention. In this way the sign becomes codified. It can also become decodified.

In the course of this process it is difficult to trace the limit at which a stimulus acquires (or loses) the status of an explicit sign. This relativity of the sign is common to most of the operational concepts of semiology; depending on each particular case, signs are *more or less* motivated, and sign systems *more or less* structured, etc.

The linguist Roman Jakobson has also lent his considerable prestige to Saussure's project of developing a general theory of signs that includes linguistics as a subbranch. Jakobson calls this theory "semiotics," by analogy to the disciplines of linguistics and semantics. Noteworthy is Jakobson's extension of semiotics to literature and poetry as "verbal arts" and to painting, sculpture, theater, and film.

6.3.3 Roman Jakobson[8]

The relationship of the science of language and languages with that of the sign and of different signs was defined briefly and explicitly by the philosopher Ernst Cassirer in his address to the New York Linguistic Circle, pointing out that "linguistics is a part of semiotics."

There is no doubt that signs belong to a field which is distinguishable in certain respects from all the other facets of our environment. All of the sectors of this field need to be explored, taking into account the generic characteristics and the convergences and divergences among the various types of signs. Any attempt to tighten the limits of semiotic research and to exclude from it certain types of signs threatens to divide the science of signs into two homonymous disciplines, namely *semiotics* in its largest sense and another province, identifically named, but taken in its narrower sense. For example, one might want to promote to a specific science the study of signs we call "arbitrary," such as those of language (so it is presumed), even though linguistic symbols, as Peirce demonstrated, can be easily related to the *icon* and to the *index*.

Those who consider the system of language signs as the only set worthy of being the object of the science of signs engage in circular reasoning (*petitio principii*). The egocentrism of linguistics who insist on excluding from the sphere of semiotics signs which are organized in a different manner than those of language, in fact reduces semiotics to a simple synonym for linguistics. However, the efforts to restrict the breadth of semiotics go even further sometimes.

At all levels and in all aspects of language, the reciprocal relationships between the two facets of sign, the *signans* and the *signatum,* remains strong, but it is evident that the character of the *signatum* and the structuring of the *signans* change according to the level of linguistic phenomenon. The privileged role of the right ear (and, more properly, that of the left hemisphere of the brain) solely in the perception of language sounds is a primary manifestation of their semiotic value, and all the phonetic

8. Roman Jakobson, "A Glance at the Development of Semiotics," in *The Framework of Language* (Ann Arbor: Michigan Studies in the Humanities, 1980), pp. 18–22. This was originally delivered as a paper in French to the First Congress of the International Association of Semiotics in 1974.

components (whether they are distinctive features, or demarcational, or stylistic, or even strictly redundant elements) function as pertinent signs, each equipped with its own *signatum*. Each level above brings new particularities of meaning: they change substantially by climbing the ladder which leads from the phoneme to the morpheme and from there to words (with all their grammatical and lexical hierarchy), then go through various levels of syntactic structures to the sentence, then to the groupings of sentences into the utterance and finally to the sequences of utterances in dialogue. *Each one* of these successive stages is characterized by its clear and specific properties and by its degree of submission to the rules of the code and to the requirements of the context. At the same time, each part participates, to the extent possible, in the meaning of the whole. The question of knowing what a morpheme means, or what a word, a sentence or a given utterance means, is equally valid for all of these units. The relative complexity of signs such as a syntactic period, a monologue or an interlocution, does not change the fact that in any phenomenon of language everything is a sign. The distinctive features or the whole of a discourse, the linguistic entities, in spite of the structural differences in function and breadth, all are subject to one common science, the science of signs.

The comparative study of natural and formalized languages, and above all those of logic and mathematics, also belong to semiotics. It is here that the analysis of the various relationships between code and context has already opened broad perspectives. In addition, the confrontation of language with "secondary modeling structures" and with mythology particular points to a rich harvest and calls upon able minds to undertake an analogous type of work which attempts to embrace the semiotics of culture.

In the semiotic research which touches upon the question of language, one will have to guard against the imprudent application of the special characteristics of language to other semiotic systems. At the same time, one must avoid denying to semiotics the study of systems of signs which have little resemblance to language and following this ostracizing activity to the point of revealing a presumably "non-semiotic" layer in language itself.

Art has long escaped semiotic analysis. Still there is no doubt that all of the arts, whether essentially temporal like music or poetry, or basically spatial like painting or sculpture, or syncretic, spatio-temporal, like theater or circus performances or film showings, are linked to the sign. To speak of the "grammar" of an art is not to employ a useless metaphor: the point is that all art implies an organization of polar and significant categories that are based on the opposition of marked and unmarked terms. All art is linked to a set of artistic conventions. Some are general; for example, let us say that we may take the number of coordinates which serve as a basis for plastic arts and create a consequential distinction between a painting and a piece of statuary. Other conventions, influential ones or even mandatory ones for the artist and for the immediate receivers of his work, are imposed by the style of the nation and of the time. The originality of the work finds itself restricted by the artistic code which dominates at a given epoch and in a given society. The artist's revolt, no less than his faithfulness to certain required rules, is conceived of by contemporaries with respect to the code that the innovator wants to shatter.

The attempted confrontation between arts and language may fail if this comparative study relates to ordinary language and not directly to the verbal art which is a transformed system of the former.

The signs of a given art can carry the imprint of each of the three semiotic modes described by Peirce; thus, they can come near to the *symbol,* to the *icon,* and to the *index,* but it is obviously above all in their artistic characteristic that their significance *(semeiosis)* is lodged.

Jakobson's extension of semiotics to the arts has received an enthusiastic reception, and increasingly semiotics has been identified with attempts to extend patterns of analysis initially derived from linguistics to such nonlinguistic art forms as film, architecture, dance, and music, and to make explicit Barthes's "great signifying unities of discourse" that provide their background. The two passages that follow illustrate the issues dealt with in recent studies. In the first, F. W. Galan reviews the special features that distinguish film as a communicative medium from language. In film, Galan contends, the signifying elements are not verbal expressions but the things themselves that are being depicted.

6.3.4 F. W. Galan[9]

The reason why cinema, rather than any of the traditional arts, helped to undermine the hegemony of the verbal sign, fostered so prominently by the belief of realistic and naturalistic literature in the mimetic potency of the word, was really quite simple. Cinema reversed the fundamental principles of artistic representation. Whereas in literature, as well as other arts, the elementary materials are signs that stand for or signify people

9. F. W. Galan, "Cinema and Semiosis," *Semiotica* 44 (1983): 21–53; the excerpt is from pp. 24, 25.

and things, in film the elementary materials are the people and things themselves, literally the furniture of the world, whether still or in motion. Thus in a novel, for instance, the verbal signs constituting the narrative organize themselves so as to recreate the world of things, but in film the world is there, very recognizably, from the very beginning. And the task of the filmmaker, therefore, is not so much to duplicate or create the semblance of the world, which is achieved by and large automatically, as it is to impose a narrative order on the randomness of the photographed reality.

How can this be done? How can there be an art whose medium is physical reality as such, and not the verbal, visual or auditory signs of literature, painting or music? An answer to this dilemma, which still leads, or misleads, some to deny the cinema's claim to art, can be found in St. Augustine, who here, too, anticipated much of modern semiotic thought. As Augustine observed, along with the signs representing objects, there are also objects that may be deployed as signs. And so Jakobson could assert, as did Tynjanov before him, that "It is precisely things, visual and auditory, transformed into signs, which are specific material of cinematic art."

The familiar film terminology of closeups, medium, full, and long shots directs our attention to the characteristically cinematic conversion of persons and objects into signs, which is in most cases by dint of part-for-whole synecdoches. Hence a closeup of marching feet can represent an army, rolling wheels an automobile, a gun a gunman, flipping calendar pages the passing of days, and so on in endless permutations. As Jakobson says, "Film works with various and varied fragments of objects which differ in magnitude, and also with fragments of time and space likewise varied; it changes the proportions of these fragments and juxtaposes them in terms of contiguity, or similarity and contrast." However, owing largely to its concrete physical nature, film mostly follows the course of metonymy as a means of linking separate shots. Filmic metaphors arise at the abrupt junctures of montage typical of the Soviet film of the 1920s, where the motivation of metaphor tended to be ideological and didactic, or in the equally outmoded technique of lap dissolves, extended filmic similes. In exceptional instances metaphor comes about through the use of closeup, as when Eisenstein photographs a pair of eyes to signify the conscience. Of more recent films, Karel Reisz's *Morgan* comes to mind as an example of a predominantly metaphoric mode, in which metaphors are produced through the hero's associating certain kinds of human physiognomy, gesture, and behavior with corresponding features in the animal kingdom: if Achilles, in the classical example, is a lion, the Morgan, in the picture, is an orangutan. But the film's subtitle, *A Suitable Case for Treatment,* indicates how farfetched this type of construction is felt to be in present-day cinema.

The second passage, by Petros Martinidis, shows the influence of Barthes's view that artistic forms must be interpreted relative to a discursive background. Martinidis notes how we can interpret the "meaning" of a piece of architecture only relative to the verbal descriptions used to describe it.

6.3.5 Petros Martinidis[10]

Architecture and Verbal Language

[That architectural language consists mainly of verbal language] does not imply that there is no meaning at all in space elements as such. Directly at first sight, and without any verbal comment, a church strikes one as different from a factory for example, and, furthermore, the same church informs its contemplators whether it is orthodox, catholic, or protestant—in the same way a single column strikes one differently according to whether it is Doric, Ionic, or Corinthian, etc. But, from there, to reduce any observable phenomenon to a "sign" and to distinguish "signifiers" and "signifieds," "denotations" and "connotations" and so on, risks its being revealed as the correct consequence of an incorrect assumption; i.e., that analysis consists of a material segmentation, finding, *in the thing itself,* objectively discrete parts to be considered as "semiotic elements." On the one hand, the thing itself may be analyzable into a class of "hypotactic" relations (defined as a superimposition of certain elements, to one or more of which it is possible to ascribe a dominant role, other elements being subordinate or dependent), but it informs of its particular identity only on the basis of a "metonymical signification" (a *contiguity* between the shape and the usual function with which it is connected) and also on the basis of a "metaphorical signification" (an *equivalence* between an element and something else—a concept or a feeling—to which ordinarily it refers). On the other hand, the "contiguity" and "equivalence" which make the above significations possible can only "work" within the frame of a society, with its habits, rites, values, and verbal evaluations.

10. Petros Martinidis, "Semiotics of Architectural Theories: Toward an Epistemology of Architecture," *Semiotica* 59 (1986): 371–86; the excerpt is from pp. 371–375.

The Doric column, for example, is not just a volume shaped differently from the volume of a column of another "order." (Slightly taller from the stubby Tuscan, or advantageously smaller and more economic than the lofty, elaborate Corinthian etc.). First, columns are not stuck in the middle of the desert; they are integrated into concrete structures, in a variety of different ways (mostly carrying their own entablature and perhaps a wall or perhaps only the eaves of a roof above it, or as "detached columns" having a wall behind them, which they just do not touch but into which their entablature is firmly built, etc.). Second, according to the ways they are integrated into different structures, columns are associated with specified types of "noble" buildings: Ionic columns supporting a pediment just above the main entrance, for eighteenth- and nineteenth-century religious buildings and state capitols; Corinthian detached columns along the walls of nineteenth- and twentieth-century railroad stations and university library buildings; "three-quarter" or "half" columns (one quarter or half of each being buried in the wall) loaded up with rustic devices, for banks and insurance offices, and so on.

Furthermore, and this is perhaps the most important point, columns are not only differently formed supporting elements connected with specific functions and building types, nor is their "order" chosen only according to the height the architect wants to cover (higher for the Composite and lower for the Tuscan), or the "intercolumniation"—the spacing of columns—he wants to achieve in order to combine a number of systems of construction (e.g., an "arcuated" and a "trabeated"). The social frame, with its verbal descriptions and evaluations, interacts in a decisive way: while Vitruvius opened the door to personalization of the orders, the Renaissance let in a lot more characterizations which, even if they are not to be taken too seriously, are not without relation to the ways columns are integrated into different structures for the last twenty centuries.

More specifically, Vitruvius saw the Doric order as exemplifying "the proportion, strength, and grace of a man's body," presumably an average well-built male. By him also, and later on by others, the Ionic order was characterized as representing "feminine slenderness," and the Corinthian as imitating "the slight figure of a girl"—which may seem not very different from the "feminine slenderness" of the Ionic. But these characterizations have been extended up until the sixteenth century, with Scamozzzi echoing Vitruvius in calling the Corinthian "virginal," Sir Henry Wotton calling it "lascivious" and "decked like a wanton courtezan" (Corinth's morals had a bad reputation anyway), and Serlio recommending the Doric to be used for churches dedicated to the more extrovert male Saints (St.

Paul, St. Peter or St. George) and to militant types in general, the Corinthian for virgins, most especially of course the Virgin Mary, while the Tuscan for prisons and fortifications.

Even if these prescriptions were not literally followed all the time, the main point remains: verbal characterizations affect the choice and use of architectural elements, and the ways these elements are integrated into whole structures. The Corinthian has always been regarded as "female" and the Doric as "male," with the Ionic in between, as something rather sexless—an aging scholar or a calm and gentle matron. And these descriptions have suggested, or even dictated, treatments of built space accordingly: types of buildings and the proper order, or combinations of orders, with the "male" Doric on the ground floor, the "sexless" Ionic on the next, and the "female" Corinthian on the uppermost story.

It is therefore seen that buildings do not communicate information about their function, and far less about their aesthetic value, as concrete and secluded elements, but as material references from human imagery and socially organized understanding—a much more generally significant situation. As Eco has argued, no communication can take place without the presence of a context in which a relation of signification is first established. It goes without saying that this "context" is provided by nothing other than human society which also provides those intellectual reflections which are the initial presuppositions for every innovation or every original "game" with the code: Panofsky has masterly proved that the expansion of scholastic philosophy is not without relation to the development of Gothic architecture; and that the way the constructors of the High Gothic cathedrals thought, in order to form the typical Gothic design, was the same as the way they thought in order to face the theological contradictions of their time. A similar dependence can be traced, for example, between the late Byzantine churches with their "roselike" domes and the contemporary, widely known psalm, praising the "rose of Heaven." And in more recent times one can also indicate the fact the a cultural center like the "Centre Pompidou" in Paris, has been built in a "factory-like" form, during a period in which art is considered in terms of "production"; some decades ago, when critics used to speak about art in terms of "creation," museums and exposition halls were constructed in church-like forms.

The obvious conclusion to be drawn from these few remarks is that the built space is shaped more in accordance with the ways it is spoken of, than it is spoken of in accordance with the ways it is shaped.

The affirmation by Sebeok for "those assemblages of objects that man has elevated to the status of sign systems as he filtered them through his languages," may also be applicable in the case of architectural objects. The nomenclature of fashion, on which Barthes has ingeniously focused our attention, is not a unique example. Architectural books, reviews, articles on interior decoration, and even advertisements, are continuously "filtering" the forms of built space through language, thus determining quite directly not only the ways of space appreciation, but the ways of its formation as well.

Still other writers under the influence of the American behavioral tradition of Watson and Morris conceive of a science of communicated signs adhering to the methods of the behavioral sciences. The following passage presents the influential view of Thomas A. Sebeok, who takes as his central task comparisons and contrasts between human language and communicative systems of lower animals. Like Jakobson, Sebeok employs the term 'semiotics' as a way of distinguishing the discipline from logic (without the plural s) and aligning it with semantics and linguistics (with the s). Sebeok follows Buhler in emphasizing comparisons and contrasts between human language and communication systems of lower animals. He thus challenges Chomsky's claim that human language is unique and without features shared with more primitive communication systems that are capable of scientific study. But Sebeok also notes the problems involved in imposing on nonverbal systems models derived from linguistics.

6.3.6 Thomas A. Sebeok[11]

The variant form *semiotics*—by analogy with *semantics* and its congeners, rather than with *logic* and its congeners—seems lately to have gained currency on the initiative of Margaret Mead, as a term that might aptly cover "patterned communications in all modalities."

As a scientific discipline, general semiotics is still in its infancy. When Saussure postulated . . . the existence of a science devoted to "la vie des signes au sein de la vie sociale," he further remarked that, since *semiologie* (as he called it then; nowadays the French term is being increasingly replaced by *semiotique,* because the former more commonly means "symptomatology") did not yet exist, no one could foretell what it would be like; one could only be certain that linguistics would be a part of it and

---

11. Thomas A. Sebeok, "Is a Comparative Semiotics Possible?" in *Contributions to the Theory of Signs* (Bloomington: Indiana University Press, 1976); the excerpted passage is from pp. 64–67.

that the laws of the former would apply to it as well. Even today, semiotics lacks a comprehensive theoretical foundation but is sustained largely as a consistently shared point of view, having as its subject matter all systems of signs irrespective of their substance and without regard to the species of emitter or receiver involved. As Mayenowa has correctly observed, since the semiotic disciplines, excepting only linguistics "are themselves of recent origin, more or less contemporary with semiotics, we cannot as yet be said to have developed adequate and universally accepted theories for sign systems, other than those developed in linguistics for the natural languages." It remains to be seen whether a general theory of semiotics can be constructed such that the problems and solutions relating to the natural languages can themselves be reformulated in an interesting way. At present, the trend continues in the opposite direction, that is, the descriptions of other sign systems tend to more or less slavishly imitate— despite occasional warnings, e.g., by Lévi-Strauss—and more often than not quite erroneously, the narrow internal models successfully employed by linguists. The literature of semiotics is thus replete with mere restatements rather than solutions of problems, and the need for different kinds of theory at different levels of "coding" appears pressing.

Man's total communicative repertoire consists of two sorts of sign systems: the anthroposemiotic, that is, those that are exclusively human, and the zoosemiotic, that is, those that can be shown to be the end-products of evolutionary series. The two are often confused, but it is important to distinguish the purely anthroposemiotic systems, found solely in man, from his zoosemiotic systems, which man shares with at least some ancestral species.

Anthroposemiotic systems are again of two types: first, language, plus those for which language provides an indispensable integrating base; and second, those for which language is merely—and perhaps mistakenly— thought to provide an infrastructure, or at least an analytical model to be approximately copied. Obvious examples of systems of the first type are furnished by any of the arts qualified, for this very reason, as verbal, where a particular natural language necessarily intervenes between the source of a message and its destination. Among such complex macrostructures, that may be considered secondary semiotic systems (cf., however, the discussion of Kristeva), belong also forms, for instance, of normative etiquette behavior, as well as those assemblages of objects that man has elevated to the status of sign systems as he filtered them through his languages. Thus clothing serves at once a protective and a communicative function, and food satisfies both a need for calories and a craving for information: the nomenclature of fashion or of cooking is the untranslatable *signans*, to be understood in relation to the use to which the objects are put in this or that society, in brief, to the corresponding transmutable *signatum*. (It is interesting to note in passing that clothing, in its duple function, is not a universal, but bodily adornment, constituting a system of signs with no evident protective function, is.)

To the contrary, such is not the case when addresser and addressee are coupled, e.g., in the acoustic channel by music, in the visual channel by chalk marks (internationally used by men's tailors), or in the chemical channel by manufactured perfumes: semiotic systems of this type, although uniquely human, do not imply any particular linguistic code. Myth and ritual, which function *in situ* as mutually redundant (although not necessarily homologous, cf. Lévi-Strauss) components of a single culture complex, illustrate, in the sense implied here, typological opposites.

Zoosemiotic systems found in man, *inter alia*, are sometimes classified under such labels as paralinguistics and kinesics, proxemics, or simply in terms of the sensory channels used, as gustation for proximal and olfaction for distal chemical signaling, or tactile, more specifically cutaneous, communication. Although there seems to be no compelling reason to assume, and some evidence (supporting intuition) to the contrary, that sign-systems of this sort are language-like in any but trivial ways—chiefly arising from the evident fact that they, like language, are classified as semiotic disciplines—yet they are often prejudicially modeled according to one fashionable theory of language or another. Thus kinesics, to take one glaring example (but others could readily be cited), was deliberately and closely drawn by analogy with a design considered temporarily serviceable by a dominant school of American descriptivists of the late 1940s. This adherence has severely constrained the presentation of a wealth of valuable data on body motion, as well as distorted, in consequence, the proper perspective on kinesics in the hierarchy of semiotic systems in general. The particularism of linguistics of the previous generation, already mentioned, has led even one of the acutest observers of human postures and movements, Birdwhistell, to deny altogether the existence of universal gestures, and this in spite of Darwin's empirical analysis of displays, including a thorough treatment of human expressions, and Birdwhistell's own avowed attitude when he first began to formulate a research strategy without the benefit of linguistics. As a matter of fact, and as one would expect *a priori*, recent pilot studies have confirmed that Darwin was quite correct in asserting that certain human expressions do occur cross-culturally and are probably universal: for instance, film documents of flirting girls from five cultures "show in principle the same type of facial expression and ambivalent behavior."

There are, indeed, compelling reasons for sharing Chomsky's skepticism for studying animal communication systems, human gestures, and language within the same framework, unless one is willing to rise to a level of abstraction where there are "plenty of other things incorporated under the same generalizations which no one would have regarded as being continuous with language or particularly relevant to the mechanisms of language." To establish this level of abstraction is precisely the challenge of semiotics, but diachronic continuities are not material to the theory. Tavolga is also quite correct when he states that it is "erroneous to use the methods and theory developed for the study of human language in the investigation of a kind of communication found in another species at a different organizational level," and in his insistence that levels of integration in behavior are qualitatively different, requiring, as such, "distinctive instrumentation, experimental operations, and theoretical approaches." Nevertheless, his assertion that "communication does not exist as a single phenomenon" simply does not follow; on the contrary, highly insightful cross-phyletic comparisons have already been made, and will, we may confidently anticipate, continue to be made, provided that the analytical framework used is that of a well developed theory of signs and not just of linguistic signs.

Sebeok's program for an inclusive behavioral science of communication obviously has a different methodological basis from Barthes and Jakobson's project of analyzing complex cultural forms on the basis of intuitions by those participating in a shared culture. Semiology, under its relatively recent label 'semiotics', seems in fact to be heading in three different and not altogether consistent directions. First, there are attempts to continue Saussure's project of constructing a comprehensive science of communication systems patterned on linguistics that specifies minimal meaningful elements and their modes of combination. Barthes's analysis of clothing, food, and material possessions as ways of conveying status is in a qualified way consistent with this project, though there has been little subsequent progress in extending linguistic models to such means of communication. Second, there are interpretive studies, such as that of Martinidis, that attempt to make explicit the discursive backgrounds of the various nonlinguistic art forms. Such studies include expression of personal insights characteristic of humanistic studies and are often inconsistent with the goal of science to reach consensus either by empirical methods appealing to public evidence or shared intuitions. And finally there is Sebeok's goal of a science embracing human and subhuman systems of communication, employing primarily the methods of the behavioral sciences, as contrasted to the linguists' method of explaining the linguistic intuitions of those using a language. The failure to sort out and resolve the differences between these three contrasting methodologies has prevented the umbrella term 'semiotics' from having a clear application and from fulfilling the ambitious goals set by those employing it.

CHAPTER SEVEN

Recent Philosophical Developments

7.1 Criticisms

Sharp contrasts between the approaches in chapters 5 and 6 and unresolved difficulties in their programs have contributed to the uncertain status of semiotic in present-day philosophy. Also contributing have been criticisms directed toward the principal assumption of semiotic—that all signs share important common features that serve to delimit a distinct field of study. This criticism is presented by Gilbert Harman as part of a commentary on a dispute between Christian Metz and Peter Wollen regarding similarities and differences between language and film as an artistic medium. Metz, in a way characteristic of the semiological tradition of Saussure, Hjelmslev, and Barthes, emphasizes the similarities and attempts to identify meaningful elements and rules for combining them. The results of these combinations are "film messages" analogous to linguistic sentences and discourse. Wollen, on the other hand, claims that film has distinctive iconic and indexical features that prevent our drawing close analogies with the linguistic.

This intramural dispute between representatives of the renamed discipline of "semiotics" is the occasion for Harman's challenge to this discipline's assumption of common sign features described by a general science of signs.

7.1.1 Gilbert Harman[1]

Most signs have more than one aspect. A sentence of English will have a symbolic aspect because of the conventions on which the meanings of its words depend. It will have an indexical aspect if it contains proper nouns, which have the significance they do because of a real connection between name and thing named. And, according to Peirce, the sentence will have an iconic aspect since its significance depends in part on its logical-grammatical structure, which is an internal property of the sentence and is relevant to what other sentences logically imply or are implied by it.

1. Gilbert Harman, "Semiotics and the Cinema," *Quarterly Review of Film Studies* 2 (1977): 15–24; the excerpt is from pp. 19–24.

A photograph has an indexical aspect; what it pictures depends to a large extent on a real connection between the picture and the object photographed. It also has an iconic aspect because of the resemblance between the picture and what is pictured. There may also be a symbolic aspect to the photograph if, for example, the subject matter is identifiable by appeal to some sort of convention or stipulation.

So far, this is simply Peirce's classification of signs. Given this classification Wollen observes, "In the cinema, it is quite clear, indexical and iconic aspects are by far the most powerful. The symbolic is limited and secondary." But, it is, according to Wollen, exactly the "submerged" secondary aspects of signs that assume importance in art. Since in the cinema "it is the symbolic which is the submerged dimension, we should therefore expect that in the 'poetry' of the cinema, this aspect will be manifested more palpably."

Metz's error, according to Wollen, is to take the linguistic analogy too seriously, thus overlooking the fact that film is primarily iconic and indexical rather than symbolic. Metz looks for conventions in film that bear some resemblance to the conventions of language. But this is to miss the point that the role of conventional symbols or codes in film is different from its role in language. The basic linguistic codes are needed for literal significance. The relevant codes in cinema primarily concern the poetic rather than the literal.

Wollen's first conclusion is, therefore, the opposite of Metz's. As film semioticists, our primary task must be to uncover the codes exploited in films in producing the sort of poetry that films can produce. We must do this, moreover, remembering that signs combine all three of Peirce's aspects of significance, iconic, indexical, and symbols.

Wollen's next point is that although signs are often used to communicate messages, they are not always used in that way and are not used that way in films. A scientist working out the implications of a theory, a mathematician doing a calculation, and a traveller planning an itinerary are all using signs, but not to communicate with anyone. They are, as it were, seeing the implications of certain signs. Similarly, a poet, an artist, and a film director are using signs but not to communicate any sort of message. To suppose that they are is simply to make a mistake about what they are doing. They, like the mathematician, scientist, and traveller, are using signs for a different purpose. Like them, they are constructing signs in order to see what the implications of those signs are.

Wollen therefore rejects Metz's idea that the purpose of film semiotics is "to study the ordering and functionings of the main signifying units used in the filmic message." Metz's proposal is due to his linguistic analogy.

Language is often used to communicate messages but film is not normally used in that way. Films have meaning and significance but they do not carry messages—any more than other works of art.

According to Wollen, works of art exploit and call attention to various codes. The greatest works "interrogate" their own codes by pitting them against each other. "We know that *Don Quixote* was destructive of the chivalric romance . . . that *Ulysses* or *Finnegans Wake* are destructive of the nineteenth century novel. . . . A valuable work, a powerful work, at least, is one which challenges codes, overthrows established ways of reading or looking, not simply to establish new ones, but to compel an unending dialogue, not at random but productively." Wollen goes on to argue that an analysis along these lines can enable us to see what is great about a director like Godard.

Both Metz and Wollen believe, then, that the theory of film must become part of semiotics, although they disagree slightly about the nature of semiotics. For Metz, "the methods of linguistics . . . provide the semiotics of the cinema with a constant and precious aid in establishing units that, although they are still very approximate, are liable over time (and, one hopes, through the work of many scholars) to become progressively refined." For Wollen, this appeal to linguistics is an error. We must rely, rather, on Peirce's general theory of signs, which allows us to see that filmic significance is very different from linguistic signification, and allows us to understand why the role of codes in films is different from the primary role that linguistic codes play in the everyday use of language. Still, Wollen endorses the idea that we ought "to dissolve cinema criticism and cinema aesthetics into a special province of the general science of signs." The differences between Wollen and Metz are then really matters of emphasis rather than anything else. Their first priorities are different. But Metz would agree with Wollen that it is important to discover the various symbolic codes that give film its importance as a work of art; and Wollen can agree that there is *some* point to specifying the significance of close-ups, zoom shots, filmic punctuation, and Metz's syntagmas.

I now want to look more closely at the idea, endorsed by both Metz and Wollen, that films exploit certain codes. What do they mean by codes?

The word *code* as it is ordinarily used is ambiguous. It can mean either cipher or standards. We speak in one sense of messages in code and in another sense of the military code and of codes of dress. Metz and Wollen use the term in a way that appears to combine both of these senses. On the one hand, they speak of decoding works of art and they take codes to be systems of signs with meanings. Here *code* would seem to mean cipher. To decode is to decipher. What would it mean to decode (in this sense) actions done in accordance with the military code? On the other hand, Metz and Wollen also speak, without any sign that they are using the term in a different sense, of codes of dress and even musical codes.

Now, in what sense are there musical codes? Certainly not in the sense of ciphers. Instrumental music does not encode messages. A piano solo does not in any obvious way have meaning. It does not represent, indicate, or signify anything. There are various musical structures, of course, and we might speak of these or of the principles of structure as codes, but that is certainly stretching a point. We would not normally speak of symphonic or fugal codes.

But then what counts as decoding music? Apparently that is supposed to be figuring out what the structure of a piece of music is, hearing it as having a certain structure, hearing what there is to hear in the music. Similarly, to decode a style of dress—the style of dress in westerns, for example—is first to uncover the dress code that is involved and then, perhaps, to indicate the meaning or significance of that code.

In this usage, then, any sort of system or structure might be called a code, to decode a work is to uncover the various structures that are relevant to it and appreciate their significance for the work in question. Furthermore, any system of assumptions, beliefs, ideology, or stereotypes that is relied on or alluded to in a film or other work of art can be called a code. For, to "decode" the work is also to see how its significance is affected by such things.

What is the point of this usage? Why call all these different things codes, especially when they are not all codes in the same sense of the term and some are not codes at all in any ordinary sense of the term? The answer is that Metz and Wollen are cheating. Their usage disguises the fact that much of aesthetics and criticism is properly concerned with something other than the significance of signs. Instrumental music is not a language, a system of signs. It has no meaning. It does not represent or signify anything. An understanding of musical structure plays a role in our appreciation of music, but that is not to say that an understanding of the significance of musical signs plays a role in our appreciation of music.

Much the same is true of our understanding and appreciation of films. To appreciate something about the structure of a film is not necessarily to appreciate something that functions as a sign. To say, for example, that the love triangle functions as a specific code in the films of Max Ophuls is to say no more than that the love triangle is a feature of many of Max Ophuls's films and to say it in a way that wrongly suggests that you are saying something semiotic. Once that is clear, it is obvious that neither

Metz nor Wollen has given any reason at all for identifying film theory with film semiotics—indeed it is or should be clear that there is nothing to be said for such an identification.

Of course, even if film theory cannot be *identified* with the semiotics of the cinema, the semiotics of the cinema might be a useful subject in its own right. But there are ample reasons for skepticism about this. Both Metz and Wollen envision a science of signs. What makes them think that there is such a science or could be one? What are its laws? Its principles? To be sure, there is Peirce's distinction between the iconic, indexical, and symbolic aspects of signs. You can spend a considerable amount of time separating out the relevant components in various cases. That can be fun, for a while, but it does not constitute a science.

Part of the problem is that Peirce's use of the term *sign* is a technical one, which counts as signs rather different sorts of things. Words are not normally signs in any ordinary sense of the term *sign*, nor are pictures or diagrams; and the sense in which road signs are signs is different from the sense in which smoke is a sign of fire. It is by no means obvious that there is a unitary phenomenon to be captured in a theory of signs in Peirce's sense.

Smoke means fire and the word *combustion* means fire, but not in the same sense of *means*. The word *mean* is ambiguous. To say smoke means fire is to say that smoke is a symptom, sign, indication, or evidence of fire. To say that the word *combustion* means fire is to say that people use the word to mean fire. The word is not normally a symptom, sign, indication, or evidence of fire; on the other hand, people do not normally use smoke to mean fire. Furthermore, there is no ordinary sense of the word *mean* in which a picture of a man means a man or means that man. This suggests that Peirce's theory of signs would comprise at least three rather different subjects: a theory of intended meaning, a theory of evidence, and a theory of pictorial depiction. There is no reason to think that these theories must contain common principles.

A fourth and different subject is also relevant— the study of representation. In our scientific, practical, and aesthetic thinking, we often let certain things stand for or represent others, so that relations among the first things can represent corresponding relations among the others. We do this for several reasons—to see the implications of a theory, to see how a battle went, or might go, and so forth. This sort of representation may seem to be exactly what Peirce had in mind when he spoke of signs, since the relation that leads us to let one thing stand for another might be iconic, indexical, conventional, or just arbitrary choice. But, in fact, this sort of representation is a much narrower phenomenon than what Peirce had in mind. Pictures do not ordinarily in this sense "stand for" what they depict; words do not "stand for" their meanings; and evidence does not "stand for" what it indicates.

Metz observes that in the film *M*, a loose balloon caught in overhead wires symbolizes the death of a girl whom we earlier saw always holding a balloon. Now, the earlier photographic images of the girl holding a balloon *depict* a girl holding a balloon but do not stand for or represent a girl with a balloon. The loose balloon by itself, without the wires, would be evidence of her capture and therefore her death, given the filmic context, but the balloon would not in that case stand for or represent her, her capture, or her death. The capturing of the balloon by the wires does stand for the capturing of the girl. The balloon stands for the girl in this context. It is not clear whether the wires stand for the man who captures her; I am inclined to think not. The capturing of the balloon by the wires does not directly stand for the death of the girl. It symbolizes the death because it represents the capture which leads to her death.

Sometimes we arbitrarily let one thing stand for another; sometimes, as in the example just described, we find that it is "natural" to take a particular thing to stand for another. We might try to discover under what conditions such representation seems "natural," although there is, in fact, no reason to suppose that we will ever be able to do this.

Harman's objections to extending the term 'sign' in a unitary sense to both smoke as a sign of fire and the word 'combustion' as meaning fire are, I think, valid and in fact were indirectly anticipated by the Stoic theory of evidential signs presented in 2.2.1. To interpret smoke as standing for fire is first to identify smoke as an instance of what is signified by the word 'smoke' and then relate it to fire by means of a linguistic generalization such as 'Whenever there is smoke there is fire'. From this generalization and assent to 'There is smoke', we infer to 'There is fire'. The occurrence of smoke as a natural event has in this way meaning for us only as identified through the use of a linguistic expression that is a term in an inference, whereas a word such as 'combustion' signifies without similar mediation. But this objection has force only because of the type of examples chosen by the tradition as natural signs. There are other events—e.g., lightning as a sign of thunder or the sight of a candle as a sign for a child of intense heat—that may be interpreted as directly signifying another event associated with it in prior experience. The nature of this association and the way these unmediated natural signs signify were described by Berkeley in 3.2.1 and Morris in 5.2.2.

There are, of course, important differences between the interpretation of a linguistic expression as a conventional sign used in communication and the interpretation of a natural event. There are also important differences between communication by means of iconic representations and by means of language. These differences seem to make impossible an empirical science of signs, either of the behavioral kind envisioned by Morris and Skinner or one modeled on linguistics using as data intuitions of sign users. For a science requires a well-defined subject matter and a methodology agreed upon by a community of investigators in terms of which there can be a steady, progressive accumulation of results. Semiotic confronts us, in contrast, with a variety of methodologies and series of programs for imposing one of them on the entire domain of signs. The lesson that seems to be taught by its recent history (chapters 5 and 6) is that a given methodology may be appropriate in a restricted domain but faces difficulties when extended by its advocates beyond it.

There remains, however, the philosophical task of making explicit the contrasts between these methodologies and examining the unique logical features that characterize one type of sign by way of contrasts and comparisons with other types. How do we distinguish natural events as signs from signs used with communicative intent? What is distinctive about conventional signs that distinguishes them from the nonconventional? The paradigm conventional sign is the sentence, with its predicate and one or more subjects. How do subjects refer? In what respects does such reference differ from that possible for more primitive linguistic expressions lacking this subject-predicate structure? How do the conditions of reference change when a sentence is placed within the context of an inference or some form of narrative discourse? Exactly how do iconic representations such as maps and drawings differ in function from linguistic descriptions?

These questions can be classified as logical, but in a wider sense of 'logic' than is applied to the evaluation of deductive inferences through the application of symbolic techniques. This sense is often expressed by the term 'philosophical logic' to contrast this study with formal semantics, deductive logic, and inductive logic. The medieval logical tradition used the term 'speculative grammar', a term Peirce takes as a synonym for 'semiotic' in 4.1.2. The discipline to which such terms refer can best be described as a functional or pragmatic logic describing basic features of the use and interpretation of sentences as constituents of inferences and other forms of discourse by way of contrasts and comparisons to the functioning of natural signs, nonconventional communicated signs, and iconic representations. A number of recent writers have made significant contributions to this study, though without explicit recognition of the semiotic tradition. Their attempts to resolve its principal issues indicate a direction semiotic as a logical discipline can take that seems more consistent with its long history than the ambitious projects to establish comprehensive sciences outlined in chapters 5 and 6.

7.2 Communicative Intent

I noted in my discussion of 2.4.1 how the medieval tradition seems to have assumed that all signs produced with communicative intent were conventional signs. Examples of natural signs, to which conventional signs were contrasted, were laughter and groans as involuntary behavior interpreted as evidence of emotional states. In the words of Peter of Spain, "Conventionally significant voice is that which represents something at the will of one who originates it" (2.4.1). H. P. Grice has developed a theory of meaning that has the effect of challenging this assumption. Grice distinguishes between the "nonnatural" meaning of an "utterance" used to communicate and "natural" meaning conveyed by evidence. Nonnatural meaning requires a complex kind of communicative intent by the speaker and recognition of this intent by an audience. Grice's definition of this latter type of meaning does not require that it be expressed by a conventional sign with a more or less constant meaning as used on a variety of occasions. Instead, the "occasion meaning" of an utterance will vary with the intentions of the agent producing it from one occasion to another. The "timeless" conventional meaning of a sentence is then derived as a generalization from variable intention-dependent meaning.[2] Critics have questioned such a derivation, noting the independence of the meaning of linguistic expressions from the varying intentions of speakers.[3]

Grice's examples of signs with natural meaning make it clear that these signs are the natural signs of the classical tradition, evidential signs that presuppose for their interpretation some linguistic generalization. They are clearly not the natural signs introduced by Charles Morris (5.2.2) and the behavioral tradition. The latter are natural occurrences that signify by virtue of some direct association in experience between a sign and what it signifies. Grice's evidential signs, in contrast, can themselves be intentionally produced, as when a person makes evidence available, e.g., drops a handkerchief at the scene of the crime in order to incriminate another. This feature leads Grice and subsequent commentators to increasingly

2. For an elaboration of this, see his "Utterer's Meaning, Sentence-Meaning, and Word-Meaning," *Foundations of Language* 4 (1968): 225–242.
   3. For this argument, see Paul Ziff, "On H. P. Grice's Account of Meaning," *Analysis* 28 (1967): 1–8.

complex conditions for a sign to have nonnatural meaning, conditions introducing successive stages of reflexive intentions. Such complexities could be avoided by the simple expedient of restricting natural signs to the non-evidential variety of Morris's.

7.2.1 H. P. Grice[4]

Consider the following sentences:
"Those spots mean (meant) measles."
"Those spots didn't mean anything to me, but to the doctor they meant measles."
"The recent budget means that we shall have a hard year."
(1) I cannot say, "Those spots meant measles, but he hadn't got measles," and I cannot say, "The recent budget means that we shall have a hard year, but we shan't have." That is to say, in cases like the above, *x meant that p* and *x means that p* entail *p*.

(2) I cannot argue from "Those spots mean (meant) measles" to any conclusion about "what is (was) meant by those spots"; for example, I am not entitled to say, "What was meant by those spots was that he had measles." Equally I cannot draw from the statement about the recent budget the conclusion "What is meant by the recent budget is that we shall have a hard year."

(3) I cannot argue from "Those spots meant measles" to any conclusion to the effect that somebody or other meant by those spots so-and-so. *Mutatis mutandis*, the same is true of the sentence about the recent budget.

(4) For none of the above examples can a restatement be found in which the verb "mean" is followed by sentence or phrase in inverted commas. Thus "Those spots meant measles" cannot be reformulated as "Those spots meant 'measles'" or as "Those spots meant 'he has measles'."

(5) On the other hand, for all these examples an approximate restatement can be found beginning with the phrase "The fact that . . ."; for example, "The fact that he had those spots meant that he had measles" and "The fact that the recent budget was as it was means that we shall have a hard year."

Now contrast the above sentences with the following:
"Those three rings on the bell (of the bus) mean that the 'bus is full'."

4. H. P. Grice, "Meaning," *Philosophical Review* 66 (1957): 377–388.

"That remark, 'Smith couldn't get on without his trouble and strife', meant that Smith found his wife indispensable."

(1) I can use the first of these and go on to say, "But it isn't in fact full—the conductor has made a mistake"; and I can use the second and go on, "But in fact Smith deserted her seven years ago." That is to say, here *x means that p* and *x meant that p* do not entail p.

(2) I can argue from the first to some statement about "what is (was) meant" by the rings on the bell and from the second to some statement about "what is (was) meant" by the quoted remark.

(3) I can argue from the first sentence to the conclusion that somebody (viz., the conductor) meant, or at any rate should have meant, by the rings that the bus is full, and I can argue analogously for the second sentence.

(4) The first sentence can be restated in a form in which the verb 'mean' is followed by a phrase in inverted commas, that is, "Those three rings on the bell mean 'the bus is full'." So also can the second sentence.

(5) Such a sentence as "The fact that the bell has been rung three times means that the bus is full" is not a restatement of the meaning of the first sentence. Both may be true, but they do not have, even approximately, the same meaning.

When the expressions 'means', 'means something', 'means that' are used in the kind of way in which they are used in the first set of sentences, I shall speak of the sense, or senses, in which they are used, as the *natural* sense, or senses, of the expressions in question. When the expressions are used in the kind of way in which they are used in the second set of sentences, I shall speak of the sense, or senses, in which they are used, as the *nonnatural* sense, or senses, of the expressions in question. I shall use the abbreviation 'means$_{nn}$' to distinguish the nonnatural sense or senses.

I propose, for convenience, also to include under the head of natural senses of "mean" such senses of "mean" as may be exemplified in sentences of the pattern "A means (meant) *to do* so-and-so (by *x*)," where A is a human agent. By contrast, as the previous examples show, I include under the head of nonnatural senses of 'mean' any senses of 'mean' found in sentences of the patterns "A means (meant) something by *x*" or "A means (meant) by *x* that . . ." (This is overrigid; but it will serve as an indication.)

I do not want to maintain that *all* our uses of 'mean' fall easily, obviously, and tidily into one of the two groups I have distinguished; but I think that in most cases we should be at least fairly strongly inclined to assimilate a use of 'mean' to one group rather than to the other. The question which now arises is this: "What more can be said about the distinction between the cases where we should say that the word is applied in a natural sense and the cases where we should say that the word is applied in an nonnatural sense?" Asking this question will not of course prohibit us from trying to give an explanation of 'meaning$_{nn}$' in terms of one or another natural sense of 'mean'.

This question about the distinction between natural and nonnatural meaning is, I think, what people are getting at when they display an interest in a distinction between "natural" and "conventional" signs. But I think my formulation is better. For some things which can mean$_{nn}$ something are not signs (e.g., words are not), and some are not conventional in any ordinary sense (e.g., certain gestures); while some things which mean naturally are not signs of what they mean (cf. the recent budget example).

I want first to consider briefly, and reject, what I might term a causal type of answer to the question, "What is meaning$_{nn}$?" We might try to say, for instance, more or less with C. L. Stevenson, that for x to mean$_{nn}$ something, x must have (roughly) a tendency to produce in an audience some attitude (cognitive or otherwise) and a tendency, in the case of a speaker, to *be* produced *by* that attitude, these tendencies being dependent on "an elaborate process of conditioning attending the use of the sign in communication." This clearly will not do.

(1) Let us consider a case where an utterance, if it qualifies at all as meaning$_{nn}$ something, will be of a descriptive or informative kind and the relevant attitude, therefore, will be a cognitive one, for example, a belief. (I use 'utterance' as a neutral word to apply to any candidate for meaning$_{nn}$; it has a convenient act-object ambiguity.) It is no doubt the case that many people have a tendency to put on a tail coat when they think they are about to go to a dance, and it is no doubt also the case that many people, on seeing someone put on a tail coat, would conclude that the person in question was about to go to a dance. Does this satisfy us that putting on a tail coat means$_{nn}$ that one is about to go to a dance (or indeed means$_{nn}$ anything at all)? Obviously not. It is no help to refer to the qualifying phrase "dependent on an elaborate process of conditioning. . . ." For if all this means is that the response to the sight of a tail coat being put on is in some way learned or acquired, it will not exclude the present case from being one of meaning$_{nn}$. But if we have to take seriously the second part of the qualifying phrase ("attending the use of the sign in communication"), then the account of meaning$_{nn}$ is obviously circular. We might just as well say, "X has meaning$_{nn}$ if it is used in communication," which, though true, is not helpful.

(2) If this is not enough, there is a difficulty—really the same difficulty, I think—which Stevenson recognizes: how we are to avoid saying, for example, that "Jones is tall" is part of what is meant by "Jones is an athlete," since to tell someone that Jones is an athlete would tend to make him believe that Jones is tall. Stevenson here resorts to invoking linguistic rules, namely, a permissive rule of language that "athletes may be nontall." This amounts to saying that we are not prohibited by rule from speaking of "nontall athletes." But why are we not prohibited? Not because it is not bad grammar, or is not impolite, and so on, but presumably because it is not meaningless (or, if this is too strong, does not in any way violate the rules of meaning for the expressions concerned). But this seems to involve us in another circle. Moreover, one wants to ask why, if it is legitimate to appeal here to rules to distinguish what is meant from what is suggested, this appeal was not made earlier, in the case of groans, for example, to deal with which Stevenson originally introduced the qualifying phrase about dependence on conditioning.

A further deficiency in a causal theory of the type just expounded seems to be that, even if we accept it as it stands, we are furnished with an analysis only of statements about the *standard* meaning, or the meaning in general, of a "sign." No provision is made for dealing with statements about what a particular speaker or writer means by a sign on a particular occasion (which may well diverge from the standard meaning of the sign); nor is it obvious how the theory could be adapted to make such provision. One might even go further in criticism and maintain that the causal theory ignores the fact that the meaning (in general) of a sign needs to be explained in terms of what users of the sign do (or should) mean by it on particular occasions; and so the latter notion, which is unexplained by the causal theory, is in fact the fundamental one. I am sympathetic to this more radical criticism, though I am aware that the point is controversial.

I do not propose to consider any further theories of the "causal-tendency" type. I suspect no such theory could avoid difficulties analogous to those I have outlined without utterly losing its claim to rank as a theory of this type.

I will now try a different and, I hope, more promising line. If we can elucidate the meaning of

"x meant$_{nn}$ something (on a particular occasion)" and
"x meant$_{nn}$ that so-and-so (on a particular occasion)"

and of

"A meant$_{nn}$ something by x (on a particular occasion)" and
"A meant$_{nn}$ by x that so-and-so (on a particular occasion),"

this might reasonably be expected to help us with

"x means$_{nn}$ (timeless) something (that so-and-so),"

"A means$_{nn}$ (timeless) by x something (that so-and- so),"

and with the explication of 'means the same as', 'understands', 'entails', and so on. Let us for the moment pretend that we have to deal only with utterances which might be informative or descriptive.

A first shot would be to suggest that "x meant$_{nn}$ something" would be true if x was intended by its utterer to induce a belief in some "audience" and that to say what the belief was would be to say what x meant$_{nn}$. This will not do. I might leave *B's* handkerchief near the scene of a murder in order to induce the detective to believe that *B* was the murderer; but we should not want to say that the handkerchief (or my leaving it there) meant$_{nn}$ anything or that I had meant$_{nn}$ by leaving it that B was the murderer. Clearly we must at least add that, for x to have meant$_{nn}$ anything, not merely must it have been "uttered" with the intention of inducing a certain belief but also the utterer must have intended an "audience" to recognize the intention behind the utterance.

This, though perhaps better, is not good enough. Consider the following cases:

(1) Herod presents Salome with the head of St. John the Baptist on a charger.

(2) Feeling faint, a child lets its mother see how pale it is (hoping that she may draw her own conclusions and help).

(3) I leave the china my daughter has broken lying around for my wife to see.

Here we seem to have cases which satisfy the conditions so far given for meaning$_{nn}$. For example, Herod intended to make Salome believe that St. John the Baptist was dead and no doubt also intended Salome to recognize that he intended her to believe that St. John the Baptist was dead. Similarly for the other cases. Yet I certainly do not think that we should want to say that we have here cases of meaning$_{nn}$.

What we want to find is the difference between, for example, "deliberately and openly letting someone know" and "telling" and between "getting someone to think" and "telling."

The way out is perhaps as follows. Compare the following two cases:

(1) I show Mr. X a photograph of Mr. Y displaying undue familiarity to Mrs. X.

(2) I draw a picture of Mr. Y behaving in this manner and show it to Mr. X.

I find that I want to deny that in (1) the photograph (or my showing it to

Mr. X) meant$_{nn}$ anything at all; while I want to assert that in (2) the picture (or my drawing and showing it) meant$_{nn}$ something (that Mr. Y had been unduly unfamiliar), or at least that I had meant$_{nn}$ by it that Mr. Y had been unduly familiar. What is the difference between the two cases? Surely that in case (1) Mr. X's recognition of my intention to make him believe that there is something between Mr. Y and Mrs. X is (more or less) irrelevant to the production of this effect by the photograph. Mr. X would be led by the photograph at least to suspect Mrs. X even if instead of showing it to him I had left it in his room by accident; and I (the photograph shower) would not be unaware of this. But it will make a difference to the effect of my picture on Mr. X whether or not he takes me to be intending to inform him (make him believe something) about Mrs. X, and not to be just doodling or trying to produce a work of art.

But now we seem to be landed in a further difficulty if we accept this account. For consider now, say, frowning. If I frown spontaneously, in the ordinary course of events, someone looking at me may well treat the frown as a natural sign of displeasure. But if I frown deliberately (to convey my displeasure), an onlooker may be expected, provided he recognizes my intention, *still* to conclude that I am displeased. Ought we not then to say, since it could not be expected to make any difference to the onlooker's reaction whether he regards my frown as spontaneous or as intended to be informative, that my frown (deliberate) does *not* mean$_{nn}$ anything? I think this difficulty can be met; for though in general a deliberate frown may have the same effect (as regards inducing belief in my displeasure) as a spontaneous frown, it can be expected to have the same effect only *provided* the audience takes it as intended to convey displeasure. That is, if we take away the recognition of intention, leaving the other circumstances (including the recognition of the frown as deliberate), the belief-producing tendency of the frown must be regarded as being impaired or destroyed.

Perhaps we may sum up what is necessary for A to mean something by x as follows. A must intend to induce by x a belief in an audience, and he must also intend his utterance to be recognized as so intended. But these intentions are not independent; the recognition is intended by A to play its part in inducing the belief, and if it does not do so something will have gone wrong with the fulfillment of A's intentions. Moreover, A's intending that the recognition should play this part implies, I think, that he assumes that there is some chance that it will in fact play this part, that he does not regard it as a foregone conclusion that the belief will be induced in the audience whether or not the intention behind the utterance is recognized. Shortly, perhaps, we may say that "A meant$_{nn}$ something by x" is roughly equivalent to "A uttered x with the intention of inducing a belief by means of the recognition of this intention." (This seems to involve a reflexive paradox, but it does not really do so.)

Now perhaps it is time to drop the pretense that we have to deal only with "informative" cases. Let us start with some examples of imperatives or quasi-imperatives. I have a very avaricious man in my room, and I want him to go; so I throw a pound note out of the window. Is there here any utterance with a meaning$_{nn}$? No, because in behaving as I did, I did not intend his recognition of my purpose to be in any way effective in getting him to go. This is parallel to the photograph case. If on the other hand I had pointed to the door or given him a little push, then my behavior might well be held to constitute a meaningful$_{nn}$ utterance, just because the recognition of my intention would be intended by me to be effective in speeding his departure. Another pair of cases would be (1) a policeman who stops a car by standing in its way and (2) a policeman who stops a car by waving.

Or, to turn briefly to another type of case, if as an examiner I fail a man, I may well cause him distress or indignation or humiliation; and if I am vindictive, I may intend this effect and even intend him to recognize my intention. But I should not be inclined to say that my failing him meant$_{nn}$ anything. On the other hand, if I cut someone in the street I do feel inclined to assimilate this to the cases of meaning$_{nn}$, and this inclination seems to me dependent on the fact that I could not reasonably expect him to be distressed (indignant, humiliated) unless he recognized my intention to affect him in this way. (Cf., if my college stopped my salary altogether I should accuse them of ruining me; if they cut it by 2/6^d I might accuse them of insulting me; with some intermediate amounts I might not know quite what to say.)

Perhaps then we may make the following generalizations.

(1) "A meant$_{nn}$ something by x" is (roughly) equivalent to "A intended the utterance of x to produce some effect in an audience by means of the recognition of this intention"; and we may add that to ask what A meant is to ask for a specification of the intended effect (though, of course, it may not always be possible to get a straight answer involving a "that" clause, for example, "a belief that. . .").

(2) "x meant something" is (roughly) equivalent to "Somebody meant$_{nn}$ something by x." Here again there will be cases where this will not quite work. I feel inclined to say that (as regards traffic lights) the change to red meant$_{nn}$ that the traffic was to stop; but it would be very unnatural to say, "Somebody (e.g., the Corporation) meant$_{nn}$ by the red-

light change that the traffic was to stop." Nevertheless, there seems to be *some* sort of reference to somebody's intentions.

(3) "*x* means$_{nn}$ (timeless) that so-and-so" might as a first shot be equated with some statement or disjunction of statements about what "people" (vague) intend (with equalifications about "recognition") to effect by *x*. I shall have a word to say about this.

Will any kind of intended effect do, or may there be cases where an effect is intended (with the required qualifications) and yet we should not want to talk of meaning$_{nn}$? Suppose I discovered some person so constituted that, when I told him that whenever I grunted in a special way I wanted him to blush or to incur some physical malady, thereafter whenever he recognized the grunt (and with it my intention), he did blush or incur the malady. Should we then want to say that the grunt meant$_{nn}$ something? I do not think so. This points to the fact that for *x* to have meaning$_{nn}$, the intended effect must be something which in some sense is within the control of the audience, or that in some sense of "reason" the recognition of the intention behind *x* is for the audience a reason and not merely a cause. It might look as if there is a sort of pun here ("reason for believing" and "reason for doing"), but I do not think this is serious. For though no doubt from one point of view questions about reasons for believing are questions about evidence and so quite different from questions about reasons for doing, nevertheless to recognize an utterer's intention in uttering *x* (descriptive utterance), to have a reason for believing that so-and-so, is at least quite like "having a motive for" accepting so-and-so. Decisions "that" seem to involve decisions "to" (and this is why we can "refuse to believe" and also be "compelled to believe"). (The "cutting" case needs slightly different treatment, for one cannot in any straightforward sense "decide" to be offended; but one can refuse to be offended.) It looks then as if the intended effect must be something within the control of the audience, or at least the *sort* of thing which is within its control.

One point before passing to an objection or two. I think it follows that from what I have said about the connection between meaning$_{nn}$ and recognition of intention that (insofar as I am right) only what I may call the primary intention of an utterer is relevant to the meaning$_{nn}$ of an utterance. For if I utter *x*, intending (with the aid of the recognition of this intention) to induce an effect E, and intend this effect E to lead to a further effect F, then insofar as the occurrence of F is thought to be dependent solely on E, I cannot regard F as in the least dependent on recognition of my intention to induce E. That is, if (say) I intend to get a man to do something by giving him some information, it cannot be regarded as relevant to the meaning$_{nn}$ of my utterance to describe what I intend him to do.

Now some question may be raised about my use, fairly free, of such words as 'intention' and 'recognition'. I must disclaim any intention of peopling all our talking life with armies of complicated psychological occurrences. I do not hope to solve any philosophical puzzles about intending, but I do want briefly to argue that no special difficulties are raised by my use of the word 'intention' in connection with meaning. First, there will be cases where an utterance is accompanied or preceded by a conscious "plan," or explicit formulation of intention (e. g., I declare how I am going to use x, or ask myself how to "get something across"). The presence of such an explicit "plan" obviously counts fairly heavily in favor of the utterer's intention (meaning) being as "planned"; though it is not, I think, conclusive; for example, a speaker who has declared an intention to use a familiar expression in an unfamiliar way may slip into the familiar use. Similarly in nonlinguistic cases: if we are asking about an agent's intention, a previous expression counts heavily; nevertheless, a man might plan to throw a letter in the dustbin and yet take it to the post; when lifting his hand he might "come to" and say *either* "I didn't intend to do this at all" *or* "I suppose I must have been intending to put it in."

Explicitly formulated linguistic (or quasi-linguistic) intentions are no doubt comparatively rare. In their absence we would seem to rely on very much the same kinds of criteria as we do in the case of nonlinguistic intentions where there is a general usage. An utterer is held to intend to convey what is normally conveyed (or normally intended to be conveyed), and we require a good reason for accepting that a particular use diverges from the general usage (e. g., he never knew or had forgotten the general usage). Similarly in nonlinguistic cases: we are presumed to intend the normal consequences of our actions.

Again, in cases where there is doubt, say, about which of two or more things an utterer intends to convey, we tend to refer to the context (linguistic or otherwise) of the utterance and ask which of the alternatives would be relevant to other things he is saying or doing, or which intention in a particular situation would fit in with some purpose he obviously has (e. g., a man who calls for a "pump" at a fire would not want a bicycle pump). Nonlinguistic parallels are obvious: context is a criterion in settling the question of why a man who has just put a cigarette in his mouth has put his hand in his pocket; relevance to an obvious end is a criterion in settling why a man is running away from a bull.

In certain linguistic cases we ask the utterer afterward about his intention, and in a few of these cases (the very difficult ones, like a philosopher asked to explain the meaning of an unclear passage in one of his works), the answer is not based on what he remembers but is more like a decision, a decision about how what he said is to be taken. I cannot find a nonlinguistic parallel here; but the case is so special as not to seem to contribute a vital difference.

All this is very obvious; but surely to show that the criteria for judging linguistic intentions are very like the criteria for judging nonlinguistic intentions is to show that linguistic intentions are very like nonlinguistic intentions.

That Grice's conditions for nonnatural meaning do not require it to be expressed by conventional signs is shown by Jonathan Bennett in his adaptation of the theory to the problem of determining communicative intent from behavior alone. His example is of a tribe of "anthropoid mammals" exhibiting two stages of behavior. In the first, members induce beliefs in one another by making evidence available. In such cases, there is no communicative intent, and by Grice's conditions the evidence has only "natural" meaning. In the second stage, one member, *U*, emits a snakelike hissing sound accompanied by a gesture of an undulating motion in the presence of another member, *A*. Bennett uses Grice's analysis of communicative intent (an agent's intent to mean something nonnaturally) to conclude that *U* intends by the sound and gesture to communicate with *A*. Notice that as his example of a nonconventional communicated sign Bennett chooses iconic representations, a sound similar to the sound of a snake, a gesture similar to its motion. The suggestion is that in the absence of a shared background of conventional rules, such iconic representations are our only vehicles for getting another to recognize what we intend to convey about states of affairs. We may recall the central role that Reid assigns to iconic representations in 3.2.3 in describing the "natural language" of men.

In the final section of this selection, Bennett turns to the problem of determining whether display behavior exhibited by lower animals (e.g., the courting dance of stickleback fish or the dance of honeybee scouts orienting other bees to a honey source) is an example of communication. Bennett concludes that it is not, and distinguishes the biological function of such behavior to transmit information by means of genetically inherited mechanisms from signs expressed with a communicative intent satisfying Grice's conditions.

7.2.2 Jonathan Bennett[5]

Having explained what I take meaning to be, I now return to the laying of behavioural foundations for it. The plan is . . . to show how someone's non-linguistic behaviour can be good evidence that he means something by what he does or utters. I shall do this through an anthropological fiction, according to which we are observing a tribe of anthropoid mammals, and will say about them only what we can soundly base on their behaviour in relation to the nature of their environments and sense-organs. We shall gradually become entitled to credit them with having a language: either because they develop one under our very eyes, or because we learn more about them. . . .

Throughout, I shall pretend that we are observing the tribe without their realizing it, so that their behaviour is not deflected by any attitude towards us, such as embarrassment or puzzlement or a desire to impress or deceive. Such deflections could be handled, for if we were affecting the tribe's behaviour, we could discover that we were doing so, and how, and adjust our account of their normal behaviour accordingly. But for simplicity's sake I shall pretend that no such problems arise.

My tribesmen are highly educable and inquisitive, their sensory organs work well, and their motor capacities are unimpaired. These stipulations are convenient, not necessary, for the programme.

We have already learned much about the tribe's intentions and beliefs. We know that they have beliefs about one anothers' intentions and beliefs, and that they sometimes try to produce intentions or beliefs in one another. For example, we know that a once thought that b intended to pull a tree down, that c intended to get d to think there were fish in the bay, that e thought that f thought that a certain noise was made by a snake, and so on. But we have never yet been in a position to apply to the tribe any concept involving language or even meaning.

So far, the only way tribesman a can reasonably intend to produce a belief in tribesman b is by revealing evidence to him. He sweeps away leaves to reveal squirrel droppings, intending to get b to think there are squirrels nearby; he turns b's head towards the sky so that he sees the rain-clouds, intending him to think that it will rain; and so on. The evidence may concern a himself, as when he belches so as to get b to think that he has recently eaten, or lets b see that he is trembling so as to convince b that there is a predator nearby. All of these cases involve

5. Jonathan Bennett, *Linguistic Behavior* (Cambridge: Cambridge University Press, 1976), pp. 137–141, 204–206.

intention-free evidence, by which I mean items whose status as evidence does not depend at all upon why the agent revealed them.

The tribesmen are highly educable, but are not yet capable of many beliefs which are so highly theoretical, so far removed from experience, that their falsity could remain undetected for a long time. So I assume that most of their beliefs are true or nearly true. I also assume that they have, and know one another to have, some interest in producing true beliefs in one another. I could do without either assumption, but they help to simplify the exposition. . . .

The First Case of Meaning

Suppose that we have reached that stage in our understanding of the tribe, without ever having grounds for thinking that any tribesman ever means anything by what he does. Then one day we observe a tribesman, U, stand in full view of another, A, and emit a snake-like hissing sound while also making with his hand a smooth, undulating, horizontal motion which resembles the movement of a snake. Why did he do this? Countless answers are possible, but our knowledge of U could lead us to one in particular. I shall assemble it by layers, to make clear how behavioural evidence could support it. We could have solid evidence that U intended

(1) to affect something other than himself,

(2) to affect A,

(3) to affect A auditorially and/or visually, or in some way arising from the audio-visual effect,

(4) to get A to believe something,

(5) to get A to believe something about a snake,

(6) to get A to believe there is a snake nearby.

As regards (1), whenever U engages in protracted, apparently connected sequences of behaviour he intends to affect something outside himself. Furthermore, it would be out of character for U to think (2) that he was affecting anything other than A, or (3) that he was having any immediate effect upon A other than an audio-visual one. Also, (4) whenever U deliberately produces a sensory change in another tribesman, it is in order to get the latter to believe something. This, like the backing for (1), could admit of classes of exceptions, so long as our present situation did not belong to any of them. As for (5): this raises the question of *what* U intended to get A to believe. Well, U's performance gave A intention-free evidence that U's hands were not paralysed, and that his lungs were working; but I stipulate that we have no evidence that U is interested in convincing A of anything like that. And that is about as far as U's performance reaches, considered as intention-free evidence. Certainly, it cannot have been offered as intention-free evidence of anything about a snake: there is no chance that U thought that A might mistake his noise and hand-movement for an actual snake. But the nature of the performance—the fact that it naturally induces the thought of a snake—forces us to conclude that if U is trying to make A believe something, it is something about a snake. So we shall tentatively conjecture that U intended (5), acknowledging that this leaves us with the problem of how U can have expected his performance to convince A of something for which the performance was not intention- free evidence.

Finally, (6) could be reached on the grounds that the only belief about snakes which U could want to produce in A on this occasion is that there is a snake nearby. This is not based on our observation that there *is* a snake there, but rather on a more general assessment of the set-up: U has not just been bitten by a snake, there are no other tribesmen in sight, U is not in a position to know of a recent snake-encounter of which A is ignorant, the proximity of snakes is a matter of interest to this tribe because they fear snakes or value them, and so on.

Note that I moved from (4) to (5) on the strength of the "iconic" aspect of U's performance, that is, its constituting a natural pointer towards the thought of a snake; and that I moved on to (6) by eliminating alternatives. These two features of my procedure seem to be inescapable. . . .

A problem remains, though; for (6), even if we have no decent alternative to it, is hardly tenable unless we can explain how U could expect his performance to produce that result. He need not be certain of success, but he must think he has some chance. . . . Well, then, what could underlie U's belief that his pantomime might lead to A's thinking there was a snake nearby?

Of many possible answers, my interest is in this one: U was relying on A's thinking that U intended to get A to believe that there was a snake nearby ("to believe P," for short); and he further expected that A would be led to believe P by his belief that U wanted him to believe P. That last move is secured if A trusts U to this limited extent: A thinks that if on this occasion U wants A to believe P, that is a reason for believing P. . . .

But what is supposed to bring A to believe that U intends (6)? Well, A has access to all our data, and so A can come to realize that nothing but (6) will do as an account of U's intention; and U can expect A to realize this. U could then expect the following: A tentatively accepts that U intends (6), as having no tenable rivals; he is led by that plus trust in U to a tentative acceptance of P; A then reflects on the route he has followed, and conjectures that U expected him to follow it; this explains how U could expect his action to produce (6), and so A is no longer tentative in accepting that that was *U*'s intention or, therefore, in accepting *P*. All that, I repeat, is what *U* intended to happen.

Summing all this up: When *U* performed his pantomime he intended to get *A* to believe there was a snake in *A*'s vicinity, and he was relying on the following mechanism: *A* recognizes that *U* intends to get *A* to believe *P*, and *A* is led by that, plus trust in *U*, to believe *P*. *U* has not intended *A* to have any false beliefs about *U*'s intentions or expectations, and indeed *U* has relied upon *A*'s getting a pretty good grasp of what *U* was up to.

All of that suffices to make the case one of meaning. By performing his pantomime, *U meant that* there was a snake nearby.

· ·

Although it would be foolish to dogmatize about this, I shall henceforth assume that the intention to communicate is not exhibited in the displays of animals in the wild. For this does *seem* to be so; yet many people confidently speak of the "languages" of non-human animals; and I want to explain why.

In a language, properly so-called, the utterance of *S* is evidence for *P* because of the utterer's intention. In animal displays, the utterance of *S* is evidence for *P*, and may produce the belief that *P*; but its being evidence for *P* is not due to any intention to communicate *P*, but rather due to the existence in that species of certain inflexible, wired-in behaviour-patterns whose instances do not exhibit intentionalness of any sort. Given that enormous difference—on the one hand an intention to communicate, on the other no intention at all—what is the similarity which many people feel so strongly?

It cannot be merely that the "displays" are in fact informative; for virtually all behaviour is informative in the sense that information could be gleaned from it. Nor can it be merely that the displays do inform; for some animal behaviour which regularly informs other animals still does not strike anyone as linguistic. When a trapped fly thrashes around in the web, it conveys "information" to the waiting spider, yet this behaviour on the fly's part does not seem like language even to those who freely credit honey-bees with language.

The linguistic feel of some animal behaviour is explained by the fact that it, like linguistic behaviour, is "for" communication in some sense; and the relevant senses are closely connected. A linguistic utterance is for communication in the sense that it is performed with the individual intention of getting a hearer to believe something. In infra-human displays, the "utterance" does not manifest an individual intention, and sometimes not even an individual goal of a lower kind; what it does manifest is a species-wide analogue of intention—namely a rigid behavioural disposition whose biological *function* is to transmit information. . . . A behaviour-pattern has the function of achieving F if it does regularly achieve F and that fact explains its becoming part of the genetic heritage of the species. I believe that the relevant explanation is always evolutionary rather than theological or something else; but, since the evolution of behaviour is hard to study directly, we must be able to discover the functions of various behaviour-patterns without having independent evidence about their origins. This can be done, though. One can base a well-founded guess about the function of a given behaviour-pattern on one's observations of how it serves the present life of the species.

I take it, then, that a behaviour-pattern has communication for its function if and only if the species evolved it because of the survival-value to them of the information-transfers which it makes possible. The movements of the trapped fly do not have communication as their function: they do communicate something to the spider, but this item occurs in the flies' genetic repertoire for a different reason, namely that flies which thrash around sometimes break free. That explains why the fly's behaviour does not feel linguistic, even to those to whom display behaviour does feel linguistic.

That explanation presupposes that the two senses of "for communication" are closely related, that is, that individual intention is significantly like biological function. So it is, despite the fact a behaviour-pattern which has a biological function may admit of a single mechanistic explanation, and thus not admit of legitimate teleological explanation. The likeliness is as follows.

Consider a species whose members do not have individual intentions: they are, then, highly inflexible or unadaptable in their behaviour. If some of them have a behaviour-pattern which proves unsuitable to their environments, they cannot modify it; but they are likely to serve their species by dying before they mature, and so those unsuitable behaviour-patterns will tend to drop out of the species' genetic repertoire. Thus, natural selection serves a species as intelligent adaptability serves an individual. There is also a similarity which does not depend upon a specifically evolutionary view of biological function. It is that intentional and functional explanations of items of behaviour, although in many ways very different, both give an explanatory role to the behaviour's being apt to produce such-and-such a result.

I prefer to reserve the terms 'meaning' and 'language' to communication-systems which manifest individual intentions to communicate. Intentional behaviour is attuned to the particular circumstances as wired-in displays frequently fail to be: displays often occur in the absence of observers, or the absence of suitable observers, or more often than they are needed, and so on. The relatively blind and mechanical look of most display behaviour puts a great behavioural gulf between it and the employment of a communication-system which reflects individuals' intentions to communicate. But the common desire to stretch the concept of language further is explicable. If we leave semantic structure out of the story, the stretch is achieved simply by replacing 'intention-dependent evidence' by something like 'display-dependent evidence'—that is, something whose force as evidence for P depends upon its being a display, which is a manifestation of a behaviour-pattern whose function is to communicate. In essence, then, the shift is just from *intention* to *function,* and they have enough in common to make the shift inviting.

7.3 Convention

The medieval tradition characterized conventional signs as "voluntarily instituted" for the purposes of communication (cf. Ockham, 2.4.2). Reid's "artificial" signs were those which "have no meaning but what is affixed to them by compact or agreement among those who use them" (3.2.3). With the exception of some scientific terminology introduced by stipulation, such an account is at variance with how words come to be introduced into languages. Linguists have noted that new words often gain currency through the play of children. Far from there being a "compact or agreement," there is introduction of an expression, often by random whim, followed by imitation that spreads to the adult population.

David Lewis has formulated a theory of convention that recognizes this feature and provides an alternative to the traditional "compact" theory. For Lewis, a convention arises when a "coordination equilibrium" is achieved as a solution to a "coordination problem." Such a problem arises when there is a need for cooperating action within a community (which may number as few as two individuals) in order to achieve a mutually desired state of affairs. Coordination equilibrium can be achieved by linguistic communication, as when two people verbally agree to meet regularly on a certain day of the week in order to exchange information. But since Lewis is interested principally in explicating the conventions governing linguistic communication, he cannot provide an account of conventions that assume the use of language. He thus concentrates on the problem of explaining how a coordination equilibrium can be achieved without communication. This can occur if the agents recognize a particular solution to a coordination problem as salient, distinguished from other possible solutions by its uniqueness. Equilibrium is achieved when a precedent is established that can be generalized in a way that serves to regulate future behavior.

7.3.1 David Lewis (1)[6]

Let us start with the simplest case of coordination by precedent and generalize in various ways. In this way we shall meet the phenomenon I call *convention*. . . .

Suppose we have been given a coordination problem, and we have reached some fairly good coordination equilibrium. Given exactly the same problem again, perhaps each of us will repeat what he did before. If so, we will reach the same solution. If you and I met yesterday—by luck, by agreement, by salience, or however—and today we find we must meet again, we might both go back to yesterday's meeting place, each hoping to find the other there. If we were cut off on the telephone and you happened to call back as I waited, then if we are cut off again in the same call, I will wait again.

We can explain the force of precedent just as we explained the force of salience. Indeed, precedent is merely the source of one important kind of salience: conspicuous uniqueness of an equilibrium because we reached it last time. We may tend to repeat the action that succeeded before if we have no strong reason to do otherwise. Whether or not any of us really has this tendency, we may somewhat expect each other to have it, or expect each other to expect each other to have it, and so on— that is, we may each have first- and higher-order expectations that the others will do their parts of the old coordination equilibrium, unless they have reason to act otherwise. Each one's expectation that the others will do their parts, strengthened perhaps by replication using his higher-order expectations, gives him some reason to do his own part. And if his original expectations of some order or other were strong enough, he will have a decisive reason to do his part. So he will do it.

I have been supposing that we are given a coordination problem, and then given the same problem again. But, of course, we could never be given exactly the same problem twice. There must be this difference at least: the second time, we can draw on our experience with the first. More generally, the two problems will differ in several independent respects. We cannot do exactly what we did before. Nothing we could do this time

6. David Lewis, *Convention* (Cambridge, Harvard University Press, 1969), pp. 36–39, 41, 42.

is exactly like what we did before—like it in every respect—because the situations are not exactly alike.

So suppose not that we are given the original problem again, but rather that we are given a new coordination problem analogous somehow to the original one. Guided by whatever analogy we notice, we tend to follow precedent by trying for a coordination equilibrium in the new problem which uniquely corresponds to the one we reached before.

There might be alternative analogies. If so, there is room for ambiguity about what would be following precedent and doing what we did before. Suppose that yesterday I called you on the telephone and I called back when we were cut off. Today you call me and we are cut off. We have a precedent in which I called back and a precedent—the same one—in which the original caller called back. But this time you are the original caller. No matter what I do this time, I do something analogous to what we did before. Our ambiguous precedent does not help us.

In fact, there are always innumerable alternative analogies. Were it not that we happen uniformly to notice some analogies and ignore others—those we call "natural" or "artificial," respectively—precedents would always be completely ambiguous and worthless. *Every* coordination equilibrium in our new problem (every other combination, too) corresponds uniquely to what we did before under *some* analogy, shares *some* distinctive description with it alone. Fortunately, most of the analogies are artificial. We ignore them; we do not tend to let them guide our choice, nor do we expect each other to have any such tendency, nor do we expect each other to expect each other to, and so on. And fortunately we have learned that all of us will mostly notice the same analogies. That is why precedents can be unambiguous in practice, and often are. If we notice only one of the analogies between our problem and the precedent, or if one of those we notice seems far more conspicuous than the others, or even if several are conspicuous but they all happen to agree in indicating the same choice, then the other analogies do not matter. We are not in trouble unless conflicting analogies force themselves on our attention.

The more respects of similarity between the new problem and the precedent, the more likely it is that different analogies will turn out to agree, the less room there will be for ambiguity, and the easier it will be to follow precedent. A precedent in which I, the original caller, called back is ambiguous given a new problem in which you are the original caller—but not given a new problem in which I am again the original caller. That is why I began by pretending that the new problem was like the precedent in all respects.

Salience in general is uniqueness of a coordination equilibrium in a preeminently conspicuous respect. The salience due to precedent is no exception: it is uniqueness of a coordination equilibrium in virtue of its preeminently conspicuous analogy to what was done successfully before.

So far I have been supposing that the agents who set the precedent are the ones who follow it. This made sure that the agents given the second problem were acquainted with the circumstances and outcome of the first, and expected each other to be, expected each other to expect each other to be, and so on. But it is not an infallible way and not the only way. For instance, if yesterday I told you a story about people who got separated in the subway and happened to meet again at Charles Street, and today we get separated in the same way, we might independently decide to go and wait at Charles Street. It makes no difference whether the story I told you was true, or whether you thought it was, or whether I thought it was, or even whether I claimed it was. A fictive precedent would be as effective as an actual one in suggesting a course of action for us, and therefore as good a source of concordant mutual expectations enabling us to meet. So let us just stipulate that somehow the agents in the new problem are acquainted with the precedent, expect each other to be acquainted with it, and so on.

So far I have been supposing that we have a single precedent to follow. But we might have several. We might all be acquainted with a class of previous coordination problems, naturally analogous to our present problem and to each other, in which analogous coordination equilibria were reached. This is to say that the agents' actions conformed to some noticeable regularity. Since our present problem is suitably analogous to the precedents, we can reach a coordination equilibrium by all conforming to this same regularity. Each of us wants to conform to it if the others do; he has a *conditional preference* for conformity. If we do conform, the explanation has the familiar pattern: we tend to follow precedent, given no particular reason to do anything else; we expect that tendency in each other; we expect each other to expect it; and so on. We have our concordant first- and higher-order expectations, and they enable us to reach a coordination equilibrium.

It does not matter *why* coordination was achieved at analogous equilibria in the previous cases. Even if it had happened by luck, we could still follow the precedent set. One likely course of events would be this: the first case, or the first few, acted as precedent for the next, those for the next, and so on. Similarly, no matter how our precedents came about, by following them this time we add this case to the stock of precedents available henceforth. . . .

Coordination by precedent, at its simplest, is this: achievement of coordination by means of shared acquaintance with the achievement of coordination in a single past case exactly like our present coordination problem. By removing inessential restrictions, we have come to this: achievement of coordination by means of shared acquaintance with a *regularity* governing the achievement of coordination in a class of past cases which bear some conspicuous analogy to one another and to our present coordination problem. Our acquaintance with this regularity comes from our experience with some of its instances, not necessarily the same ones for everybody.

Given a regularity in past cases, we may reasonably extrapolate it into the (near) future. For we are entitled to expect that when agents acquainted with the past regularity are confronted by an analogous new coordination problem, they will succeed in achieving coordination by following precedent and continuing to conform to the same regularity. We come to expect conforming actions not only in past cases but in future ones as well. We acquire a general belief, unrestricted as to time, that members of a certain population conform to a certain regularity in a certain kind of recurring coordination problem for the sake of coordination.

Each new action in conformity to the regularity adds to our experience of general conformity. Our experience of general conformity in the past leads us, by force of precedent, to expect a like conformity in the future. And our expectation of future conformity is a reason to go on conforming, since to conform if others do is to achieve a coordination equilibrium and to satisfy one's own preferences. And so it goes—we're here because we're here because we're here because we're here. Once the process gets started, we have a metastable self-perpetuating system of preferences, expectations, and actions capable of persisting indefinitely. As long as uniform conformity is a coordination equilibrium, so that each wants to conform conditionally upon conformity by the others, conforming action produces expectation of conforming action and expectation of conforming action produces conforming action.

This is the phenomenon I call convention. Our first, rough, definition is:

> A regularity R in the behavior of members of a population P when they are agents in a recurrent situation S is a *convention* if and only if, in any instance of S among members of P,
> (1) everyone conforms to R;
> (2) everyone expects everyone else to conform to R;

(3) everyone prefers to conform to R on condition that the others do, since S is a coordination problem and uniform conformity to R is a coordination equilibrium in S.

Lewis then proceeds to amend his statement of the necessary and sufficient conditions for a regularity of behavior constituting a convention by adding the requirement that there be common knowledge within the community that the conditions just listed are satisfied.

7.3.2 David Lewis (2)[7]

Let us say that it is *common knowledge* in a population P that ____ if and only if some state of affairs A holds such that:
(1) everyone in P has reason to believe that A holds.
(2) A indicates to everyone in P that everyone in P has reason to believe that A holds.
(3) A indicates to everyone in P that ____ .
We can call any such state of affairs A a *basis* for common knowledge in P that ____ . A provides the members of P with part of what they need to form expectations of arbitrarily high order, regarding sequences of members of P, that ____ . The part it gives them is the part peculiar to the content ____ . The rest of what they need is what they need to form *any* higher-order expectations in the way we are considering: mutual ascription of some common inductive standards and background information, rationality, mutual ascription of rationality, and so on.

Let us return to our example and consider the state of affairs A more completely. Suppose that as part of A we manifest our conditional preferences for returning to the meeting place. Then A may also indicate to us that we both have such preferences. If so, A can serve as a basis not only for common knowledge that you will return, but also as a basis each of us prefers to return if the other does. Suppose also that as part of A we somehow manifest a modicum of rationality. Then A may indicate to us, and be a basis for common knowledge of, our possession of this modicum of rationality. By now A—our incident of agreeing to return—is generating all the higher-order expectations that contribute to our success in solving our coordination problem by means of replication.

A basis for common knowledge generates higher-order expectations with the aid of pre-existing higher-order expectations of rationality. Can these themselves be generated by some basis for common knowledge?

7. Lewis, *Convention*, pp. 56–59.

Yes, because all the higher-order expectations of rationality needed to generate an nth-order expectation are themselves of less than nth-order. What cuts off the generation of higher-order expectations is the limited amount of rationality indicated by any basis—not any difficulty in generating higher-order expectations of as much rationality as *is* indicated by a basis.

Agreement to do one's part of coordination equilibrium is a basis for common knowledge that everyone will do his part. Salience is another basis for common knowledge that everyone will do his part of a coordination equilibrium; but it is a weaker basis, in general, and generates weaker higher-order expectations, since the salience of an equilibrium is not a very strong indication that agents will tend to choose it. Precedents also are a basis for common knowledge that everyone will do his part of a coordination equilibrium; and, in particular, past conformity to a convention is a basis for common knowledge of a tendency to go on conforming. Consider a conventional regularity R in a population P. Everyone in P has reason to believe that members of P have conformed to R in the past. The fact that members of P have conformed to R in the past indicates to everyone in P that everyone in P has reason to believe that members of P have conformed to R in the past. And the fact that members of P have conformed to R in the past indicates to everyone in P that they will to do so in the future as well.

For example, drivers in the United States have hitherto driven on the right. All of us have reason to believe that this is so. And the fact that this is so indicates to all of us that all of us have reason to believe that drivers in the United States have hitherto driven on the right and also that drivers in the United States will tend to drive on the right henceforth.

Our defining conditions for the existence of a convention consist of a regularity in behavior, a system of mutual expectations, and a system of preferences. I propose to amend the definition: not only must these conditions be satisfied, but also it must be common knowledge in the population that they are. Our amended definition is:

> A regularity R in the behavior of members of a population P when they are agents in a recurrent situation S is a *convention* if and only if it is true that, and it is common knowledge in P that, in any instance of S among members of P,
> (1) everyone conforms to R;
> (2) everyone expects everyone else to conform to R;
> (3) everyone prefers to conform to R on condition that the others do, since S is a coordination problem and uniform conformity to R is a coordination equilibrium in S.

Thus there is to be some state of affairs *A* (such that *A* holds, everyone in *P* has reason to believe that A holds, and A indicates to everyone in *P* that a everyone in *P* has reason to believe that *A* holds) which indicates to everyone in *P* that members of *P* conform to *R*, that they expect each other to conform to *R*, and that they have preferences which make uniform conformity to *R* a coordination equilibrium.

Lewis states conditions for conventional rules solely in terms of the preferences of members of a community and regularities of behavior. This "regularity theory" of convention can be criticized for ignoring the normative aspect of following a rule. What seems characteristic of a conventional rule governing the use of a linguistic expression is that misapplications of it are corrected as "wrong" and contrasted with "correct" applications. That behavior exhibits regularity, even if this regularity fulfills social purposes, will not constitute it as rule-following behavior if such normative terms have no application.

7.4 Reference

With the development of natural languages comprising a lexicon of words as conventional signs and grammatical rules for combining them came the ability to form sentences. The basic logical constituents of a sentence are its predicate and one or more subjects. With a distinct subject term, the scope of reference can be extended far beyond the present and the immediate environment. If someone says 'Red', she must directly point to or otherwise indicate a nearby object to which the adjective is being ascribed. However, to say, 'The apple on the shelf is red' may be to say what could be understood without the apple being present. Proper and common nouns typically occur as subjects referring to particular objects that can be reidentified on different occasions. It is this ability to reidentify that makes possible the extension of reference beyond what occurs in the immediate future and in a region spatially proximate to speaker and hearer. This extension of reference is characteristic of the use and interpretation of sentences.

In the passage that follows, P. F. Strawson contrasts the use of ordinary common nouns standing for concrete objects, e.g., 'cat' and 'apple', to so-called mass nouns like 'snow' and 'water', standing for kinds of undifferentiated matter. Mass nouns, as Strawson points out, lack the criteria for distinguishing and reidentifying characteristic of those nouns we typically use as referring subjects. The feature-placing sentences in which they occur are thus a primitive type of sentence that by way of contrast helps us to understand what is characteristic of linguistic reference. It also helps us to understand (in a way Strawson himself does not elaborate on) the type of reference characteristic of all prelinguistic signs, including nonconventional communicated signs such as gestures and the natural signs of the behaviorists signifying by virtue of some direct association.

Strawson follows traditional logic in distinguishing three types of terms: (1) terms expressing or "introducing" "characterizing universals," e.g., adjectives and verbs such as 'red' and 'runs', which can occur only in the predicate position of a sentence; (2) terms introducing "sortal universals," e.g., concrete nouns such as 'man' and 'cat', which can occur as both subjects (as in 'All men are mortal') and predicates of sentences ('Socrates is a man'); and (3) terms introducing "feature-universals," which constitute a "primitive pre-particular level of thought" at which are absent criteria for reidentifying and distinguishing. Without such criteria, the feature-placing sentences in which they occur can refer only to spatial locations, not objects, and the reference is necessarily restricted in scope to the immediate environment.

7.4.1 P. F. Strawson[8]

> As examples [of feature-placing statements] I suggest the following:
> Now it is raining
> Snow is falling
> There is coal here
> There is gold here
> There is water here.

The universal terms introduced into these propositions do not function as characterizing universals. *Snow, water, coal,* and *gold,* for example, are general kinds of stuff, not properties or characteristics of particulars; though *being made of snow* or *being made of gold* are characteristics of particulars. Nor are the universal terms introduced into these propositions sortal universals. No one of them of itself provides a principle for distinguishing, enumerating and reidentifying particulars of a sort. But each can be very easily modified so as to yield several such principles: we can distinguish, count, and reidentify *veins* or *grains, lumps* or *dumps* of coal, and *flakes, falls, drifts* or *expanses* of snow. Such phrases as 'lump of coal' or 'fall of snow' introduce sortal universals; but 'coal' and 'snow' *simpliciter* do not. These sentences, then, neither contain any part which introduces a particular, nor any expression used in such a way that its

8. P. F. Strawson, *Individuals* (London: Methuen, 1959), pp. 208–214.

use presupposes the use of expressions to introduce particulars. Of course, when these sentences are used, the combination of the circumstances of their use with the tense of the verb and the demonstrative adverbs, if any, which they contain, yields a statement of the incidence of the universal feature they introduce. For this much at least is essential to any language in which singular empirical statements could be made at all: viz. the introduction of general concepts and the indication of their incidence. But it is an important fact that this can be done by means of statements which neither bring particulars into our discourse nor presuppose other areas of discourse in which particulars are brought in.

Languages imagined on the model of such languages as these are sometimes called 'property-location' languages. But this is an unfortunate name: the universal terms which figure in my examples are not properties; indeed the idea of a property belongs to a level of logical complexity which we are trying to get below. This is why I have chosen to use the less philosophically committed word 'feature', and to speak of 'feature-placing' sentences.

Though feature-placing sentences do not introduce particulars into our discourse, they provide a basis for this introduction. The facts they state are presupposed, in the required sense, by the introduction of certain kinds of particular. That there should be facts statable by means of such sentences as 'There is water here', 'It is snowing', is a condition of there being propositions into which particulars are introduced, by means of such expressions as 'This pool of water', 'This fall of snow'. In general, the transition from facts of the presupposed kind to the introduction of the particulars for which they supply the basis involves a conceptual complication: it involves the adoption of criteria of distinctness and, where applicable, criteria of reidentification for particulars of the kind in question, as well as the use of characterizing universals which can be tied to a particular of that kind. A *basis* for criteria of distinctness may indeed already exist at the feature-placing level. For where we can say 'There is snow here' or 'There is gold here', we can also, perhaps, say, 'There is snow (gold) *here*—and—*here*—and *here*'. Factors which determine multiplicity of placing may become, when we introduce particulars, criteria for distinguishing one particular from another. Of criteria of reidentification I shall say more later.

It might now reasonably be said that it is by no means sufficient, for the general theory of presuppositions, to find just some class of presupposed facts which qualify for the terminal stage of the regress, the stage at which no particulars are introduced at all. For if the theory is to work in general, then any route, and not merely specially chosen routes, through the regress, should lead, in the end, to facts of such a class. It is reasonable enough to claim that facts of the class just illustrated supply a basis for the introduction of certain kinds of particulars. But it would be highly unplausible to claim that particulars of these kinds supply, together with the characterizing universals which attach to them, a basis for the introduction of all other kinds of particulars whatever. In the first chapter of this book, it was argued that certain kinds of particular are, from the point of view of identification, the basic particulars of our conceptual scheme. These were, roughly, those directly locatable particulars which were or possessed material bodies. If we could find, for a reasonable selection of particulars of this class, presupposed facts in the statement of which particulars were not introduced, then, perhaps, we might regard the general theory as vindicated. For facts involving basic particulars may be presumed to provide, directly or indirectly, a basis for the introduction of most types of non-basic particular. The apparent exceptions are those non-basic particulars, such as public auditory or visual phenomena like flashes and bangs, which are directly locatable, but are not conceived of by us as necessarily e.g. events happening to, or states of, particulars of other types. But if these raise any problem, it is likely to be a problem of secondary importance.

It appears, however, that basic particulars themselves raise a serious problem. For whilst particulars like pools of water, lumps of gold etc. do certainly belong to the class of basic particulars, they can scarcely be said to constitute a fair or reasonable selection from that class. The sortal universals of which they are instances (*pool of water, lump of gold*) are alike in this: that their names incorporate, as a part, the names of kinds of stuff (*water, gold*) which seem supremely, or even uniquely, well adapted to be introduced as universal terms into feature-placing sentences. That is why it is so easy to find, in ordinary language, convincing examples of cases where we operate, not with the notion of particular instances of, e.g., gold or snow, but merely with the notion of the universal feature itself and the notion of placing. But the sortal universals of which basic particulars are more characteristically instances (e.g., men, mountains, apples, cats, trees) do not thus happily separate into indications of a particularizing division, such as *pool* or *lump,* on the one hand, and general features, such as *water* or *gold,* on the other. It is easy to see the ground of this difference. For particulars such as heaps of snow could be physically lumped together to yield one particular mass of snow; but we could not lump particular cats together to yield one enormous cat. It must surely be more difficult, therefore, to envisage a situation in which, instead of operating with the notion of the sortal universal, *cat* or *apple,* and hence with the notion of particular cats or apples, we operate with the notion of a corresponding feature and of placing. Ordinary language does not seem to provide us with a name for a universal term which could count as the required feature in the case of, say, cats. Is it not perhaps the essential difference between, say, cats and snow, that there *could* be no concept of the 'cat-feature' such as the theory seems to require, that any general idea of cat *must* be the idea of *a* cat, i.e., must already involve criteria of distinctness and reidentification for cats as particulars?

These difficulties, though important, are not decisive. For they do not show that it is logically absurd to suppose that there might be a level of thought at which we recognize the presence of cat, or signs of the past or future presence of cat, yet do not think identifyingly of particular cats. Let us suppose that the idea of such a level of thought is coherent; and let us introduce, as its linguistic counterpart, the idea of a form of linguistic activity which, if we are to speak of language-games, might be called *"the naming-game."* Playing the naming-game may be compared with one of the earliest things which children do with language—when they utter the general name for a kind of thing in the presence of a thing of that kind, saying 'duck' when there is a duck, 'ball' when there is a ball &c. Now it may be said that these utterances have the force of 'There is a duck', 'There is a ball' &c., i.e. they have the force of forms which have the place in language which they do have only because expressions used to make identifying references to particulars have the place in language which *they* have. But anyone for whom these utterances have this force is not playing the naming-game. This remark indeed deprives me of the right to appeal to the alleged fact that the naming-game is played. But no such appeal is necessary. All that is required is the admission that the concept of the naming-game is coherent, the admission that the ability to make identifying references to such things as balls and ducks includes the ability to recognize the corresponding features, whereas it is logically possible that one should recognize the features without possessing the conceptual resources for identifying reference to the corresponding particulars. Granted this, it does not matter whether naming-game utterances, or feature- placing utterances in general, are common or ordinary or not. We can readily enough acknowledge that the introduction of particulars is so fundamental a conceptual step as to leave the primitive pre-particular level of thought as, at most, no more than vestigial in language.

But is the idea of the naming-game a coherent and distinct idea—distinct, that is, from the idea of bringing a particular under a sortal universal? To answer this, we must say more about the criteria of distinctness and reidentification involved in the conceptual move to particulars.

I referred just now to a possible argument to the effect that there *could* be no idea of a cat-feature which would be distinct from, yet yield a basis for, the sortal universal, *cat,* as the general feature, *snow,* is distinct from, yet yields a basis for, the sortal universals, *patch of snow* or *fall of snow;* for in the case of cats there is no general feature which can be thought of as divided in different ways to yield different sortal universals, as the general feature, snow, can be thought of as divided in different ways to yield different sortal universals. What this argument shows, however, is not that the required type of general concept of cat is impossible, but rather that the concept must already include in itself the *basis* for the criteria of *distinctness* which we apply to particular cats. Roughly, the idea of the cat-feature, unlike that of snow, must include the idea of a characteristic shape, a characteristic pattern of occupation of space.

But now what of the criteria of reidentification? Does the concept of the cat-feature include a *basis* for this? If so, what is the substance of the phrase, 'a basis for criteria'? Is it not merely an attempt to persuade us that there is a difference, where there is none, between the concept of the cat-feature and the sortal universal, cat? This is the crucial question. I think the answer to it is as follows. The concept of the cat-feature does indeed provide a basis for the idea of reidentification of particular cats. For that concept includes the idea of a characteristic shape, of a characteristic pattern for the occupation of space; and this idea leads naturally enough to that of a continuous path traced through space and time by such a characteristic pattern; and this idea in its turn provides the core of the idea of particular-identity for basic particulars. But this is not to say that the possession of the concept of the cat-feature entails the possession of this idea. Operating with the idea of reidentifiable particular cats, we distinguish between the case in which a particular cat appears, departs and reappears, and the case in which a particular cat appears and departs and a different cat appears. But one could play the naming-game without making this distinction. Someone playing the naming-game can correctly say 'More cat' or 'cat again' in both cases; but someone operating with the idea of particular cats would be in error if he said 'Another cat' in the first case, or 'The same cat again' in the second. *The decisive conceptual step to cat-particulars is taken when the case of 'more cat' or 'cat again' is subdivided into the case of 'another cat' and the case of 'the same cat again'.*

7.5 Iconic Representation

As the final example of work in recent philosophy that deals with issues developed in the history of semiotic, I choose Nelson Goodman's comparison between the way an iconic representation such as a picture stands for or denotes an object and the way a symbolic linguistic description denotes. For object A to be a pictorial representation of some other B is not simply for A to resemble B. It must instead stand for B in some respect in a way that Goodman regards as analogous to the way linguistic descriptions stand for objects.

7.5.1 Nelson Goodman[9]

Denotation

Whether a picture ought to be a representation or not is a question much less crucial than might appear from current bitter battles among artists, critics, and propagandists. Nevertheless, the nature of representation wants early study in any philosophical examination of the ways symbols function in and out of the arts. That representation is frequent in some arts, such as painting, and infrequent in others, such as music, threatens trouble for a unified aesthetics; and confusion over how pictorial representation as a mode of signification is allied to and distinguished from verbal description on the one hand and, say, facial expression on the other is fatal to any general theory of symbols.

The most naive view of representation might perhaps be put somewhat like this: "*A* represents *B* if and only if *A* appreciably resembles *B*," or "*A* represents *B* to the extent that *A* resembles *B*." Vestiges of this view, with assorted refinements, persist in most writing on representation. Yet more error could hardly be compressed into so short a formula.

Some of the faults are obvious enough. An object resembles itself to the maximum degree but rarely represents itself; resemblance, unlike representation, is reflexive. Again, unlike representation, resemblance is symmetric: *B* is as much like *A* as *A* is like *B*, but while a painting may represent the Duke of Wellington, the Duke doesn't represent the painting. Furthermore, in many cases neither one of a pair of very like objects represents the other: none of the automobiles off an assembly line is a picture of any of the rest; and a man is not normally a representation of another man, even his twin brother. Plainly, resemblance in any degree is no sufficient condition for representation.

Just what correction to make in the formula is not so obvious. We may attempt less, and prefix the condition "If *A* is a picture, . . ." Of course,

9. Nelson Goodman, *Languages of Art* (Indianapolis: Bobbs- Merrill, 1968), ch. 1, secs. 1 and 6, pp. 3–6, 27–31.

if we then construe "picture" as "representation," we resign a large part of the question: namely, what constitutes a representation. But even if we construe "picture" broadly enough to cover all paintings, the formula is wide of the mark in other ways. A Constable painting of Marlborough Castle is more like any other picture than it is like the Castle, yet it represents the Castle and not another picture—not even the closest copy. To add the requirement that *B* must not be a picture would be desperate and futile; for a picture may represent another, and indeed each of the once popular paintings of art galleries represents many others.

The plain fact is that a picture, to represent an object, must be a symbol for it, stand for it, refer to it; and that no degree of resemblance is sufficient to establish the requisite relationship of reference. Nor is resemblance *necessary* for reference; almost anything may stand for almost anything else. A picture that represents—like a passage that describes—an object refers to and, more particularly, *denotes* it. Denotation is the core of representation and is independent of resemblance.

If the relation between a picture and what it represents is thus assimilated to the relation between a predicate and what it applies to, we must examine the characteristics of representation as a special kind of denotation. What does pictorial denotation have in common with, and how does it differ from, verbal or diagrammatic denotation? One not implausible answer is that resemblance, while no sufficient condition for representation, is just the feature that distinguishes representation from denotation of other kinds. Is it perhaps the case that if *A* denotes B, then *A* represents *B* just to the extent that *A* resembles *B*? I think even this watered-down and innocuous-looking version of our initial formula betrays a grave misconception of the nature of representation. . . .

Representation-as

The locution 'represents . . . as' has two quite different uses. To say that a picture represents the Duke of Wellington as an infant, or as an adult, or as the victor at Waterloo is often merely to say that the picture represents the Duke at a given time or period—that it represents a certain (long or short, continuous or broken) temporal part or "time-slice" of him. Here 'as . . .' combines with the *noun* 'the Duke of Wellington' to form a description of one portion of the whole extended individual. Such a description can always be replaced by another like 'the infant Duke of Wellington' or 'the Duke of Wellington upon the occasion of his victory at Waterloo'. Thus these cases raise no difficulty; all that is being said is that the picture represents the object so described.

The second use is illustrated when we say that a given picture represents Winston Churchill as an infant, where the picture does not represent the infant Churchill but rather represents the adult Churchill as an infant. Here, as well as when we say that other pictures represent the adult Churchill as an adult, the 'as . . .' combines with and modifies the *verb;* and we have genuine cases of *representation-as.* Such representation-as wants now to be distinguished from and related to representation.

A picture that represents a man denotes him; a picture that represents a fictional man is a man-picture; and a picture that represents a man as a man is a man-picture denoting him. Thus while the first case concerns only what the picture denotes, and the second only what kind of picture it is, the third concerns both the denotation and the classification.

More accurate formulation takes some care. What a picture is said to represent may be denoted by the picture as a whole or by a part of it. Likewise, a picture may be a soandso-picture as a whole or merely through containing a soandso-picture. Consider an ordinary portrait of the Duke and Duchess of Wellington. The picture (as a whole) denotes the couple, and (in part) denotes the Duke. Furthermore, it is (as a whole) a two-person-picture, and (in part) a man-picture. The picture represents the Duke and Duchess as two persons, and represents the Duke as a man. But although it represents the Duke, and is a two-person-picture, it obviously does not represent the Duke as two persons; and although it represents two persons and is a man-picture, it does not represent the two as a man. For the picture neither is nor contains any picture that as a whole both represents the Duke and is a two-man-picture, or that as a whole both represents two persons and is a man-picture.

In general, then, an object k is represented as a soandso by a picture p if and only if p is or contains a picture that as a whole both represents k and is a soandso-picture. Many of the modifiers that have had to be included here may, however, be omitted as understood in what follows; for example, "is or contains a picture that as a whole both represents Churchill and is an adult-picture" may be shortened to "is an adult-picture representing Churchill."

Everyday usage is often careless about the distinction between representation and representation-as. Cases have already been cited where in saying that a picture represents a soandso we mean not that it denotes a soandso but that it is a soandso-picture. In other cases, we may mean both. If I tell you I have a picture of a certain black horse, and then I produce a snapshot in which he has come out a light speck in the distance, you can hardly convict me of lying; but you may well feel that I misled you. You understandably took me to mean a picture of the black horse as such; and you therefore expected the picture not only to denote the horse in question but to be a black-horse-picture. Not inconceivably, saying a picture represents the black horse might on other occasions mean that it represents the horse as black (i.e., that it is a black-thing-picture representing the horse) or that it represents the black thing in question as a horse (i.e., that it is a horse-picture representing the black thing).

The ambiguities of ordinary use do not end there. To say that the adult Churchill is represented as an infant (or as an adult) is to say that the picture in question is an infant-picture (or an adult-picture). But to say that Pickwick is represented as a clown (or as Don Quixote) cannot mean that the picture is a clown-picture (or Don Quixote-picture) representing Pickwick; for there is no Pickwick. Rather, what is being said is that the picture belongs to a certain rather narrow class of pictures that may be described as Pickwick-as-clown-pictures (or Pickwick-as-Don-Quixote-pictures).

Distinctions obscured in much informal discourse thus need to be carefully marked for our purposes here. Being a matter of monadic classi-fication, representation-as differs drastically from dyadic denotative repre-sentation. If a picture represents k as a (or the) soandso, then it denotes k and is a soandso-picture. If k is identical with h, the picture also denotes and represents h. And if k is a suchandsuch, the picture also represents a (or the) suchandsuch, but not necessarily as a (or the) suchandsuch. To represent the first Duke of Wellington is to represent Arthur Wellesley and also to represent a soldier, but not necessarily to represent him *as* a soldier; for some pictures of him are civilian-pictures.

Representations, then, are pictures that function in somewhat the same way as descriptions. Just as objects are classified by means of, or under, various verbal labels, so also are objects classified by or under various pictorial labels. And the labels themselves, verbal or pictorial, are in turn classified under labels, verbal or nonverbal. Objects are classified under 'desk', 'table', etc., and also under pictures representing them. Descriptions are classified under 'desk-description', 'centaur-description', 'Cicero-name', etc.; and pictures under 'desk-picture', 'Pickwick-picture', etc. The labeling of labels does not depend upon what they are labels for. Some, like 'unicorn', apply to nothing; and as we have noted, not all pictures of soldiers are soldier-pictures. Thus with a picture as with any other label, there are always two questions: what it represents (or de-scribes) and the sort of representation (or description) it is. The first question asks what objects, if any, it applies to as a label; and the second asks about which among certain labels apply to it. In representing, a picture at once picks out a class of objects and belongs to a certain class or classes of pictures.

Goodman's use of the term 'denotes' masks some serious difficulties with this account. In logic it is customary to define the denotation of a term as the class of objects to which it can be truly ascribed. Thus, the denotation of the term 'tree' is the class of trees, that of 'Socrates' the individual Socrates. But the evaluative term 'true' seems applicable only to conventional signs with accepted rules for their use, rules that fix the respect in which the sign must stand for its object. The sentence 'Reagan is our oldest living former president' may be said to express a true proposition. But it makes no sense to say of a nonconventional icon such as a portrait of Reagan that it is true or false. It is instead a more or less faithful copy of the person it purports to represent, a resemblance admitting of degrees that stands in contrast to the all-or-nothing character of truth.

The term 'denotes' can also be regarded as a synonym of 'refers' as a function of the subjects of a sentence. In this sense it also seems clear that iconic representations such as pictures or diagrams do not denote. A portrait of Reagan would not by itself refer to the former president, though we may recognize it as depicting him. Reference would have to be supplied by a verbal caption such as 'Ronald Reagan' occurring on the portrait, its frame, or some accompanying label. Similarly, a child may produce a drawing of his dog, and we may recognize it as such a drawing. But reference to the dog must be supplied by a caption such as 'my dog' or an accompanying pointing gesture. Like any communicated sign, iconic representations can refer beyond the immediate environment only insofar as they are embedded in some accompanying verbal context containing subject terms. Independent of such a context, they are tied to the here and now.

While Goodman's account of iconic representations faces such difficulties, it does successfully draw attention to the problem of clearly contrasting and comparing the way these signs function in communication with the functioning of linguistic expressions. In this respect it is a valuable contribution to semiotic as a continuing, viable part of present-day philosophy.

WORKS CITED

INDEX

WORKS CITED

Aristotle. *De Interpretatione*. Translated by H. G. Apostle. In *Aristotle's Categories and Propositions*. Grinnell: Peripatetic Press, 1980.

———. *Rhetorica*. Translated by W. Rhys Roberts. In *The Basic Works of Aristotle*, edited by R. McKeon.New York: Random House, 1941.

Arnauld, Antoine. *The Art of Thinking*. Translated by J. Dickoff and P. James. Indianapolis: Bobbs-Merrill, 1964.

Augustine. *On Christian Doctrine*. Translated by D. W. Robertson, Jr. New York: Macmillan, 1986.

———. *On the Trinity*. Translated by A. W. Haddan. Vol. 2 in *Basic Writings of Saint Augustine*, edited by W. J. Oates. New York: Random House, 1948.

Barthes, Roland. *Elements of Semiology*. Translated by A. Laverson and C. Smith. New York: Hill and Wang, 1968.

Bennett, Jonathan. *Linguistic Behaviour*. Cambridge: Cambridge University Press, 1976.

Berkeley, George. *A New Theory of Vision*. New York: Dutton, 1910.

———. *Three Dialogues between Hylas and Philonous*. New York: Dutton, 1910.

Blonsky, Marshall, ed. *On Signs*. Baltimore: Johns Hopkins University Press, 1985.

Bonaventure. *Commentary on the Four Books of Sentences of Peter Lombard*. Translated by R. McKeon. Vol. 2 in *Selections from Medieval Philosophers*. New York: Scribner's, 1930.

Buhler, Karl. "The Axiomatization of the Language Sciences." In R. E. Innis, *Karl Buhler*. New York: Plenum Press, 1982.

Carnap, Rudolph. "Meaning and Synonymy in Natural Languages." Appendix D of *Meaning and Necessity*. Chicago: University of Chicago Press, 1947.

Chisholm, Roderick. "Intentionality and the Theory of Signs." *Philosophical Studies* 3 (1952): 56–63.

Chomsky, Noam. "Review of B. F. Skinner's *Verbal Behavior*." *Language* 35 (1959): 25–58.

Clarke, D. S., Jr. *Principles of Semiotic*. London: Routledge and Kegan Paul, 1987.

Deely, John. *Introducing Semiotic*. Bloomington: Indiana University Press, 1982.

Eco, Umberto. *Semiotics and the Philosophy of Language*. Bloomington: Indiana University Press, 1984.

Galan, F. W. "Cinema and Semiosis." *Semiotica* 44 (1983): 21–53.

Gérando, Joseph Marie de. *The Observation of Savage Peoples*. Translated by F. C. T. Moore. Berkeley: University of California Press, 1969.

Goodman, Nelson. *Languages of Art*. Indianapolis: Bobbs-Merrill, 1968.

Grice, H. P. "Meaning." *Philosophical Review* 66 (1957): 377–88.

———. "Utterer's Meaning, Sentence-Meaning, and Word-Meaning." *Foundations of Language* 4(1968): 225–42.

Guiraud, Pierre. *Semiology*. Translated by G. Gross. London: Routledge and Kegan Paul, 1975.

Hacking, Ian. *The Emergence of Probability*. London: Cambridge University Press, 1975.

Harman, Gilbert. "Semiotics and the Cinema." *Quarterly Review of Film Studies* 2 (1977): 15–24.

Hippocrates. *Prognostic*. Translated by W. H. S. Jones. Vol. 2 in *Hippocrates*. Cambridge: Harvard University Press, 1923.

Hjelmslev, Louis. *Prolegomena to a Theory of Language*. Translated by F. Whitfield. Madison: University of Wisconsin Press, 1963.

Hobbes, Thomas. *De Corpore*. Translated by A. Martinich. In *Thomas Hobbes: Computatio Sive Logica*. NewYork: Abaris Books, 1981.

Innis, Robert, ed. *Semiotics*. Bloomington: Indiana University Press, 1985.

Jakobson, Roman. "A Glance at the Development of Semiotics." In *The Framework of Language*. Ann Arbor: Michigan Studies in the Humanities, 1980.

John of St. Thomas. *Ars Logica*. Translated by John Deely. In *Tractatus de Signis: The Semiotic of John Poinsot*. Berkeley: University of California Press, 1985.

Kant, Immanuel. *Anthropology from a Pragmatic Point of View*. Translated by V. L. Dowdell; Edited by H. Rudnick. Carbondale: Southern Illinois University Press, 1978.

Kremper, M. et al. *Classics of Semiotics*. New York: Plenum, 1981.

Lewis, David. *Convention*. Cambridge: Harvard University Press, 1969.

Locke, John. *Essay Concerning Human Understanding*. New York: Dover, 1959.

Martinidis, Petros. "Semiotics of Architectural Theories: Toward an Epistemology of Architecture."*Semiotica* 59 (1986): 371–86.

Mead, George Herbert. *Mind, Self and Society*. Edited by C. W. Morris. Chicago: University of Chicago Press, 1934.

Morris, Charles. *Signs, Language and Behavior*. New York: Braziller, 1946.

Ogden, C. K., and I. A. Richards. *The Meaning of Meaning*. New York: Harcourt and Brace, 1923.

Osgood, C. E., G. Succi, and P. Tannenbaum. "The Logic of Semantic

Differentiation." In *Psycholinguistics,* edited by S. Saporta. New York: Holt, 1965.

Peirce, Charles. *The Collected Papers of Charles Saunders Peirce.* Edited by C. Hartshorne and P. Weiss. 6 vols.Cambridge: Harvard University Press, 1934–1936.

Peter of Spain. *The Summulae Logicales.* Translated by I. M. Bochenski. In *A History of Formal Logic.* South Bend: Notre Dame University Press, 1961.

Quine, W. V. O. *Word and Object.* Cambridge: M.I.T. Press, 1960.

Quintilian, Marcus Fabius. *Institutio Oratoria.* Translated by C. Little. In *The Institutio Oratoria of Marcus Fabius Quintiliamus.* Nashville: George Peabody College for Teachers, 1951.

Reid, Thomas. *An Inquiry into the Human Mind.* Vol. 1 in *Philosophical Works.* Hildesheim: Olms, 1967.

Rollins, Bernard. *Natural and Conventional Meaning.* The Hague: Mouton, 1976.

Russell, Bertrand. *An Inquiry into Meaning and Truth.* London: Allen and Unwin, 1940.

Saussure, Ferdinand de. *Course in General Linguistics.* Edited by C. Bally and A. Sechehtrans in collaboration with A. Riedlinger. Translated by W. Baskin. New York: Philosophical Library, 1959.

Sebeok, Thomas A. "Is a Comparative Semiotics Possible?" In *Contributions to the Doctrine of Signs.*Bloomington: Indiana University Press, 1976.

––––––. "Semiotics: A Survey of the State of the Art." In *Contributions to the Doctrine of Signs.* Bloomington: Indiana University Press, 1976.

Sextus Empiricus. *Against the Logicians.* Translated by R. G. Bury. Vol 2 in *Sextus Empiricus,* Loeb Classical Library. Cambridge: Harvard University Press, 1935.

Skinner, B. F. *Verbal Behavior.* New York: Appleton-Century-Croft, 1957.

Strawson, P. F. *Individuals.* London: Methuen, 1959.

Uldall, H. J. *Outline of Glossematics.* Part I. Copenhagen: Nodisk Sprog- og Kulturforlag, 1957.

Watson, John. *Behaviorism.* Chicago: University of Chicago Press, 1930.

William of Ockham. *Summa Totius Logicae.* Translated by S. Tornay. In *Ockham: Studies and Selections.* LaSalle: Open Court, 1938.

––––––. *Super Quatuor Libros Sententarium Subtilissimae Earumdenque Decisiones.*Translated by S. Tornay. In *Ockham: Studies and Selections.* LaSalle: Open Court, 1938.

Ziff, Paul. "On H. P. Grice's Account of Meaning." *Analysis* 28 (1967): 1–8.

D. S. Clarke, Jr., received his doctorate from Emory University, where he wrote his dissertation on Charles Peirce under the direction of Charles Hartshorne. He is currently Professor of Philosophy at Southern Illinois University at Carbondale. He is the author of *Deductive Logic* (1974), *Practical Inferences* (1985), *Principles of Semiotic* (1987), and *Rational Acceptance and Purpose* (1989), and numerous articles on logic and the philosophy of language.